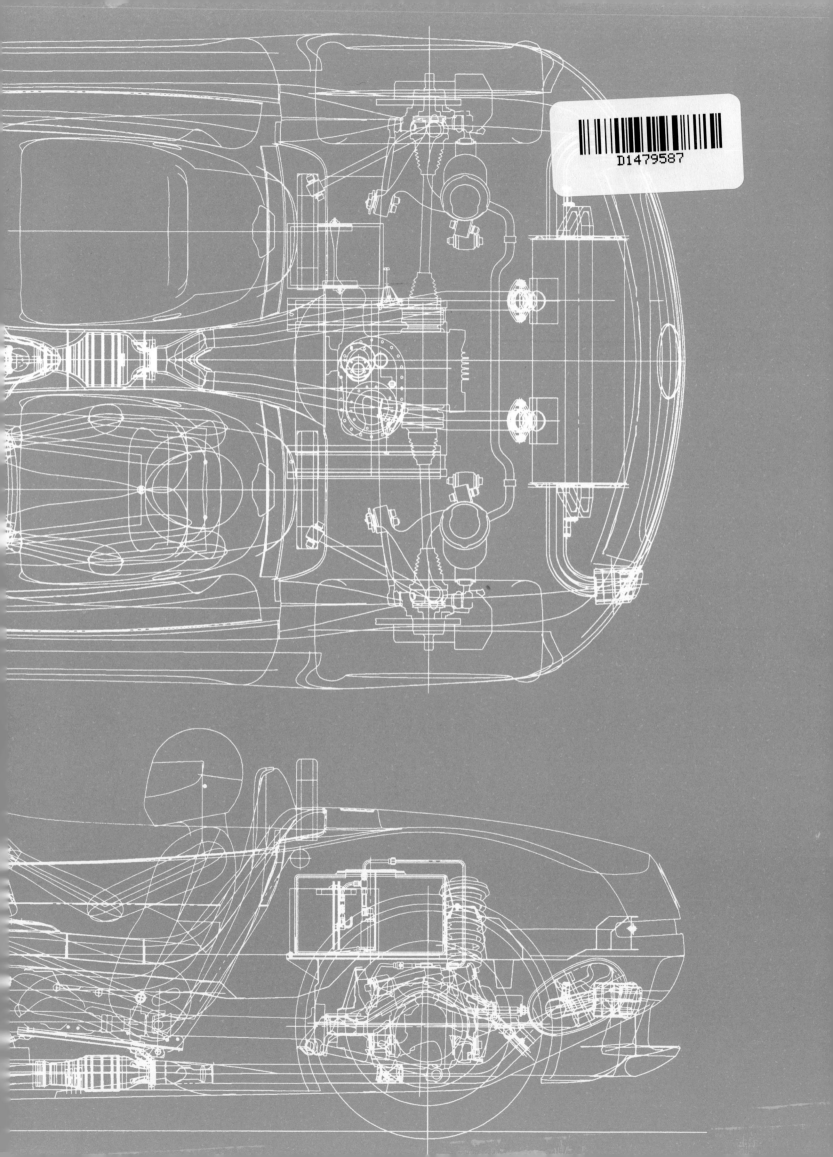

CONCEPT
CARS

CONCEPT CARS

DESIGNING FOR THE FUTURE

RICHARD DREDGE

THUNDER BAY
P·R·E·S·S

San Diego, California

Thunder Bay Press
An imprint of the Advantage Publishers Group
5880 Oberlin Drive, San Diego, CA 92121-4794
www.thunderbaybooks.com

Library of Congress Cataloging-in-Publication Data available upon request.

ISBN 1-59223-324-4

Editorial and design by
Amber Books Ltd
Bradley's Close
74–77 White Lion Street
London N1 9PF
England
www.amberbooks.co.uk

Project Editor: Michael Spilling
Designer: Jerry Williams
Picture Research: Natasha Jones, Sandra Assersohn

Printed in China

1 2 3 4 5 08 07 06 05 04

Contents

Designing the Dream

For more than half a century, the dream-makers have been hard at work, creating wheeled fantasies to entice that most fickle group of people – car buyers. The world of fashion comes and goes, and concept cars are merely another branch of fashion; one year promotes huge wheels, the next year puts the focus on rear doors. Only one thing never changes, and that is the importance of the concept car.

Few concepts ever make it into production, although elements of most of them eventually reach the showrooms. So the concept car lets the marketing departments promise virtually anything – and deliver virtually nothing. As everybody knows, this is just an ideas car; nobody expects to be able to buy it in the form shown. So what, you may ask, is the point? Again, like any branch of the fashion world, the point

is to push out the boundaries: not until you have gone too far do you know just how far you can go. True, many concepts could hardly be labelled adventurous, but there are some that are pretty challenging to say the least.

Paul Horrell summed up the situation well when writing for *Car* magazine. There are, he suggested, five reasons for concept cars, the first being to promote an Italian design house. And while concept cars are not exclusively an Italian preserve, Italian designers do account for more than most. The next reason is to prepare the public for an impending production car, while the third reason is to create a distraction while churning out dull cars that do nothing for the company's image. Rejected design proposals and major shifts in a company's design direction are the final two reasons for a company producing a concept car. In fact, you would be hard-pressed to come up with a concept that does not fit into at least one of these categories.

Certainly, that was the case with what is considered to be the first true concept car – the Buick Y Job of 1938. Designed by Harley Earl of General Motors, this was a car which owed nothing to what had gone before – it was smooth, sleek, aerodynamic and impossibly stylish. It also remained a one-off, as it was simply too daring for pre-war car buyers.

The Y Job is usually given the credit for launching the very concept of concept cars, though it is possible to argue that the world's first concept car was, in fact, launched five years previously – the Venus Bilo. Unveiled in November

The Venus Bilo pre-dated the world's first official concept car, the Buick Y Job, by half a decade. But where the American car still survives, the Bilo quickly disappeared without trace.

The GM Motoramas of the 1950s and 1960s were lavish affairs, a celebration of the car and the freedom it offers. In the foreground is the Firebird I at the 1954 event.

1933, the concept was initiated by Volvo, which initially refused any involvement in its creation. Indeed, it was built by an independent coachbuilder using a Volvo PV653 chassis, and only later did Volvo admit that the car had been built to test reactions to its advanced styling. The Venus Bilo took inspiration from contemporary aircraft design and experimented with interior space utilization. Finished in a bright blue with beige stripes, it also examined the idea of removable panels, which could be replaced in the event of an accident. Once on display, the Venus Bilo drew a very mixed reaction.

And only when the Y Job was shown five years later were the floodgates opened for a whole raft of concepts, which were usually referred to as 'dream cars'. These mostly hailed from the United States, and Harley Earl of General Motors was responsible for many of them. His Le Sabre arrived in 1951 and was

every bit as jaw-dropping as its predecessor. Inspired by jet-fighter aircraft (this was the start of the jet age), the Le Sabre made all contemporary production cars look dated overnight.

Cashing in

As the dream car phenomenon gained momentum, General Motors cashed in by setting up a series of events around the United States. Each year, the corporation held what it termed a 'Motorama', where it could show off its latest production models as well as the concepts that flowed from its design centre. The events were full of glitz and glamour, and they ran between 1949 and 1961 in cities such as New York, Miami, Chicago, Detroit, Boston and San Francisco.

It was at these Motoramas that the Firebird series of cars was shown, of which there were four in total. These were also inspired by jet fighters, each one looking like an aircraft on wheels, and each version more radical than the last.

With General Motors whipping car buyers into a frenzy, its major rivals had to compete if they were not

to be left behind. By 1941, Chrysler was also unveiling dream cars, including the Thunderbolt. Just the name was exciting – and, like the GM cars, its design owed little to anything that was available.

The designer of this concept was Alex Tremulis, who also designed such masterpieces as the Tucker Torpedo and Cord 812 – cars which made their mark in history by going their own way. But it was Virgil Exner who really put Chrysler on the concept car map. He had worked with Harley Earl at General Motors in the 1930s and was later hired by Chrysler to lead its design studios. By 1950, his first concept was on display – the rather awkward-looking XX-500. Throughout the 1950s he worked with the Italian coachbuilding company Ghia to produce a series of concepts. Some were beautiful, some looked especially awkward, but they all had one thing in common: they kept pushing the barriers, to see just what was acceptable to a car-buying public.

European concepts

While America's Big Three (Chrysler, General Motors and Ford) were churning out dream cars to wow their own car buyers, things were very different in Europe. Although the first European motor shows took place immediately after World War II, it was not until well into the 1950s that the various coachbuilders began to produce their own concepts. The first important

concept to be built in Europe was to be the Bertone-produced BAT 5, the first of a trio of concepts designed to explore aerodynamics further. BAT was short for Berlina Aerodynamica Technica, or streamlined, closed touring car, and all three cars were built on Alfa Romeo mechanicals. After the BAT 5 of 1953 came the BAT 7 of 1954 and the BAT 9 of 1955 – all three cars still exist and their significance to the automotive world remains enormous.

Throughout the 1950s, various concepts were produced in Europe; however, whereas the cars on display at the American auto shows were very much pie-in-the-sky and far removed from reality, the European cars were generally used as the basis for research. This was especially true for the Italians, who already had a strong coachbuilding tradition. Fiat and Alfa Romeo were busy testing aerodynamics and gas turbine engines while Ghia, which would later be swallowed up by Ford, was constructing many of Chrysler's concepts.

Throughout the 1950s it was left to the Americans to produce most of the seminal concepts, but in 1960 Pininfarina built the X, which featured four wheels in a diamond formation, sported huge rear fins, and also threw away the rule book in terms of vehicle packaging and aerodynamics. This was the car as art – a concept which was largely alien to the European car makers and coachbuilders at that time. By the mid-1960s, however, Bertone, Pininfarina and Ghia were all building concepts, which bore their own badges and which were usually – but not exclusively – based on European mechanicals.

By the second half of the 1960s, the Italian concepts were coming thick and fast – but few were being built in other European countries. Cars such as the Marzal (a Bertone design that wore Lamborghini badges), the Bertone Carabo and the Ferrari 512S (a Pininfarina design) were significant concepts. Unveiled in the late 1960s, they were all outlandish supercars. It is true that some concepts being produced were more accessible, but these were very much in the minority.

This remained the case throughout much of the 1970s, despite the arrival of the safety car at the start of that decade. This accounted for a large chunk of the prototypes that were shown at European motor shows. Indeed, concepts with huge bumpers, massive crash resistance and hugely padded interiors seemed to mushroom overnight. This was the car makers' attempt to build cars which would look after their occupants no matter what – the problem was that, without exception, they were ugly, awful to drive and

expensive to produce, and, because they were usually heavier than normal, they were often more thirsty.

By the mid-1970s, safety cars were just a bad memory, and cars which were more acceptably styled, yet still safer than their predecessors, were becoming more common. Many of the concepts being churned out were still no-compromise supercars, but vehicles such as the Citroën Camargue and NSU Trapeze aimed to inject a bit of style into the mass-market sector by planting two- or three-door bodyshells onto the platforms of relatively ordinary cars. The Camargue was based on the Citroën GS, the Trapeze used the NSU Ro80 as its basis. While the Trapeze was hardly run-of-the-mill with its clutchless manual gearbox, rotary engine and wind-cheating bodyshell, it was pretty ordinary in terms of its basic configuration.

The 1970s also marked the turning of the tables in terms of where the important concepts were being produced. After the hedonism of the 1950s and 1960s, all went very quiet in the United States while the focus turned to Europe. Ford had bought the very important Ghia design studio in 1973, and the cars produced after that were seen as European in origin

The Oldsmobile Golden Rocket of 1956 was about much more than exterior design. When one of the doors was opened, the roof rose automatically, to allow easier entry and exit.

despite the American ownership. Other European coachbuilders (almost exclusively Italian) continued to rebody production cars, as well as to produce bespoke designs. Such companies included Bertone, Zagato and Pininfarina, and, although many of their creations were definitely brand-building exercises, some of them were touted as production-ready cars in the hope that one of the major car makers might buy an off-the-shelf creation.

Small is beautiful

At the end of the 1970s came another noticeable shift in emphasis: small car concepts became more common. Such production cars had been very popular in the 1950s, when the microcar market had taken off. But most concepts until this point had been about luxury and performance, or were at the very least a reinterpretation of something that was to be reasonably desirable in production form. As the environmental movement had started to gain momentum, this move towards creating concepts which were more environmentally aware suggested the car makers were being forced to display a social conscience.

Makers such as Fiat (best known for its small cars) had understood this much earlier and continued with vehicles such as the electrically powered Ecos of 1978. Pininfarina took a Peugeot 104 and turned it into a lightweight, low-cost barchetta (roadster) called the Peugette, to demonstrate that having fun need not mean a heavy car with lots of power and equipment. Even Porsche got in on the act with its Long Life car of 1975, which aimed to reduce the amount of vehicles scrapped each year by making them last much longer.

Opposite: At the top is the 1951 Buick Le Sabre, the follow-up to arguably the most important concept car ever, the Buick Y Job. That car is shown in the lower two pictures, and the 13-year difference between them is clear, as the jet age approached.

But the emphasis was not only on paring back to the minimum – there were still plenty of ground-breaking concepts rolled out, which pointed to a motoring future that was full of excitement and driving pleasure, not to mention technology. Mercedes produced a series of supercars wearing the C-111 tag, experimenting with different types of engine, including diesel and rotary. This series experimented with various rotary engines, and, although these ultimately came to nothing, it took the production of such cars to evaluate whether certain technologies were worth pursuing or not.

Aerodynamic technology

The 1970s was also the decade which focused on new aerodynamic technologies. Although wind-cheating shapes had been produced several decades before, cars such as the Pininfarina CNR explored the boundaries of just how slippery it was possible to make a car while still allowing it to carry people and luggage. Madly impractical cars with incredibly low drag coefficients had been produced before, but these had tended to be single-seaters, in which the occupant had to drive while semi-reclining. Innovations such as flush glazing, more compact power units and transmissions, and lightweight but strong materials now allowed these concepts to be produced. Even so, these were not suitable for production. That would come later.

Throughout the 1980s and 1990s, wildly impractical concepts continued to be built and shown, though

society had changed since the early days. The car still represented freedom on wheels, but social responsibility had now become a factor. As the environmental and safety movements gathered pace, concepts that were safer and kinder to the environment became increasingly commonplace. This movement had begun in the 1970s, but by the 1980s the terms 'economical' or 'environmentally friendly' no longer meant stripped out or basic.

Later, the advent of new methods of propulsion and lightweight materials would improve the situation still further, but the 1980s saw its fair share of genuinely desirable cars that could conceivably also be affordable and practical. In 1981, Mercedes built the Auto 2000, and Citroën built its Eco 2000 in 1984. Both of these offered practical solutions for transporting families, while also being frugal with fuel and incorporating safety systems which would later become commonplace.

Showing concepts that resembled models which would actually reach production was still rare in the 1980s, but it did become more common. This had previously been the preserve of supercars, which were built by hand in tiny numbers. But the early 1980s saw the unveiling of cars such as the Peugeot VERA and Volvo VCC, which would later be available in the showrooms as the 309 and 700-Series, respectively.

Other designs were predicted for production, but never made it, the Italdesign Maya being a classic

International Automotive Design's Alien was quite unlike anything ever devised before. Enthusiasts hoped it would be put into production (it deserved it), but the company did not survive.

example. This was built with a mid-mounted 3l V6 engine, the aim being to put it into the showrooms within at least a couple of years of its 1984 debut. More of a sports car than a supercar, it had everything needed to carry it off, but Ford got cold feet and dropped the project.

Japanese concepts

Perhaps the most significant change of emphasis that occurred in the 1980s was the arrival of Japanese concept cars en masse. Although Mazda, Toyota and Nissan had all produced concepts as long ago as the 1960s, these had not been shown in Europe or the United States, and the country's motoring industry was not considered a force to be reckoned with. But that had all changed by the 1980s, as Japanese car sales took off around the world. The companies became richer and were better able to invest in dream cars that showcased their talents – and, because they were also being taken more seriously in the first place, their efforts were not dismissed out of hand.

In the early 1980s, many of the major Japanese companies began building credible concepts, and in many ways they overtook the American and European builders. Although the styling (and the names!) often left a lot to be desired, the engineering and technology within these cars moved the game on apace. As Japanese companies developed electronics to the point where hugely complex equipment could reliably be installed in cars, concepts suddenly leapt forward. For the first time, it was possible to fit liquid crystal displays and computer-controlled systems in cars.

Low-cost technology

By the 1990s, technological costs had tumbled. Cars could now do more than offer 'guaranteed reliability'; even the most basic production car had computerized systems. Concepts were becoming increasingly complex, while the materials being used in concept car construction had also progressed enormously. As reliability improved, the likelihood of drive-by-wire systems being used also increased. This allowed more efficient packaging of interiors, and made things much safer by eradicating mechanical linkages.

Proving that even when the sky is the limit it's still possible to go beyond, the Rinspeed X-Dream made no sense whatsoever, with its built-in jet ski, motorbike and submersible.

So, it looks as though the concept car is definitely here to stay, and thirst for the shock of the new remains unabated. Each year, there are as many motor shows around the world as there have ever been. Some that used to be less prominent – such as Detroit – are now among the biggest in the calendar. That means that they get their fair share of concepts both mild and wild, and the good news is that, at long last, many of those concepts are American once more. Although the United States had slipped back into the habit of building more concepts in the 1990s, many of them were not especially ground-breaking, and it was the Japanese and Europeans who produced the most interesting examples.

More than 70 years since the introduction of the first concept car, things have certainly advanced. Back then, Volvo would not even admit to being involved in that initial project, a concept that revolved around nothing more than an exterior design and a bit of alternative packaging. Now we routinely see concepts with new methods of propulsion, new bodystyles, innovative transmissions and mind-bending levels of equipment. Long may it continue!

Sports Cars

So exactly where do these particular types of car fit in the spectrum that makes up the world of motoring? In truth, sports models are the link between the real-world concepts and the outrageous supercars, as they include elements of both. Although some of these sports cars are closer to one side of the divide than the other, they do all share one thing – they are designed to be fun to drive above all else.

From the brutal BMW Z9 to the feline curves of the Jaguar F-Type, all these sports cars put pleasure before practicality. Some are definitely more outrageous than others, but even the most radical keeps at least one wheel in the real world. Yet some would not look out of place on the roads of today.

Attempting to inject some of the pleasure back into driving is one of the key reasons for producing a concept car. While the reality might not be quite as delicious as marketing departments would have us believe, simply the promise of escapism means that sports cars will always be a popular genre when it comes to concepts – boundaries can be explored while little more than a token nod is made towards reality.

Occasionally a designer will display a social conscience and a sportscar concept will be wheeled out with an ultra-clean engine that burns virtually no fuel while claiming to offer the most amazing driving experience. Thankfully, though, the full-fat offering is still the norm, and this chapter contains some of the most enticing sports car concepts from recent years.

Making the leap

Although none of these cars was to see production in the form in which it is shown here, elements of some of them did progress beyond the concept stage. Sadly, the Alfa Romeo Nuvola, Peugeot RC and Bertone Birusa cannot be counted among this number, but how exciting they were.

All too often, this type of concept fails to really push those boundaries, but occasionally it does happen – even in the unlikeliest of places. Just such a car was the Mercedes-Benz F300; one of the most innovative ideas cars of the past two decades, the F300 was devised by one of the world's most conservative car makers. Other cars that deserved to be on sale include the SEAT Formula and the Jaguar F-Type.

Still, who knows? Concepts will continue to be exhibited at motor shows around the world, and some may just make that leap from concept to reality.

In the late 1990s, the open-topped Mercedes SLK proved to be a phenomenal success for Mercedes; the natural progression was to produce a smaller convertible based on the A-Class that even more drivers could afford. Sadly, this compact version remained a one-off.

Alfa Romeo Nuvola

The Alfa Romeo Nuvola looks fantastic at first glance, but is quite a fussy design when examined more closely. The front end incorporates all types of fine details, yet still manages to look balanced.

Although the grille clearly identifies the maker of the Nuvola, it is those alloy wheels that offer the strongest clue as to the corporate identity of this vehicle.

There is plenty of leather and aluminium inside the Nuvola, to give the car a luxurious, upmarket feel. It is also modern, although the wood-rimmed steering wheel is somewhat nostalgic in style.

The Nuvola's spaceframe chassis was constructed in such a way that it was possible for virtually any configuration of bodyshell to be fitted onto it – from a convertible to an estate (station wagon).

With a 2.5l V6 engine developing a healthy 224kW (300bhp), the Nuvola was no slouch. With four-wheel drive, the car was capable of sprinting to 96km/h (60mph) in less than five seconds.

With distinct overtones of the BMW Z07 styling exercise that was to become the well-recognized Z8, Alfa Romeo's Nuvola was an odd concept. It was designed and built to celebrate the 1930s, while also offering a strong hint of what the future might bring, and whichever angle it was viewed from, there was something new to see in it.

With a mix of traditional styling themes and radical new ones, the Nuvola was one of those cars that's hard to pigeon-hole. It had the classic Alfa Romeo grille, but also tiny inset headlights that looked as if they came

The quartet of exhaust pipes that can be seen on the rear of the car suggested there was a large-capacity V8 nestling up front, but the Nuvola would have been fitted with nothing bigger than a 3l V6.

from the future – although they had been used on the GTV and Spider from the same manufacturer. The 45.7cm (18in) wheels filled the arches wonderfully and made the car look purposeful, yet it also featured more subtle design details: the small, flush-fitted side repeaters in the front wings were very neat for the mid-1990s, and the flush-fitting rear lights and front indicators gave the car an integrated look.

Such styling cues would become more common on the roads as the decade progressed, helped along by new technology such as light-emitting diodes, which are very bright despite being far more compact than conventional bulbs. Something that was to become less popular, though, was the low rear end seen on the Nuvola – high-tailed wedge shapes were becoming increasingly common, offering better luggage capacity while also improving aerodynamics.

Curvy interior

The interior was just as much of a mix of old and new. There were plenty of curves, and the layout was simple, yet thoroughly modern. Reminiscent of classic Alfas were a wood-rimmed steering wheel and banked instruments in individual nacelles. Everything was

Alfa Romeo Nuvola

Debut:	Paris 1996
Engine capacity:	2492cc (152ci) twin-turbo
Configuration:	Front-mounted V6, petrol
Power:	224kW (300bhp)
Top speed:	267km/h (166mph)
Transmission:	6-speed manual, 4WD
Length:	4286mm (169in)
Width:	1859mm (73in)
Designer:	Walter de Silva

trimmed in soft, hand-stitched leather, and much of the cabin detailing was executed in aluminium, which was either brushed or polished.

The big story where the Nuvola was concerned, however, was not its looks, but the technology that it showcased. The concept was to test the possibility of producing a spaceframe chassis that would become available to coachbuilders to clothe in a variety of bodystyles, namely roadster or coupé bodystyles. (The long bonnet and fixed wheelbase meant other, more roomy bodystyles would not really have been possible.) Although such an idea harked back to the pre-war era, the technology which was used in the Nuvola's chassis construction meant that this spaceframe was anything but archaic – from the materials utilized to the method of production.

Paying homage

Being an Alfa Romeo, the Nuvola also had to be something pretty special to drive – the marque is renowned for the driving experience its cars offer, and this concept could be no different. To that end, there was independent suspension all round with double wishbones. The six-speed manual gearbox transmitted the power to all four wheels, and a twin-turbo 2.5l V6 meant that there was plenty of power on offer. That long bonnet housed a transversely located engine, and this, if given its head, was capable of powering the Nuvola all the way up to a massive 267km/h (166mph), while scorching from 0–96km (0–60mph) in just 4.7 seconds along the way.

To anyone who speaks Italian, the name 'Nuvola' may seem a somewhat odd choice, as the word means 'cloud'. Alfa wanted the car to be a tribute to legendary 1930s racing driver Tazio Nuvolari, but the company was not allowed to call its new concept by either his first name or his last. As a compromise, the name Nuvola was selected, which in itself combines paying homage to a glorious Alfa Romeo of the past while also looking to the future.

In typical Italian fashion, the Nuvola's dashboard was stocked with plenty of gauges, each one set into its own individual nacelle. It was set off beautifully with leather everywhere.

Bertone Birusa

The Bertone Birusa's exterior design initially looks very simple, but there are plenty of clever touches to prevent it from looking bland – look closely, and you will find something new each time.

The Birusa was based on BMW's Z8, complete with its 4l V8 engine that developed 298kW (400bhp). This also meant a six-speed manual gearbox and rear-wheel drive.

Most of the Birusa's roof was made of glass, to give the cabin an unconstricted feel. To keep the occupants comfortable in hot weather, climate control was fitted.

Much of the vehicle's interior was trimmed in Alcantara – an expensive, suedelike material. There was also lots of equipment, much of it controlled by a multilingual voice activation system.

TV cameras in place of external mirrors helped to keep the car's lines very clean. The aluminium flash that swept along the car's flanks housed the door buttons.

The styling house Bertone can always be relied upon to come up with something remarkable for any of the major European motor shows. The Birusa is a case in point. Not only does it look sensational, but it also looks like the sort of car that could actually reach the showroom. Indeed, Bertone claimed that something similar to the Birusa could realistically enter production soon after its introduction at the Geneva motor show in 2003 – although numbers would necessarily be limited as the concept was based on BMW's mega-expensive Z8. Using the Z8's floorpan and mechanicals meant a front-mounted 5.0l V8 engine was part of the package, complete with 298kW (400bhp) channelled through a six-speed manual gearbox to the rear wheels.

The design of the Birusa conveyed energy and aggression, with its smooth, low-slung two-door coupé profile. At the front was a hint of BMW's corporate grille, with inset indicators, while at the rear was a single full-width rear light, which incorporated the tail and brake lights as well as the indicators. As was becoming increasingly common with concept cars of the time, the rearview mirrors were replaced by small cameras mounted in the rear panels of the car – these relayed pictures to a monitor on the dash. An aluminium flash swept along much of the car's profile,

The doors of the Bertone Birusa were somewhere between beetle-wing and gullwing, and when opened they gave the car a striking appearance when viewed head-on.

Although the overall design is very clean and uncluttered, there are actually a lot of details in there: vents, grilles, lights and panel creases. Subtle, but effective.

housing the door push buttons; there were also air vents to allow the engine bay to keep its cool. The gullwing doors were made entirely of carbon fibre, ensuring they were incredibly light, yet at the same time very stiff.

Despite their low weight, the doors were still electrically assisted, and the rear window, which was made of heat-resistant glass, consisted of two panels that slid under the boot (trunk) lid, to open up the cabin like a large sunroof.

Grand tourer

The interior was built for grand touring, although the cradle-style design of the seats was inspired by that of racing cars. A large central tunnel bisected the cabin, and, to help the driver get in and out, the seat slid backwards when the door was opened, so that the steering wheel did not get in the way. The Birusa was developed in conjunction with Trend & Design, the newly founded styling division of Alcantara SpA, so there were plenty of surfaces trimmed in suedelike Alcantara. To keep the cabin cool, climate control was fitted, and the interior was guaranteed to seem light and airy at all times, thanks to a roof made of laminated safety glass – which also filtered out the sun's UV rays.

Operating the glass roof, and a multitude of other functions, was a voice-activated control system. This responded only to registered users, so unauthorized

users were unable to activate any of the on-board systems. Developed by Loquendo VoxDrive, the technology was called the Loquendo Automatic Speech Recognition System; it was multilingual and featured a safety net that ensured nothing was activated without the operator first confirming that it should be activated.

Bose was also involved in the construction of the Birusa's interior, with the fitment of two bass modules and 11 speakers throughout the cabin, to offer a powerful, focused sound.

Transportation module

So far, so predictable, but the Birusa also featured something never offered before – the facility to carry a Segway Human Transporter. These are two-wheeled, short-range transportation modules controlled by gyroscopes, and their wheels are set either side of each other, rather than in tandem. Not content just to provide a space in the boot for the Segway, Bertone worked in conjunction with Segway to produce an example of the Transporter that mirrored the Birusa. Hence it was fitted with a Bose sound system, plenty of Alcantara and a navigation unit. Funny how the concept has never caught on …

And if you are wondering why the name 'Birusa' was chosen – it comes from the Piedmontese word 'biross', a brilliant, extremely resourceful person.

Bertone Birusa	
Debut:	Geneva 2003
Engine capacity:	4941cc (302ci)
Configuration:	Front-mounted V8, petrol
Power:	298kW (400bhp)
Top speed:	N/A
Transmission:	6-speed manual, RWD
Length:	4400mm (173in)
Width:	1900mm (75in)
Designer:	N/A

Bertone Zabrus

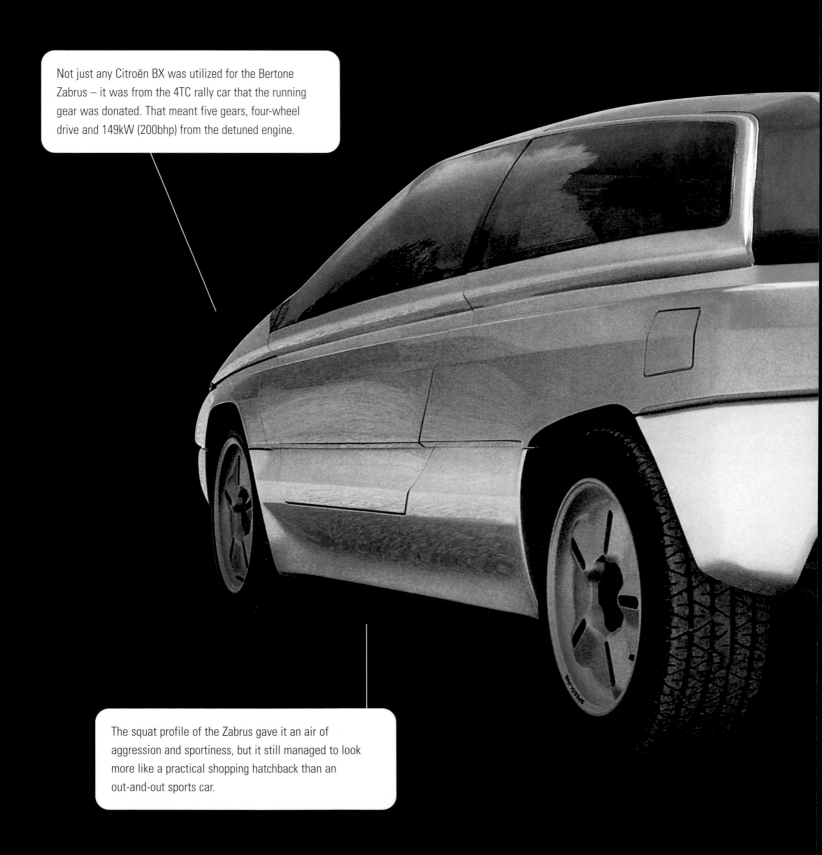

Not just any Citroën BX was utilized for the Bertone Zabrus – it was from the 4TC rally car that the running gear was donated. That meant five gears, four-wheel drive and 149kW (200bhp) from the detuned engine.

The squat profile of the Zabrus gave it an air of aggression and sportiness, but it still managed to look more like a practical shopping hatchback than an out-and-out sports car.

The cabin was designed for comfort and safety. The front seats swivelled for easy entry and exit, and adjusted automatically to allow the driver optimum visibility.

Bertone argued that a car's interior should be like that of a house – ornate rather than bland. For that reason, a mosaic was incorporated within the car's headlining.

It was easy to see that the Zabrus was based on the Citroën BX. Those angular lines made the car look like a three-door estate (station wagon) version of the Bertone-designed hatchback.

While it is true that the planes and angles of Zabrus gave it a very 1980s look, it does show what might have been. This is the car that could have been a sporting Citroën BX–based estate.

Take away the badges and you would have no trouble guessing which manufacturer supplied the car that provided the basis for Bertone's Zabrus. The boxy, angular shape was heavily inspired by the Bertone-designed Citroën BX upon which this 1986 concept was based. Nor was it any old BX. Rather, the floorpan and drivetrain were that of the BX 4TC, which was Citroën's Group B contender for the World Rally Championship.

Whereas some Group B cars – such as the Ford RS200, MG Metro 6R4 and Peugeot 205T16 – have passed into legend, the Citroën is largely forgotten. But, like its rivals, the BX 4TC was potentially hugely powerful, featured four-wheel drive to get the power down and was packed with hi-tech gadgetry to keep everything working while being thrashed along a badly surfaced rally stage at high speed. In the rally car the turbocharged 2141cc (131ci), in-line, four-cylinder powerplant provided a storming 283kW (380bhp) or so, helped along the way by fuel injection and an intercooler. But Bertone did not want such a highly stressed engine in the Zabrus, so the unit was de-tuned to around 150kW (200bhp) to make it more driveable, with the power being transmitted to all the wheels via a five-speed manual gearbox.

Comfortable cruiser

Despite such rugged underpinnings, the Zabrus was not intended to be anything more than a sure-footed, civilized, high-speed luxury cruiser. It used the concept of a relatively compact three-door sporting estate, in the mould of the Reliant Scimitar – or the

more recent Volvo 480ES – which meant plenty of style and a healthy dose of practicality. To that end, there was a split folding tailgate to get into the load bay while the doors opened scissor-style – hardly the most practical or durable configuration, but essential for attracting attention on the Bertone stand when the car was exhibited.

Comfort and safety were also high on the list of priorities, with a clever system of infrared cells built into the interior of the Zabrus. These measured where the driver's eyes were and adjusted the seat accordingly – something which the Volvo Safety Concept Car would do, in a rather more complex way, more than a decade later. The front seats were able to swivel to become rear-facing, although the aim of this facility was really to ensure easier entry and exit by turning the seats to face the doors.

The Zabrus's interior was designed to be as usable as possible, with all the instruments grouped together

Bertone Zabrus	
Debut:	Turin 1986
Engine capacity:	2141cc (131ci), turbocharged
Configuration:	Front-mounted in-line four, petrol
Power:	150kW (200bhp)
Top speed:	222km/h (138mph)
Transmission:	5-speed manual, 4WD
Length:	4300mm (169in)
Width:	1880mm (74in)
Designer:	N/A

as far forward and high up as possible so that the driver did not have to take his or her eyes far from the road ahead. Meanwhile, all the switchgear and other controls were clustered together within easy reach, on a special console. So much instrumentation meant that it had to be split into three sets of displays, with each cluster focusing on one type of information. Closest to the driver was everything relating to the speed, engine revs, trip mileage and other such functions. In the centre was everything which related to mechanical and signalling functions, while furthest away were all the navigational aids.

The Zabrus's beetle-wing doors were an unusual feature, although they have since become popular among a number of models. Bertone, however, had utilized them more than a decade earlier, on the Lamborghini Countach.

Cutting-edge technology

With compact disc technology in its infancy, it was only right that the Zabrus should feature an in-car CD player, appropriately enough engineered by Pioneer. The CD player could also act as a satellite-navigation

tool – something which would eventually become commonplace, but which in 1986 was in the realms of pure fantasy. Another extraordinary feature was the headlining, which was a leather mosaic. Bertone argued that pictures adorn the walls of any home, so why should the Zabrus not follow suit? After all, a car can be seen an extension of a person just as much as their home. Funny how that one failed to catch on – nor did the Kangaroo-finish leather which was used for the rest of the cabin …

With the Zabrus, there were as many straight lines on the inside as there were on the outside. This is the aspect of the car that has dated the most quickly, but in 1986 it was considered cutting-edge stuff.

BMW xCoupé

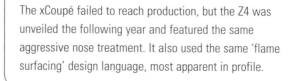

The xCoupé failed to reach production, but the Z4 was unveiled the following year and featured the same aggressive nose treatment. It also used the same 'flame surfacing' design language, most apparent in profile.

BMW's xCoupé's headlights swivelled with the front wheels to light the car's way – but instead of a link to the steering system, it was all controlled by GPS.

Four-wheel drive and a 3l, straight-six, diesel engine were borrowed from the BMW X5. That gave the vehicle strong performance and astonishing fuel economy for the class of car it was.

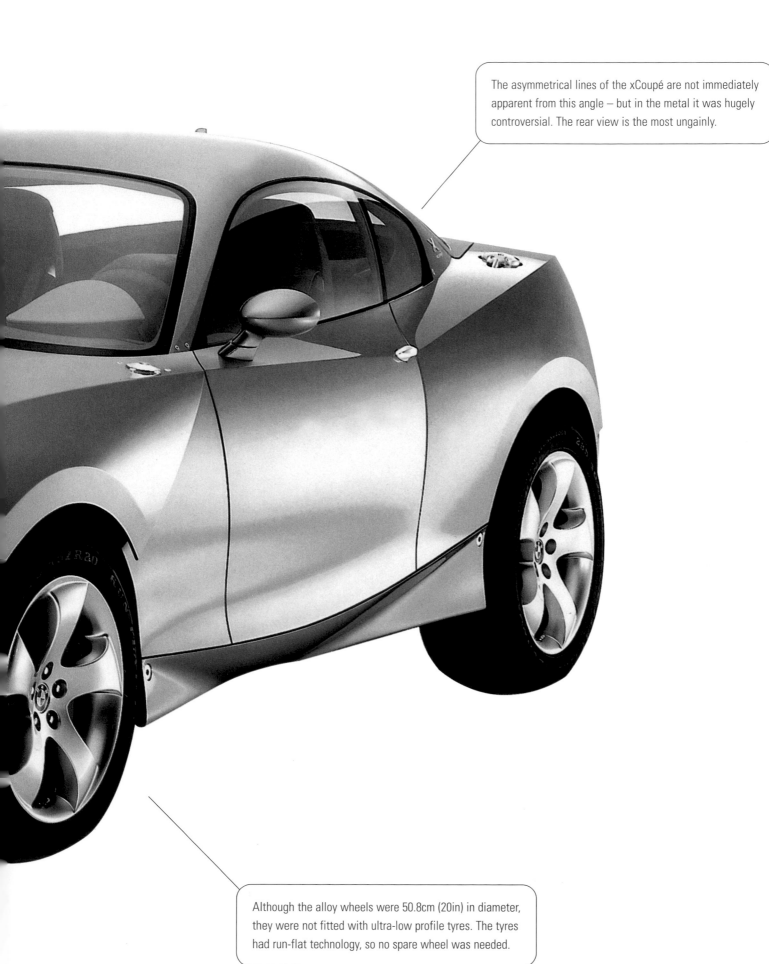

The asymmetrical lines of the xCoupé are not immediately apparent from this angle — but in the metal it was hugely controversial. The rear view is the most ungainly.

Although the alloy wheels were 50.8cm (20in) in diameter, they were not fitted with ultra-low profile tyres. The tyres had run-flat technology, so no spare wheel was needed.

When the xCoupé was first seen at the 2001 Detroit motor show, the general consensus was that BMW had lost the plot. The company was renowned for good-looking cars which were understated and elegant, and the xCoupé was anything but. The culprit was the 'flame surfacing' so beloved of BMW design chief Chris Bangle – and few others. Also, the lines were so disjointed that some reckoned the car looked as if it had been in an accident. Nor did it help that the near side of the xCoupé was different from the offside, with a full-width door on the passenger side to help with entry and exit to the rear seats, but a much shorter door fitted on the driver's side.

There were several classic BMW styling cues in evidence, the most noticeable being the double-kidney grille. But whereas this item was usually understated on models, the xCoupé's featured a startling perforated aluminium finish. The 'hockey stick' C-pillar that has long been a BMW trademark was still there – but only

BMW xCoupé	
Debut:	Detroit 2001
Engine capacity:	2926cc (179ci) turbocharged
Configuration:	Front-mounted in-line six, diesel
Power:	137kW (184bhp)
Top speed:	201km/h (125mph)
Transmission:	5-speed auto, 4WD
Length:	N/A
Width:	N/A
Designer:	Chris Bangle

Gauges mounted in the leading edge of the front door trim were not unprecedented, but they were an unusual idea. The dash was otherwise very simply laid out.

on the driver's side – and the asymmetrical styling meant that the rear end was rather less even than it first appeared. The boot (trunk) lid was rear-hinged and, when opened, took the rear wing with it on the nearside, but on the offside the rear wing remained in place. Such a strange arrangement meant the rear lights

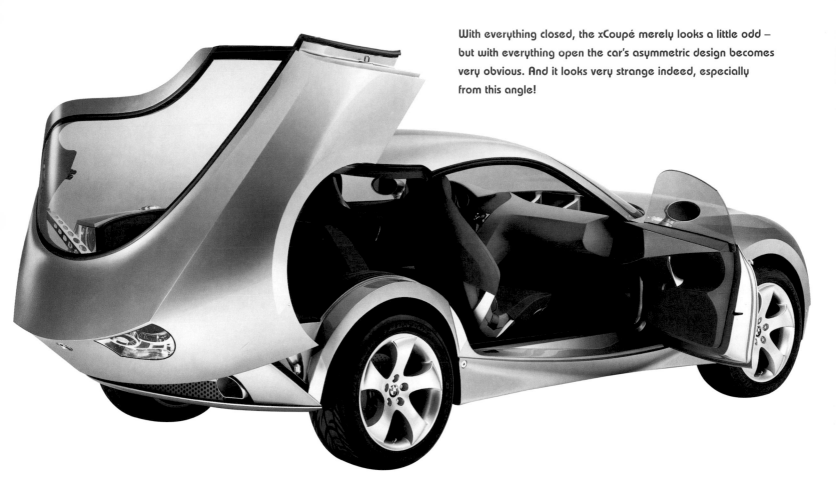

had to be different from each other, but according to BMW, 'Mild asymmetry is more pleasant than stringent mathematical symmetry.' Few observers agreed.

Radical interior

Under the skin, the BMW xCoupé proved equally radical. Instead of a rear-wheel drive layout with a powerful petrol engine at the front, there was a four-wheel drive system taken from the X5 and the six-cylinder diesel powerplant taken from the 330d. Lightweight aluminium bodywork meant the xCoupé was able to make the most of the 137kW (184bhp) and 46kg-m (332lb-ft) of torque on offer, and BMW claimed that the car was theoretically capable of 201km/h (125mph) and a 0–96km/h (0–60mph) time of around 7.5 seconds.

And although Tarmac looked like the natural home for the xCoupé, BMW asserted that the car was able to go off-roading without coming unstuck, despite having no more ground clearance than is found on any other sporting coupé. That said, the fitment of traction control and hill descent control does not an off-roader make, so it is probably just as well that such a test was never performed.

Other highlights to be featured on the show car included 50.8cm (20in) alloy wheels, which were not fitted with the usual rubber-band tyres normally found on show stars. Instead, 255/50 rubber was fitted at the front, which was relatively high profile for a concept of the twenty-first century, and at the rear were 285/45 tyres. The inclusion of run-flat technology meant that a spare wheel need not be housed.

The five-speed Steptronic transmission was something carried over from BMW's production cars, complete with steering wheel-mounted paddle shift to put some of the fun back into the driving experience.

High technology

Helping to keep the car on the road was a rear spoiler, which popped up at anything over 109km/h (68mph), and another innovation was headlights which turned with the front wheels – although the system relied on nothing so prosaic as sensors or hydraulics. Instead, the whole set-up was controlled by GPS, which could read the road ahead before the car had even got there. BMW declared that the xCoupé would go into production only if enough interest were shown.

This had also been true of the BMW Z1. Unlike the xCoupé, however, that possessed the advantage of being a good-looking car. Still, the concept did have some sort of an afterlife: when the Z4 was revealed the following year, its front end was very similar to the one seen on the xCoupé. Thankfully, the similarities did not go much further than that.

BMW Z9

The BMW Z9 aimed to dispel a few myths about sports cars, one particular one being the notion that petrol power was the only possible form of motive power; the Z9 used diesel instead.

The arrival of the BMW Z9 brought with it a new nose treatment that would subsequently be used on production cars. At first few observers liked it; however, today it has become more accepted.

The BMW Z9 was heavily criticized for its over-fussy styling – all those curves, scallops and swage lines made it look very untidy to the purist, particularly those who were expecting BMW's usual classic lines.

Although the BMW Z9 certainly introduced the world to a new way of thinking about BMW, there were still some familiar styling cues to be found, such as the kinked C-pillar and prominent swage line.

The BMW Z9 bucked the trend in many ways, overturning the popular misconception that grand touring-style vehicles have to be very heavy; aluminium and carbon fibre were used to keep the car's weight down.

At first glance, the BMW Z9 concept may look like the work of BMW head of design Chris Bangle: it is not especially easy on the eye, and it certainly needs time to grow on you. Yet it was not the controversial Bangle who penned the car, but Adrian van Hooydonk, one of BMW's in-house designers.

The Z9 Gran Turismo burst onto the scene at the 1999 Frankfurt motor show, and it was one of the first BMW cars to replace the customary elegant and graceful look for something far more controversial. With an aggressive nose that offered a total rethink of the BMW corporate grille, there were also sculpted headlights and a particularly deep air dam that gave the car a distinct air of sportiness. Minimal ground clearance reinforced that sporty feel, as did beefy, seven-spoke, deeply dished, alloy wheels, which were shod in ultra-low profile tyres. At the front, the wheels were 50.8cm (20in) in diameter (with 245/45 rubber), while at the back they were 53.3cm (21in) and shod with 285/45 tyres. The wheelarches were heavily flared to house those huge wheels, and were also sharply tapered at the front. In true BMW fashion, a prominent swage line ran the length of the car's flanks,

Perhaps the most challenging view of BMW's Z9 was its rear end, thanks to the boot (trunk) lid that looked as though it were made for a completely different type of car.

and the classic kinked C-pillar was also in evidence. Rather less predictable was the door arrangement, which allowed for either side to be opened conventionally or in gullwing fashion. By locking the window frame in place, the door could be opened by its hinges along the top; if the frame was left unlocked, it was possible to use the hinges along the front. The former mode offered much better access to the rear seats, while the latter arrangement was best if the car was being used as a two-seater.

Keeping the car's weight down was an aluminium spaceframe, around which was wrapped a bodyshell made of aluminium and carbon fibre. That not only helped to keep emissions down (while at the same time increasing fuel economy), but helped to make the car more agile as well. And BMW claimed that this method of construction also offered major cost advantages over a conventional monocoque, considering the relatively small numbers in which the car would be built if it were ever offered for sale.

Under the hood

Powering the Z9 was the 3.9l, V8 turbodiesel normally found in the production 740d. With common rail fuel injection and 32 valves, this unit offered as much efficiency and cleanliness as it was possible to get in a production oil-burning engine, and it was also one

The car's simple interior featured BMW's I-Drive system to control many of the major functions. Gears were changed by a simple steering column–mounted lever.

of the few truly large diesel-powered units available anywhere. Generating 180kW (241bhp), it also made available a monster 57kg-m (413lb-ft) of torque, all of which was transmitted to the rear wheels via a five-speed automatic transmission. Instead of a conventional gearstick, the ratios were changed (when not in fully automatic mode) by the use of a lever on the steering column, which worked in much the same way as the SMG (Sequential Manual Gearshift) system that had been introduced on the BMW M3 soon before.

Inside, there were plenty of hard edges, rather than flowing curves, which was not especially elegant. Instrumentation was kept to a minimum, while in the centre of the fascia was a 22.8cm (9in) screen, which displayed the satellite navigation, climate control and stereo information.

More than four years after the Z9 Gran Turismo had been shown, BMW showed the first pictures of its all-new 6-Series coupé. As had become customary with

BMW and its show cars, it became evident that the new production car incorporated many of the fundamental design themes of the earlier concept. The Z9 may have been difficult to understand, but it was not emasculated in the transition to the showroom. Whether or not that is a good thing is open to debate!

BMW Z9

Debut:	Frankfurt 1999
Engine capacity:	3901cc (238ci), turbocharged
Configuration:	Front-mounted, V8, diesel
Power:	180kW (241bhp)
Top speed:	155 (limited)
Transmission:	5-speed semi-auto, 4WD
Length:	4840mm (190.5in)
Width:	1950mm (76.8in)
Designer:	Adrian van Hooydonk

Cadillac Evoq

The Evoq was part of the Cadillac renaissance – not only did it look incredibly sharp, but it went beyond concept stage as well and entered production virtually unchanged on the outside.

As all good American cars should, the Evoq packed a V8 engine. Displacing 4.2l (256ci) was a healthy 302kW (405bhp) – enough to propel it to 96km/h (60mph) in just 4.5 seconds.

Plenty of state-of-the-art technology was to be found inside the Evoq, including a head-up display and a comprehensive multimedia system that offered concert-hall clarity when listening to music.

It may look like a coupé, but the Evoq was actually a convertible, with a folding metal hard top. Although that did increase the car's refinement and security, it also compromised the overall package.

As if the Evoq's front wheels were not big enough at 48.2cm (19in) in diameter, the rear ones were a massive 53.3cm (21in) across. And all four were wrapped in Michelin PAX run-flat tyres.

Cadillac built some of the most over-the-top cars of the twentieth century, but as a new millennium was dawning, the company had a reputation for building overweight cars for retired bank managers – fine if all you wanted was comfort, but drivers looking for anything else simply ignored them. What Cadillac needed was something to appeal to younger buyers, who would then get hooked on the marque much earlier in their lives, and keep on buying. The answer was to inject a bit of excitement into the brand – something that drove as well as it looked, with razor-sharp lines and slingshot performance.

That was where the Evoq came in – a roadster blending a seriously wedgy profile with sharp-edged styling and a drop-dead drop-top body style. However, displaying a concept and hoping its lines would be enough to get people into the showrooms to buy the latest Eldorado were obviously a waste of time – what was needed were promises that such stunning concepts would make it into the showrooms, and fast. So when it was first shown at the 1999 Detroit motor show the word was that the Evoq would be in the showrooms by 2002. The date was not met, but at least the basic promise was kept because, by 2003, the production version of the Evoq was unveiled, as the XLR. And even better, its lines had barely changed in the translation.

The Evoq's profile was especially eye-catching thanks to the ultra-low profile tyres fitted: at the front were 48.2cm (19in) wheels; at the back, these were a

The Evoq was a new design departure for this traditional car manufacturer. Curves were out when Cadillac devised its new look for the twenty-first century. Instead there were sharp edges and plenty of straight lines that gave its cars amazing presence.

monstrous 53.3cm (21in); and at each corner, there was a Michelin Pax run-flat tyre so that a spare wheel did not need to be carried. The car's looks were also helped by the clean, uncluttered design whether the roof was up or down – and to keep it all contemporary, a folding hard top was used. Ultra-slim neon rear lights contributed greatly to these clean lines, without having to sacrifice brightness.

Cadillac Evoq	
Debut:	Detroit 1999
Engine capacity:	4228cc (258ci)
Configuration:	Front-mounted V8, petrol
Power:	302kW (405bhp)
Top speed:	249km/h (55mph)
Transmission:	4-speed automatic, RWD
Length:	4282mm (169in)
Width:	1834mm (72in)
Designer:	Kip Wasenko

Following the US maxim of there being no substitute for cubic inches, the Evoq had a V8 delivering 302kW (405bhp). Aided by a supercharger, it was able to dash from a standing start to 96km/h (60mph) in just 4.5 seconds and 249km/h (155mph) was possible – although the straight-line performance was only the start. Cadillac's reputation for stodgy handling meant that the company also made sure the car was fun to drive, fitting double-wishbone suspension at the front and a multi-link rear axle, both of which were derived from the standard production Corvette.

Thermal imaging

Although the running gear was (at least on paper) nothing revolutionary, there were plenty of new technologies on show. The most important was the Night Vision system, which used thermal imaging to warn the driver of anything potentially dangerous in the road, in the area ahead of the car's headlights. Anything that could cause problems was shown on a head-up display, which Cadillac called the 'EyeCue', and the Evoq also introduced the Communiport, a new

multimedia communication and entertainment system. This latter function was helped by a 425-watt Bose stereo, which was capable of concert-quality sound whether the roof was stowed or raised, while the instrumentation was of the cathode-ray tube type for incredible clarity. Even the Evoq's paint scheme was something a bit different, with the all-steel bodyshell being painted Argentanium. This was a pearlescent-effect pewter colour, which varied in hue depending on the intensity and angle of the lighting.

The windows were also bronze-tinted to blend the glass area with the rest of the bodywork, and to keep the car's lines as clean as possible there were no rear-view mirrors. Instead, there were small pop-up cameras which sprouted from the doors when the ignition was activated, and complementing these were parking sensors in the rear bumper to ensure reversing collisions were minimized.

The Evoq's straight lines continued on the inside, along with lots of leather to give the cabin a luxurious feel. Aluminium trim brought the car right up to date.

Fioravanti Vola

Under that low bonnet line was the glorious 3l V6 that was seen throughout the Alfa Romeo range. With 163kw (218bhp) on tap, this powerplant offered strong performance and a fantastic noise.

Its V-shaped grille and heavily tapered nose made the Fioravanti Vola reminiscent of the car on which it was based – the Alfa Romeo GTV.

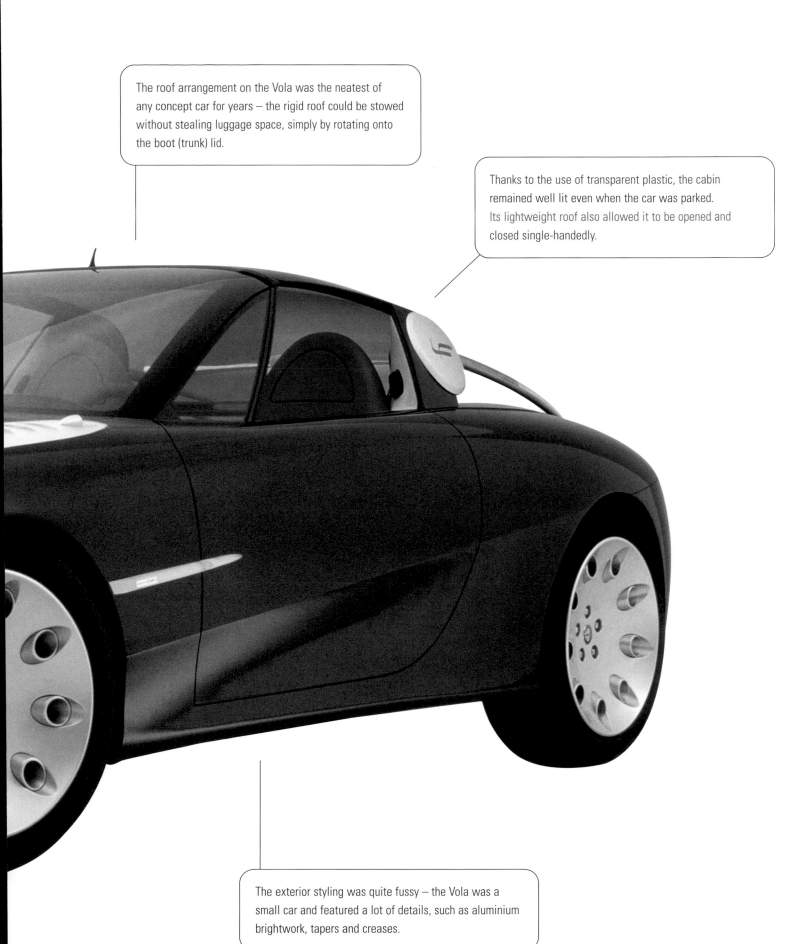

The roof arrangement on the Vola was the neatest of any concept car for years – the rigid roof could be stowed without stealing luggage space, simply by rotating onto the boot (trunk) lid.

Thanks to the use of transparent plastic, the cabin remained well lit even when the car was parked. Its lightweight roof also allowed it to be opened and closed single-handedly.

The exterior styling was quite fussy – the Vola was a small car and featured a lot of details, such as aluminium brightwork, tapers and creases.

You could hardly accuse Alfa Romeo of producing a derivative design for its GTV and Spider, but when those cars were lined up alongside the Fioravanti Vola, they suddenly seemed anything but adventurous. And while the Vola was not actually an Alfa Romeo, it was the Fioravanti design house's vision of what a sporting Alfa Romeo of the future could look like. That is why the traditional Alfa Romeo grille was incorporated into the Vola's nose and also why the overall lines were reminiscent of the GTV.

But it was not the basic silhouette that was important as far as the Vola was concerned – it was the rather

The folding roof of the Vola was simplicity itself – it simply turned through 180° to convert from a closed coupé to an open targa, without the usual roof storage problems.

neat roof design with which Fioravanti broke new ground. The problem that Fioravanti was trying to overcome was how to build an open-topped sports car without the inherent shortcomings so typical of the genre. By using a fabric roof, the packaging would be neat and tidy whether the roof was up or down, but this offered little security, and too much wind noise at speed when the roof was raised.

The arrival of the Mercedes SLK in 1993 had started a new way of thinking; however, there were serious shortcomings with the packaging of a folding metal roof. While it may have offered security and refinement when raised, the stowage of such a roof caused major problems when it came to the provision of luggage space. To overcome all these issues, Fioravanti wanted to come up with something completely different.

Pivotal point

Bearing in mind that the brief was to come up with a roof that offered security and low noise levels when in place, but which did not affect boot (trunk) space (particularly when it was stowed), something pretty radical was called for – or perhaps something very simple. After all, it is often the simple solutions which

Fioravanti Vola

Debut:	Geneva 2001
Engine capacity:	2959cc (181ci)
Configuration:	Front-mounted V6, petrol
Power:	163kW (218bhp)
Top speed:	N/A
Transmission:	N/A
Length:	4160mm (164in)
Width:	1810mm (71in)
Designer:	N/A

are the neatest. And the solution that was utilized in the Vola was certainly simple because it was nothing more than a revolving roof panel which pivoted around the top of the rear window.

When closed, the roof was secured along the top of the windscreen header rail. As it was not actually removable, there was no need to engineer any catches along the back of the panel. Nor was there any need to find anywhere to stow the roof when open-topped driving was required. Opening up the Vola's interior meant simply releasing the roof panel at the front, turning it through 180° and clipping it into place along the top of the luggage bay.

The roof itself was supported by a carbon-fibre frame, so only one person was needed to transform the Vola from closed coupé into open-topped sportster. Even when the roof was closed, the cabin remained light and airy thanks to the panel being made of

Devoid of unnecessary decoration, the Vola's cabin was trimmed in two-tone leather and featured a wide central console. The F symbol in the roundel behind the door is Fioravanti's logo.

transparent plastic – a material that did not protect against ultraviolet rays. But perhaps the most ingenious thing about the Vola's roof arrangement was its very simplicity. Indeed, so simple was it that automating it required none of the hydraulics that are so common in – and which weigh down – most production cars featuring powered folding roofs.

Uncluttered cabin

Inside the Vola, things were equally simple, despite the fact that all the gadgets expected in a modern sports car were fitted. Satellite navigation was joined by climate control, a telephone and a powerful stereo – and everything was nicely integrated into the centre console so that it looked particularly uncluttered. The outside was kept simple, too, with long, slender headlights, behind which were the louvres to let hot air out of the engine bay.

Although the Vola was in the end a non-runner, the assumption was that it would be fitted with a 3.0l Alfa Romeo V6, as fitted to the GTV and Spider. That would have been quite a car.

Jaguar F-type

Despite the F-type looking as though it were fitted with a massive and hugely powerful engine, it actually housed just a 3l V6, rated at 179kW (240bhp).

The oval grille and those faired-in headlights were inspired by the very first E-types. The same went for the muscular haunches over the rear wheels.

The showcar F-type featured no form of weather protection at all – making a tonneau would have been easy enough, but engineering a full roof would have meant spoiling the car's lines.

The F-type's interior was as simple as the exterior, but that did not mean it looked cheap. Rather, there was plenty of aluminium trim, machined from solid billets and then polished to the highest standards.

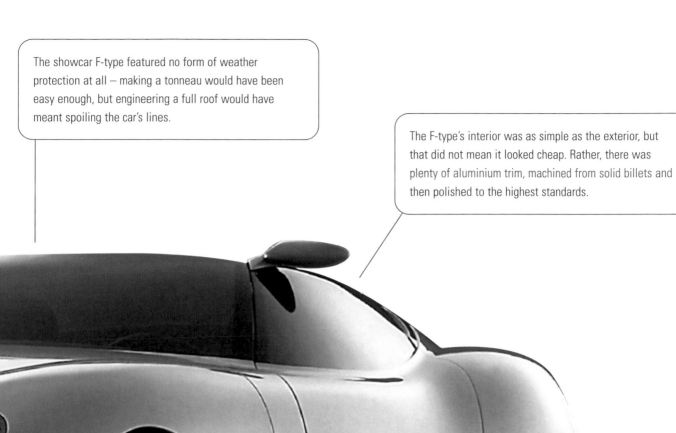

Using all the classic Jaguar styling cues, the F-type was just as curvaceous and inviting as the E-type which had been launched nearly 40 years before it.

When it comes to seminal sports cars, there can be none more iconic than the Jaguar E-type, first seen in 1961 and now one of the world's most recognizable automotive shapes. But where do you go from there? Do you try to cash in on such a revered car or do you attempt to move on by barely acknowledging it? If you are in any doubt, look at the F-type's name to get the answer – although it has to be admitted that the concept owed more to the XK8 then in production, and rather less to the E-type, which had bowed out more than two decades before the F-type's debut at the 2000 Detroit motor show.

A lightweight cat

The F-type was a development of the XK180 concept shown a year before. But whereas the XK8, and Jaguars in general, had become rather portly thanks to somewhat generous dimensions, the F-type intended to reverse the trend. The F-type began life as a project overseen by Jaguar's head of design Geoff Lawson. However, he died suddenly in June 1999, and Keith Helfet became the design project leader. The result of his team's efforts was one of the most beautiful and curvaceous concepts ever seen.

The reasoning behind the F-type was that it should provide a British competitor to the Porsche Boxster,

Jaguar F-type	
Debut:	Detroit 2000
Engine capacity:	2967cc (181ci)
Configuration:	Front-engined V6, petrol
Power:	179kW (240bhp)
Top speed:	N/A
Transmission:	5-speed auto, RWD
Length:	4115mm (162in)
Width:	1732mm (68in)
Designer:	Keith Helfet

Mercedes SLK, BMW Z3 and Audi TT Roadster – a market then worth 150,000 cars annually. Although any production model would have to be eminently practical, the show car did not need to worry about such boring details, which is why there was no weather protection of any kind. There was also no engine or running gear for the show car, but it was envisaged that a 2.5l or 3.0l V6, as seen in the X-type, would fit the bill nicely. In standard form, this would produce in the order of 179kW (240bhp), but the

The F-type had a lot to live up to, having been created in the shadow of the E-type. It was every bit as beautiful, but Jaguar did not have the money to develop it into a production car.

The dash of the F-type was as retro as the exterior, with individual dials set into an alloy dash. It was all set off beautifully by black leather on just about every surface.

addition of a supercharger would mean that a very healthy 224kW (300bhp) could easily be realized. Manual or automatic gearboxes would be available with rear-wheel drive being standard – although four-wheel drive would probably have been an option on the more powerful models.

Clean lines

The F-type was to be a sports car capable of high speeds, so it is surprising that there were no skirts, spoilers or other aerodynamic distractions on the bodywork. Whether or not the car would have proved stable at high speed with such smooth lines is not known, but the diffuser at the back of the car combined with a smooth underbody should have done their bit to maintain stability as the speed built. At the front was a very subtle adjustable air dam, which would be lowered automatically at high speed to reduce lift. But despite the best efforts of the design team, there would still have been major problems with turbulence over the car's occupants as speeds rose because of the total absence of any kind of roof.

Inside the F-type was a simple but hi-tech approach, most of the work being done by Adam Hatton and Pasi Pennanen. Aluminium abounded, with much of it machined from solid, then polished to perfection – virtually all of the switchgear was made from solid pieces of alloy to give a beautifully engineered, tactile quality. There were lightweight accents running across the dashboard, steering wheel, pedals, door panels, the seats and even the floor.

In the end, the F-type's chances of making it into production were scuppered by the need for a bespoke platform if it were to retain its compact dimensions. Engineering a floorpan just for the one model would have been prohibitively expensive, and there was no way Jaguar would have got its money back from such a move. By basing the car on an existing platform, it would have become a quite different car – and when Porsche tried to do that with its 911-based Boxster, something was lost between the concept and production stages. Jaguar was keen to avoid that trap.

Mercedes-Benz F300 Lifejet

The F300 was essentially a three-wheeled motorbike, with two seats set in tandem. But it drove much more like a conventional four-wheeled car, and was safer than a typical motorbike.

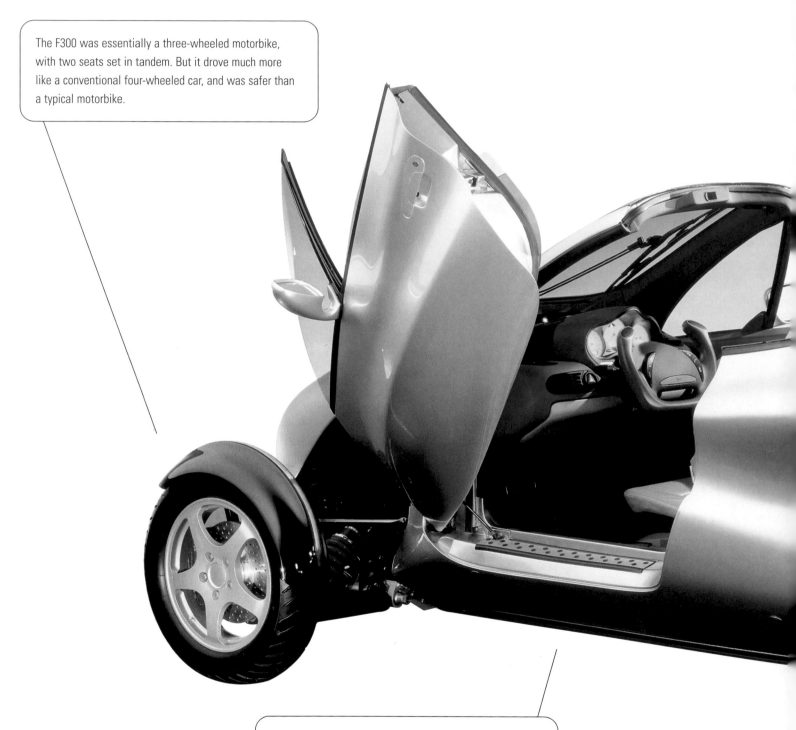

To help make the footwells less cramped, there were only two pedals, as a five-speed automatic/sequential manual transmission was fitted. This allowed ratios to be changed remarkably quickly.

The engine was borrowed from the Mercedes-Benz A-Class, in 1.6l form. That gave 76kw (102bhp), which was enough to achieve 212km/h (132mph) and a 0–100km/h (0–62mph) time of less than eight seconds.

For a company that was renowned for its conservative image, Mercedes pulled out all the stops with the F300 to produce a design as gloriously irrelevant as possible.

Active Tilt Control was fitted, which meant hydraulically controlled suspension. That allowed the car to be preprogrammed to react in a variety of ways to braking and steering inputs.

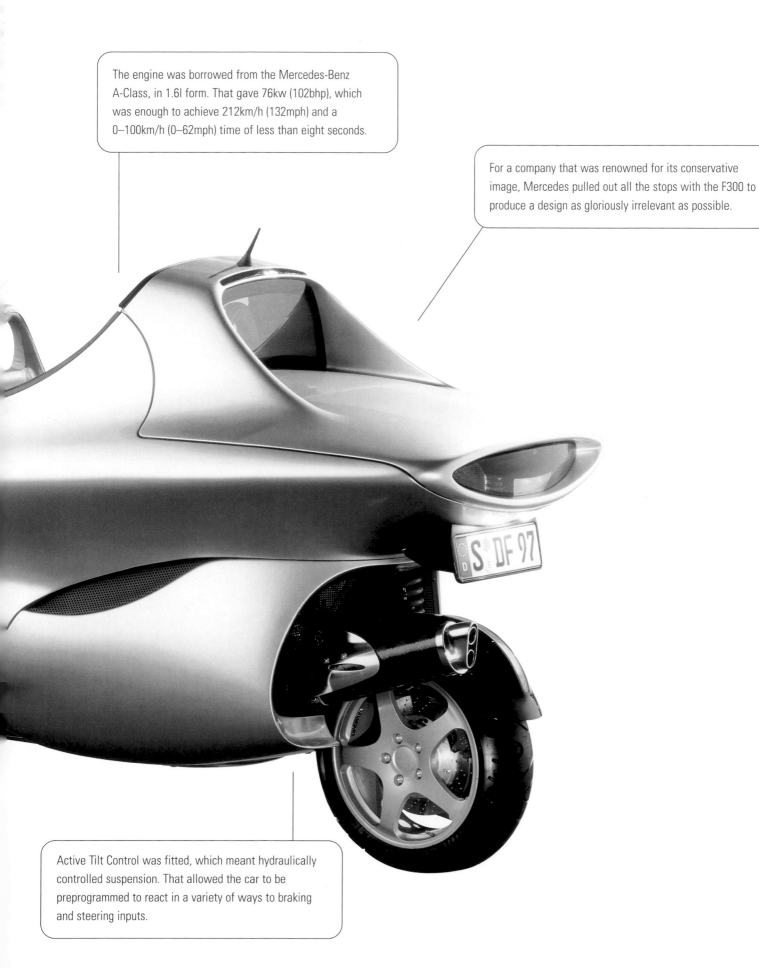

The F300 was supposed to feel like a motorbike to drive, while offering higher levels of practicality and safety. To a car driver, the tilting sensation felt most odd.

When Mercedes-Benz launched its F300 Life-Jet at the 1997 motor show, everybody laughed: there was no way anybody would ever build a car anything like this one because it was just too wacky. Looking like a cross between a motorbike and a car, the three-wheeled contraption featured a narrow body that leaned as the car turned a corner. But fast forward to 2003 and just such a car has made production – a Dutch vehicle called the Vandenbrink Carver.

Such a concept was unusually lighthearted for a company as serious as Mercedes, which is better known for testing ideas to make cars safer, more comfortable or more economical. The F300 was about none of those things. Instead, it was about having fun in a way that was impossible in anything else.

Although the F300 was just a two-seater with a narrow bodyshell featuring seats set in tandem, it was nonetheless actually quite a large car. The F300 was bigger than an A-class, the 1800l engine and

transmission of which it borrowed. But with a weight of 800kg (1764lb) – which was pretty heavy for what it was – the F300 could easily beat the A-class when it came to performance. It could sprint from a standing start to 100km/h (62mph) in less than eight seconds and was capable of more than 209km/h (130mph) – perhaps not as fast as a motorbike, but definitely safer.

Car or motorbike?

To keep with the motorbike theme, the F300 was fitted with a body which was normally open to the elements. But for those inclement moments, there was always the option of a fitted hard top, which was a less neat solution than a well-engineered folding roof. The interior should perhaps have featured a motorbike-style twist grip, but the controls to drive the F300 were the same as on any conventional car, including what was closer to being a steering wheel than handlebars. The transmission was a five-speed sequential manual that allowed ultra-fast gearchanges and did away with the need for a manually operated clutch – such transmissions were just starting to become commonplace as the F300 was being shown.

Something that was unlikely to have made it into production, even if the car had got that far, was the single headlight. To make it as effective as a conventional twin-headlight system, there were three reflector zones and two bulbs – and just in case this was not enough, there was an extra lamp built in, which would illuminate if the car was leaning too heavily into a corner.

Above everything else, it was this tilt mechanism which allowed the F300 to defy convention the most comprehensively. Whereas a motorcycle rider would be used to leaning into a bend, the F300's electronics and hydraulics allowed it to lean out of the bend. Anyone who drove it agreed that such a situation was bizarre in the extreme, and also complicated, as drivers had difficulty judging when the limits of adhesion were being reached because there was no communication of what the wheels were doing. Everything was controlled by a system called Active Tilt Control, which consisted of a series of sensors that could detect all the car's angles. And by controlling everything via a series of hydraulic rams, it was possible to engineer the F300 to react in just about any way imaginable to steering and braking inputs.

A high-quality interior aimed to offer the refinement levels of a luxury car, although the agility of the F300 was intended to be more typical of a two-wheeled vehicle.

Mercedes-Benz F300 Lifejet	
Debut:	Frankfurt 1997
Engine capacity:	1598cc (98ci)
Configuration:	Rear-mounted, in-line four, petrol
Power:	76kW (102bhp)
Top speed:	212km/h (132mph)
Transmission:	5-speed sequential manual
Length:	3954mm (156in)
Width:	1730mm (68in)
Designer:	N/A

To help make the F300 as manouevrable as possible, the vehicle's weight was kept to a minimum. The dual-wishbone front axle was made of plastic reinforced with carbon fibre while the chassis was built of aluminium and weighed just 89kg (196lb). Such a move ensured that fuel consumption was minimal while performance was optimized – but, of course, Mercedes would never even consider series production for something as bizarre as the F300 Lifejet. In the end, it was just too much fun for a company as conservative as Mercedes.

Peugeot RC

Of the two engines, the diesel promised the better drive because of its superior torque. The turbocharged 2.2l 'four' gave 41kg-m (295lb-ft) – or nearly double what the petrol engine gave.

The front end featured typical Peugeot styling cues, most notably those teardrop-shaped headlights. More unusual were the heavily kinked A-pillars, which were there to help with front three-quarter visibility.

The interiors of both cars featured red and black leather, with lots of aluminium and stainless steel highlights all round to bring it to life.

Despite the powerplants being mid-mounted, both of the concepts were four-seaters. But there was little room for the poor passengers relegated to the back seats …

Two versions of the RC were built. The Diamonds, the red one, featured a diesel engine, while the Spades, which was the black one, was fitted with a petrol unit.

Whereas many show cars are little more than mock-ups designed to last just a week or two under the glare of the spotlights, some have to earn their keep. The two RC concepts built by Peugeot in 2002 were definitely in the latter category: not only were they runners, but they were also handed over to various journalists from around the world, to be put through their paces, as well.

Designed by Peugeot's Nicolas Brissoneau, the two concepts were named the RC Spades and the RC Diamonds, both cars being essentially the same with the exception of their motive power. Whereas the RC Spades was painted black and packed a 2.0l petrol

It may look like poor panel fit, but those front wings and the leading edge of the sills on the Peugeot RC were so shaped to keep the car on the road at high speeds.

engine, the RC Diamonds was painted red and featured a 2.2l diesel powerplant.

Driving pleasure

The purpose of Peugeot's RC concepts was to create a sporting 2+2 coupé, while also challenging the thinking that it was unacceptable to use an oil-burning engine for a car the main point of which was driving pleasure. That was why two concepts were built – direct comparisons could be made between them, proving once and for all that the diesel-engined car was no longer the poor relation.

Driving pleasure was the key to both these cars, and, although they were described as being 2+2s (a fact which probably compromised them in the eyes of some), each also featured a mid-mounted engine. That factor gave them an excellent weight distribution and hence very neutral handling. Light weight also played its part in making the RC concepts fun to drive, and also helping to achieve this were the cars' structures, which were made of carbon impregnated directly onto honeycomb panels. These were then formed and baked in an autoclave. This meant that, although a roll cage was incorporated into the structure, the bodyshells themselves were already massively strong while at the same time very light.

Peugeot RC	
Debut:	Geneva 2002
Engine capacity:	2168cc (132ci)
Configuration:	Mid-mounted, in-line 4-cylinder, diesel
Power:	129kW (173bhp)
Top speed:	230km/h (143mph)
Transmission:	6-speed manual, RWD
Length:	4300mm (169in)
Width:	1800mm (71in)
Designer:	Nicolas Brissoneau

The design itself was recognizably Peugeot, the teardrop-shaped headlights being reminiscent of the company's production cars, as well as most of its previous concepts. In profile and from the rear, there was not such a strong Peugeot identity. This mattered little, however, as the cars looked all the better for it. Trying to fit in four seats and a mid-mounted engine meant the passenger cell had to be pretty far forward, which is why practicality featured rather low on the concepts' list of priorities – that bodywork in front of the windscreen was given over more to crash protection than to luggage space.

Kinky A-pillar

The RC's strangely kinked A-pillar allowed for an especially panoramic windscreen, and to eliminate the potentially unreliable (and space-wasting) conventionally linked wiper arms, each wiper arm was fitted with its own electric motor. Synchronized electronically, each arm was also fitted with a rain sensor so that they could be switched to come on automatically when it started to rain.

The cabins were pretty straightforward, with little in the way of clutter, although there was a very prominent console running the whole length of the cabin. Red and black leather covered most surfaces, while aluminium and stainless-steel detailing offered some welcome highlights.

Both cars were equipped with a six-speed sequential manual gearbox, which also offered an automatic mode, while the suspension, steering and brakes were identical. That meant double wishbones were fitted front and rear, suspending 10-spoke 57.7cm (18in) magnesium alloy wheels wrapped in 245/45 R18 Michelin Sport tyres. The RC Spades packed a 1997cc (122ci) petrol engine, which developed 133kW (178bhp) and 21kg-m (149lb-ft) of torque. This was an in-line four cylinder engine with twin overhead camshafts and 16 valves – just the same as the unit in the RC Diamonds. But the latter engine was fed on a diet of diesel, and its 2168cc turbocharged displacement meant that it was able to generate 129kW (173bhp) and 41kg-m (295lb-ft) of torque – making it anything but the poor relation next to the RC Spades.

Beautifully trimmed in red and black leather, the RC's cabin featured seating for four. But this was necessarily compromised by the mid-mounted engine, which ate into the available space.

Peugeot Feline

The Peugeot Feline included lots of glass, which gave the car, and those in it, a unique sense of space. The Feline took the idea to extremes, bringing the occupants closer to the elements.

Huge alloy wheels followed racing car practice as they were retained by a single central bolt. The wheelarches followed the wheel lines unusually closely, making the Feline look even more aggressive.

By grafting those teardrop-shaped headlights onto the nose, Peugeot was able instantly to give its concept the trademark family look. That theme continued at the rear, with those slender light units.

A true sports car should feature a long bonnet to hint at the huge powerhouse lurking below. And the Peugeot Feline's bonnet was very exaggerated indeed, despite its relatively small engine.

Despite the Feline being a compact two-seater roadster, it was nonetheless based on Peugeot's largest saloon car. That gave the Feline a 3l engine and a long wheelbase for extra agility.

There is a school of thought that says to have a truly sporty car – or at least one that looks truly sporting – a long bonnet is essential, as is a cabin set well back into the wheelbase. If you follow that to an extreme, the Peugeot Feline is exactly what you will get, thanks to its bonnet accounting for nearly half of the car's 4m (13ft) length. Not only that, but perched at the back was a passenger cell that took up only about a third of the car; practicality was not a priority for this concept.

If the Feline looked unlikely, the car on which it was based was even more so. The Peugeot 607 was not regarded as a driver's car, and because it was a rather large saloon, its platform was not the obvious one on which to base a focused driving machine. But none of this was as mad as it seemed, because the 607 had a long wheelbase, which allowed those extreme proportions to be incorporated. Not only that, but there was a 3l, V6 engine mounted up the front, which gave the car a decent dose of power, endowing it with a healthy turn of speed.

The powerplant was taken wholesale from the 607, which meant it had 157kW (210bhp) on offer. While

The Peugeot Feline's compact cabin was trimmed in red leather, and, in the best traditions of the focused lightweight sports car, there was little in the way of equipment.

Peugeot Feline	
Debut:	Geneva 2000
Engine capacity:	2946cc (180ci)
Configuration:	Front-mounted V6, petrol
Power:	157kW (210bhp)
Top speed:	N/A
Transmission:	5-speed manual, FWD
Length:	4070mm (160.2in)
Width:	1880mm (74in)
Designer:	N/A

that might not be a huge amount for an enthusiast's car, it is more than enough when allied to an all-in weight of just 875kg (1929lb). The engine itself was mounted longitudinally, which was partly why the bonnet was so long, and such proportions also allowed the unit to be mounted relatively far back to aid the handling. The power on offer, allied to the car's low weight, meant that the Feline was blessed with a power to weight ratio of 179kw (240bhp) per tonne,

which put it up against some very expensive exotica from the likes of Porsche and Ferrari.

The reason for the low weight was that the Feline's bodyshell was made of carbon fibre. This was vacuum-formed from the same type of honeycomb panels used on aircraft, providing immense strength with very low weight. Giving the Feline its fantastically purposeful stance, and also contributing greatly to its driveability, was a wheelbase that pushed the wheels to the very corners of the car. Measuring 2.85m (9.4ft), this not only gave the car a cosseting ride, but also allowed it to be placed extremely accurately when being driven at high speed.

Wonder wings

The wheels themselves were of the usual huge alloy variety and wrapped in Michelin PAX run-flat tyres, as was the norm on such concepts. Taking their cue from racing car technology, these wheels were held in place by a single bolt. But perhaps the most amazing feature was the way the bodywork appeared to hug the wheels. The front and rear wings seemed to be stretched over the wheels, following their form. And because the wheels also dictated the car's length, this illusion was especially strong.

Positioned almost over the rear wheels were the car's two occupants, who sat under a glass bubble-shaped roof. To get into the Feline, the doors were slid almost entirely into the front wings. The windscreen then had

Something that looked as radical as the Feline would never stand any chance of making it into even limited production – which was a tragedy as it was an amazing-looking machine.

to be moved 50cm (19.7in) on its frame between the passenger compartment and the bonnet, while the rear portion of the bubble had to be slid back 12cm (4.7in). While all this might sound like rather a long-winded process, it was in practice no more complex to use than many more conventional door arrangements. Even better, it was possible to enjoy some open-topped motoring, thanks to the ability to remove the rear part of the roof, which could then be stowed in a housing behind the two seats. The seats themselves, along with the rest of the interior, were trimmed in red leather. The dashboard was stocked with the bare minimum of instrumentation, although there were the obligatory stereo, telephone and climate control.

The Feline could be transformed from a closed coupé into a fully open roadster, as the roof could be removed altogether. It could even be driven with the doors fully open.

Pininfarina Osée

Apart from the Maserati-engined SM of the 1970s, the French company Citroën had not dabbled with sports cars very much. Like that car, this concept was fitted with a 3l V6 powerplant.

With the Citroën chevrons on the nose, there was no mistaking the parentage of the Pininfarina Osée. Dotted about there were also more subtle references to the French car maker.

There's a school of thought in the motoring world that says a car needs to be wedge-shaped if it is going to look sporting. Looking at the Osée, the Italian design house Pininfarina would seem to agree.

Despite the Osée's supercar looks, it definitely was not in the same league as its (mainly) Italian rivals. With less than 150kW (200bhp) on tap, the Osée promised only moderate performance.

In true Citroën Fashion, the Pininfarina Osée was fitted with decidedly unconventional fluid-controlled suspension. That gave the car an unusual balance between sharp handling and a soft ride.

You do not have to look too closely to see what forms the basis of the Pininfarina Osée, what with all those chevrons to be found in both the interior and exterior design. But although the Citroën logo was very much in evidence, this concept did not carry much of the Citroën family look. In fact, from some angles it looked more like it had Teutonic origins, with overtones of the Audi Rosemeyer. But none of that mattered – what was much more important was the fact that it had glitz and glamour aplenty, and was just the thing to generate plenty of traffic on the Pininfarina stand at the 2001 Geneva motor show.

The reason for the Osée was simply the fact that Pininfarina had never before been involved in any collaborations with the French car maker. But a relationship with Peugeot went back several decades, and as both Citroën and Peugeot were two parts of the same (PSA) company, it made sense for the Italian design house to try something new. As new ideas were being put forward, it was also suggested that a type of car with which Citroën was not normally associated would be a good idea. This mid-engined sports car was the result.

Despite being a 21st-century creation, the Pininfarina Osée borrowed certain styling elements from three decades earlier – in particular and not very wisely the appalling rear visibility due to the absence of a back window.

Although the lines suggest that the Osée could justifiably be called a supercar, it was fitted with only a 3l, V6 Citroën powerplant, developing just 145kW (194bhp). Undeniably fast it was (although the top speed was never disclosed), but this was not a car to take on the likes of Ferrari or Lamborghini. Instead, it was a junior supercar, which was as madly impractical as most supercars, but more affordable and less extreme than those Italian offerings.

All classic, nothing borrowed

The Osée appeared to borrow little from Citroën's existing or previous designs, but several details were, in fact, inspired by all-time classic models such as the DS and SM. The most important of these was the long bonnet, with the cabin sited relatively far back in the wheelbase, giving the car its proportions. Another feature was the pointed front end, especially obvious when seen in plan view. A sloping rear end, as well as air intakes positioned in the lower part of the car's nose, were other retro-inspired details. When all these were put together, the Osée was the result.

The reason for its sportscar (rather than supercar) status was that Pininfarina stuck to Citroën's principle of putting comfort and smoothness first, rather than outright speed and ultimate dynamic prowess. As Pininfarina put it, the Osée offered non-aggressive performance, gliding along the road thanks to its

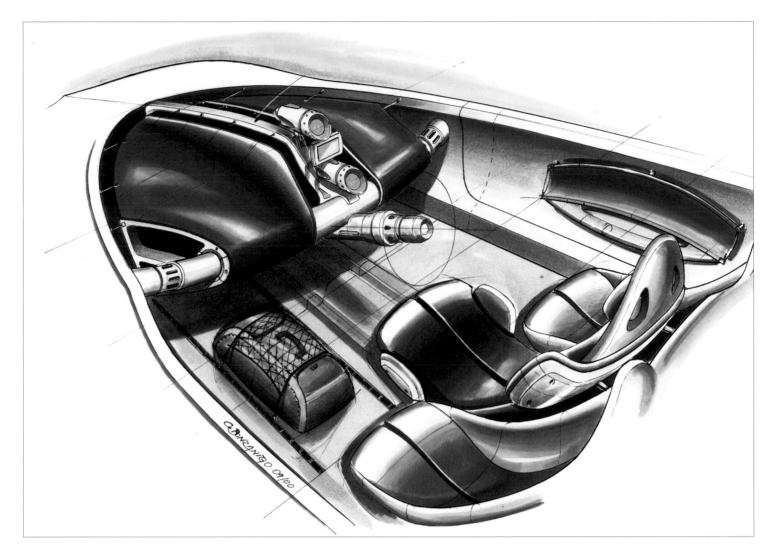

Hydractive fluid-controlled suspension, which gave it more of a smooth ride than any sportscar driver could usually expect. The hard part with any car is giving it a distinctive styling that does not look like it has been cloned from something else. The Osée was not able to avoid this entirely, but it did at least manage not to

The central driving position allowed seating for three, offering a 50 per cent improvement over the typical sports car. It also meant left- and right-hand drive cars did not have to be made.

look like all the other sports cars out there. In true concept-car style, practicality was tossed aside in the quest for a method of entry and egress, and there was a canopy which encompassed the entire width of the car. Very short overhangs, both front and rear, gave the Osée a particularly dynamic look, and the resulting long wheelbase helped the car to both ride and handle especially nicely. The positioning of the engine meant that the cabin had to be positioned quite far forward, and the whole package was kept deliberately free of fussy detailing.

Inside had seating for three, with the driver sitting slightly ahead of the two passengers, who sat either side. This gave a central driving position, McLaren F1–style, and the dash consisted of a tubular element that ran across the car's width. Stretched over this was a piece of cloth resembling a sail, which meant the bare minimum of switchgear or instrumentation. Subtle this was not, but it was very effective.

Pininfarina Osée

Debut:	Geneva 2001
Engine capacity:	2946cc (180ci)
Configuration:	Mid-mounted V6, petrol
Power:	145kW (194bhp)
Top speed:	N/A
Transmission:	5-speed auto, RWD
Length:	4150mm (163.4in)
Width:	1895mm (74.6in)
Designer:	N/A

SEAT Formula

The interior of the SEAT Formula is very simple, with no carpeting and no more than the bare minimum of trim. This made a star of the beautifully crafted aluminium tub.

Distinctive air vents in the rear wings fed air into the engine bay, but there were still plenty of scoops and slats at the front end of the car.

SEAT's Formula followed the same back-to-basics theme as its contemporary, the Lotus Elise, and made driving pleasure the first priority. Weight was cut in every possible area to maintain purity.

Ensuring strong performance was a 179kW (240bhp), 2l, turbocharged petrol engine, linked to a six-speed sequential manual gearbox. The adoption of rear-wheel drive meant oversteering was a problem.

Apart from the large SEAT badge on the grille, there were few clues to the origins of the Formula – but there was no denying the car was distinctive.

At a time when many manufacturers were embarrassed into being more socially aware, SEAT bucked the trend at the 1999 Geneva motor show, where it unveiled its Formula concept. This was described as 'bringing the excitement of competition driving to the highway, while not overlooking the comforts needed for more conventional driving'.

Two-seater roadster

The reality was that the Formula was just another two-seater roadster – though this did not make it any less tempting a prospect. With SEAT part of the Volkswagen empire, it was only natural that the mechanicals would be familiar to countless numbers of VW, Audi and Skoda drivers. To that end, the Formula used a 186kW (240bhp) 2.0l turbocharged petrol engine along with a six-speed sequential manual gearbox.

This powerplant was a development of the excellent 1.8l unit, and in 2.0l form it was derived from the high-performing SEAT Cordoba World Rally Car. Front-wheel drive was also dispensed with, leaving the rear wheels in control and meaning that the Formula would have been every bit as much fun to drive as its looks implied.

As if the concept of a two-seater roadster were not eye-catching enough, SEAT also opted to paint the car fluorescent yellow to make sure it was noticed. Wheels of the largest possible diameter were the norm around this

SEAT Formula	
Debut:	Geneva 1999
Engine capacity:	2.0l (122ci)
Configuration:	Mid-mounted turbo in-line four, petrol
Power:	186kW (240bhp)
Top speed:	240km/h (149mph)
Transmission:	6-speed sequential manual, RWD
Length:	3943mm (155in)
Width:	1758mm (69in)
Designer:	N/A

time – on road cars as well as concepts – so the Formula was equipped with 50.8cm (20in) alloy items. The doors opened upwards, being hinged at the front, while the aluminium body tub meant there were huge sills, which gave the car its strength and torsional stiffness. Such a construction meant the handling would be predictable, while the adoption of active cooling and aerodynamic systems ensured there was little chance of problems arising.

Above 50km/h (30mph), the rear spoiler popped up to maintain downforce (and hence stability), while at the front end, adjustable cooling intakes channelled

For a company that had been building Fiat's cast-offs only a few years before, SEAT's Formula was a huge leap forward, establishing the Spanish car maker as a serious player in the sportscar market. This project was the result of Volkswagen's influence, which had recently taken over SEAT.

just the right amount of air to the engine to make sure that it did not overheat – while also maintaining a high running temperature for maximum efficiency.

The minimalist approach

SEAT cut no corners in trying to create a lightweight sportster that would be great fun to drive, so in a bid to reduce weight, the chassis was built of aluminium. And rather than hide away such a beautifully crafted piece of engineering, this was proudly displayed within the cockpit. The rest of the cabin followed a minimalist approach – there was no point weighing the car down with unnecessary trim or equipment. Despite this – and although the car's interior was exposed to the elements – a climate control unit was fitted. The final weight was less than 1 tonne (1.1 tons) and, when this was combined with the 179kW (240bhp) on offer, there was never any doubt that performance would be electrifying – 0–100km/h (0–62mph) was possible in just 4.8 seconds.

Instrumentation was also kept to a minimum, and to change gear there was a conventionally located gear

The lightweight design of the SEAT Formula was flaunted rather than hidden away – the aluminium beams that made up its structure were an integral part of the cabin design.

lever, while paddles on the steering wheel allowed ratios to be selected. Whichever option was chosen, it was all done electronically without the need for a conventional clutch.

In many ways, the concept of the Formula is very much like that of the Lotus Elise, a fact which is no coincidence – Julian Thomson, the Lotus designer, was an integral part of the whole project, having joined the team as head of exterior design. He worked out how to package everything, but one thing he failed to do was introduce any form of weather protection.

Utilizing an Elise-style tensioned fabric roof would have been easy enough, but such a tight production schedule for the car's introduction meant that there was simply no time. In the event, the car did not reach production, but it did open the world's eyes to the notion that SEAT was the sporty division of the VW/Audi Group.

Toyota FXS

Strong performance was guaranteed, with the 4.3l V8 of the Lexus LS430 in that curvy front end. And 0–100km/h (0–62mph) in little more than six seconds and 246km/h (155mph) were on offer.

It may look like no Toyota ever seen before, but the FXS was built as a runner so that in theory it could enter production in some form.

Although the styling of the Toyota FXS was very clean, there were some wonderful details, such as the strip headlights, gaping front grilles and curved aeroscreen.

Inside the Toyota FXS was as radical as the outside, with blue-backlit instruments and what appeared to be a small postwar jukebox on the fascia. Tasteless, yes, but certainly a talking point.

Practicality was low on the list of priorities – there was seating for just two people and no weather protection. But it was certainly an eye-catcher!

Proving that you can have too much of a good thing, the FXS was one of 17 concepts unveiled on the Toyota stand at the 2001 Tokyo motor show. And with some far more improbable vehicles parked around it, that meant the FXS was always overlooked. Despite its 4.3l V8 and impractical two-seater roadster configuration, the FXS was actually quite a sensible car, even if it did appear to be pretty way out.

In keeping with the practice of giving all its concepts a design theme, Toyota reckoned that the FXS was a car that featured a 'simple and sexy form with a sense of presence'. Considering that this was a vaguely understandable brief, it was pretty good for Toyota – even if the finished result was a vehicle that from the front bore a close resemblance to the Batmobile from the film *Batman Forever*.

Seeing the lights

At the front were strip headlights, which climbed up the outside edges of the front panel just before they met the wings. Although there was no grille, there were three large vents sitting just above the front spoiler – all in all, it was pretty radical. But in profile

the FXS was less controversial, and at the rear it was somewhat understated – almost to the point of being bland. A strip light that ran across the whole width of the rear panel incorporated the tail lights, brake lights, indicators and reversing lights, and poking out of the rear valance was a pair of exhausts.

The three-spoke chromed alloy wheels on which the FXS sat were hardly considered the last word in good taste in Europe, but the United States was the biggest and most important market and the car was designed with US buyers in mind. The wheels did at least show off the meaty ventilated disc brakes very well, and also looked very purposeful because they were wrapped in 245/40R18 tyres at the front and 285/35R18s items at the rear.

Paddle-shifted sequential manual gearboxes were beginning to become fashionable in mainstream cars by the time the FXS made its debut, so Toyota developed a new system to fit to its new baby. With

All that silver with blue neon lighting was rather harsh on the eye, but certainly nobody could accuse the normally sober Toyota of being boring with the design of the FXS.

six ratios to choose between, the transmission was operated by buttons behind the steering wheel. The rest of the cabin was surprisingly featureless, with very little to distract the occupants as they whizzed along. A cluster of instruments was assembled directly in front of the driver, indicating road speed, engine revs, fuel level and oil pressure – but there was no multimedia system or other gadgetry. Everything was blue backlit, and, in a rather bizarre move, the centre console was trimmed in such a way that it looked as if a 1950s jukebox had been grafted on. That was not the intention, of course …

Helping to ensure that the car's handling was decently sporting, the FXS was suspended by double

The three-spoke polished chrome wheels on the FXS were just the sort of thing that European buyers would have found garish, but US and Japanese buyers would love.

wishbones at both ends, while great attention was paid to bodyshell rigidity, allowing the handling to remain predictable even when the car was being pushed to the limit.

Heavy metal
Although there was never any suggestion that the Toyota FXS could become a replacement for the Lexus SC430, the underpinnings of the former were most definitely based on those of the latter, which is why its all-aluminium V8 petrol engine was equipped with 32 valves and a pair of overhead camshafts. In standard showroom spec, this delivered 210kW (282bhp) and 58kg-m (419lb-ft) of torque, which was enough to take the Lexus SC430 from rest to 100km/h (62mph) in just 6.4 seconds, before topping out at an electronically limited 250km/h (155mph).

The FXS was never performance tested; however, considering the similarities in dimensions and weight between the cars, it would be a safe bet to say that both top speed and acceleration would have been much the same. The FXS was blessed with a perfect 50:50 front:rear weight distribution, so the handling of the FXS should have been even. But then, as the SC430 had always been criticized for its dynamics, the FXS – by contrast – could probably not have been any less fun to drive!

Toyota FXS

Debut:	Tokyo 2001
Engine capacity:	4293cc (262ci)
Configuration:	Front-mounted V8, petrol
Power:	210kW (282bhp)
Top speed:	N/A
Transmission:	6-speed sequential manual, RWD
Length:	4150mm (163in)
Width:	1870mm (74in)
Designer:	N/A

Supercar Concepts

When money is no object and power is everything, it is time to build a supercar concept. Some of these deserved to progress beyond the drawing board, and some of them were intended to do so. But the costs for these cars are always necessarily high, and it is rare that the sums add up. Economic or not, supercars are some of the most spectacular concepts ever to be designed.

If there is one area where concepts can be as frivolous as the designer likes, it is that of supercars. These 'money-no-object' image-builders are constructed for maximum impact on the show stand, and they do not have to be affordable or practical. What they do have to be, however, is radical, exciting, ultra-fast and hugely desirable. For these are 'halo-effect' cars: they do not need to reach production, but just have to make sure that some of their magic rubs off on the real-world cars which are actually available from the manufacturer in question.

Since the first car was built in the late nineteenth century, there have been those who feel that too far is not enough. More power and greater speeds are always possible – it just depends how much money is available. The problem is the law of diminishing returns: just to go that little bit faster takes even more

investment in materials technology to reduce vehicle weights. It also means squeezing ever more power out of engines that are already performing closer and closer to the limits of efficiency. Then there are the aerodynamic considerations – it is possible to go only so far in making the car more slippery while also carrying people and all the mechanicals that it needs to travel at warp speed.

Taking the challenge

Thankfully, despite all these limitations, there are plenty of car makers prepared to pick up the challenge. They know only too well that the sums almost certainly do not add up; they accept that if the car ever makes it to production, it will be as a loss leader. The point to remember is what it will do for its manufacturer's standing just by sitting in the showroom among the mass-market hatchbacks and saloons (sedans).

This is the reason for cars such as the Volkswagen W12, Audi Avus and Ford GT90. And ultimately the reason they did not reach production. The makers thought they could beat the system, but it was only a matter of time before the harsh realities hit home.

Volkswagen intended to put the VW W12 concept into production; the car was developed to an advanced stage, including subjecting it to endurance testing. But interest in a VW supercar was never that great, and the concept never went beyond development stage.

Audi Avus

Aluminium construction was a technology that few other makers were even considering when the Audi Avus was unveiled in 1991. The car was left unpainted to highlight the build material.

Trying to transmit 380kW (509bhp) to the road needs a special transmission, so the Avus was fitted with permanent four-wheel drive to keep the car on the road.

The Avus's low, swoopy body made for high drama, and most of the classic supercar styling cues also featured – a cab-forward stance, minimal ground clearance and a mid-engined layout.

Audi wanted to make the most of the special powerplant that was located behind the car's two occupants, so the engine cover was made of glass.

Another thing that nobody else was working on at the time of the Avus was a W-configuration engine. The powerplant was a W12, with a displacement of 6l (366ci).

In a world where few car manufacturers have a truly unique selling point – other than their brand – Audi can claim to have pioneered one. This is the use of aluminium in volume car production, and Audi's quattro four-wheel drive system, bringing the availability of all-wheel drive to 'normal' saloon (sedan) and estate (station wagon) cars, is perhaps another.

By the time the Avus concept was first shown at the 1991 Tokyo motor show, Audi was already committed to volume aluminium car production with its A8 luxury car. The A8 was launched in 1994, but it was several years before this that Audi had signed a deal with the Aluminium Company of America (ALCOA) to engineer a car that broke convention in terms of materials selected for monocoque-bodied cars.

Technological innovations

The Avus was a radical concept that followed in the footsteps of the Spyder, which had first been shown a month earlier at the 1991 Frankfurt motor show. Whereas the Spyder was initially slated for production, the Avus was a technological *tour de force*

With everything trimmed in black, the interior of the Avus was a sombre place to be. That is why the roof was made of glass – it opened the car up, making it feel lighter and more spacious.

showcasing just what Audi could do. As well as its 380kW (509bhp), 5.9l W12 engine, it featured four-wheel drive and – most importantly – that aluminium bodyshell. To make sure that nobody missed the fact that what was usually steel was in fact aluminium, the bodyshell was left unpainted and was instead highly polished. For yet more emphasis, there were beautiful curves everywhere – from any angle you chose, you were hard-pressed to find a straight line.

There was no need for even the slightest nod to practicality, so the Avus was a strict two-seater with no real space for luggage. In true supercar fashion, the doors featured a scissor action and the rear-view mirrors were located at the top of the A-pillar for maximum effect.

When a company has created a W12 engine, it makes sure everybody appreciates this, so rather than being fitted with a conventional engine cover, the rear of the

Avus fitted extensive glass panelling at the rear to show off the powerplant.

And if you are wondering what a W12 engine looks like, it has two banks of four cylinders set like a V8, and a third bank of four combustion chambers sitting upright in between. Such a configuration leads to a far more compact design than a V12 because this is the length of four cylinders, rather than six. To complicate things even further, each cylinder was equipped with five valves, all operated by a pair of camshafts for each bank of cylinders. Despite all the power that was on offer, however, Audi claimed that the Avus would pass all of the then-current regulations concerning road car emissions, thanks to the use of electrically heated exhaust catalysts, exhaust gas recirculation and air injection.

Light and minimalistic

It was British designer Martin Smith who was responsible for the look of the Audi Avus, which was heavily inspired by the Auto Union racers of the 1930s. Auto Union was one of the four companies that merged to become Audi (hence the four rings), and the Avus was a famous Berlin race track where those original racers fought close battles.

The interior of the Avus was no less daring than the exterior, but not overdesigned in the way many concepts are. The materials used were simple, with leather, wood and woollen textiles being the most

Audi Avus	
Debut:	Tokyo 1991
Engine capacity:	5998cc (366ci)
Configuration:	Mid-mounted W12, petrol
Power:	380kW (509bhp)
Top speed:	338km/h (210mph)
Transmission:	4WD
Length:	4470mm (176in)
Width:	2006mm (79in)
Designer:	Martin Smith

common – having saved weight by using a lightweight bodyshell, there was no point in filling the car with unnecessary equipment that would just blunt performance. By keeping weight to a minimum, the top speed was reckoned to be 338km/h (210mph), while Audi claimed that the car was capable of completing the 0–96km/h (0–60mph) sprint in just three seconds. Unfortunately, the company's timing was all wrong – the global economy was in tatters, so the plug was pulled on the project. Now the Avus sits in Audi's museum at Ingolstadt.

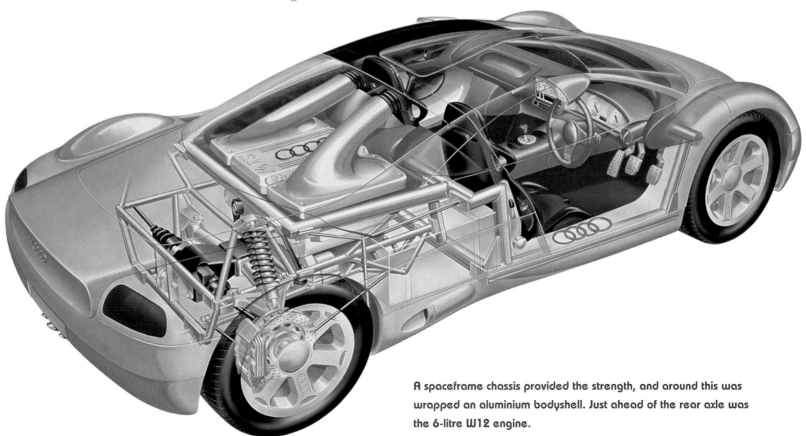

A spaceframe chassis provided the strength, and around this was wrapped an aluminium bodyshell. Just ahead of the rear axle was the 6-litre W12 engine.

Bentley Hunaudières

That V16 engine was a masterpiece, with its 465kW (623bhp) and 78kg-m (561lb-ft) of torque. Transmitting that to the road safely meant four-wheel drive was a necessity for the Hunaudières.

Masses of curves gave the car real presence. However, the tiny projector headlights and large, accentuated grille did not gel with the overall lines.

Although Bentley was renowned for building sporting cars, it had not previously built a supercar – so the Hunaudières, with its 8l, mid-mounted V16 engine was a break from tradition.

Although the Hunaudières was a big car with a big engine, Bentley attempted to keep the weight down as much as possible by using carbon fibre and aluminium in its construction.

Although low-profile tyres had been fashionable before the Hunaudières made its debut, the concept's 50.8cm (20in) wheels took things to extremes – which certainly made it look dramatic.

When the Hunaudières concept was shown at the 1999 Geneva motor show, it was not hard to see that Bentley had been absorbed into the VW/Audi empire. Bugatti and Lamborghini were also part of the huge German multinational, and it was uncanny how similar their show cars were starting to look to Bentley's. It was also uncanny how they all sported mid-mounted powerplants with huge displacements and strange configurations such as W12 and V16. If the American expression that there is no substitute for cubic inches is correct, Bentley was certainly on to a winner.

In a world where the production version of the 6.0l Bentley Continental GT is now a reality, the Hunaudières does not seem so incongruous. When it was first shown, however, this was the first time a car from the Crewe-based marque had featured a mid-mounted engine and four-wheel drive. And while the Continental has its engine at the front, the concept of any type of impractical supercar (rather than a grand cruiser) from Bentley was anathema.

By the end of the twentieth century, Rolls-Royce and Bentley were reduced to producing little more than badge-engineered versions of each other's cars.

The pre-war cars that Bentley produced in tiny numbers, by hand, were often fitted with a turned aluminium dash. In a nod towards the venerable car maker's history, the interior of the Hunaudières was inspired by this tradition.

What was needed was for the two marques to split, taking separate identities – Bentley producing the sporting cars and Rolls-Royce building gentlemen's carriages. Rather than be shy about it, Bentley decided to go for broke, producing something that would recapture the glory days of Bentley when it was a force to be reckoned with at racing venues such as Le Mans. To help things along, the Hunaudières took its name from the famous high-speed straight at the renowned circuit.

Mid-mounted monster

Clearly a name alone would not recapture past glories, so the car was given a set of clothes that were in keeping with a supercar. A mid-mounted engine allowed the front end to be kept as low as possible, while there was minimal ground clearance, a cab-forward stance and a surprisingly simple silhouette.

Bentley Hunaudières

Debut:	Geneva 1999
Engine capacity:	8004cc (488ci)
Configuration:	Mid-mounted V16
Power:	465kW (623bhp)
Top speed:	320km/h (200mph)
Transmission:	5-speed manual, 4WD
Length:	4432mm (174in)
Width:	1985mm (78in)
Designer:	N/A

In true Bentley fashion, the engine was anything but tame. Harking back to the days of the Bentley Boys at Le Mans, the powerplant featured a capacity of 8.0l – enough to develop 458kW (623bhp) and a monstrous 78km-m (561lb-ft) of torque. Helping to produce such huge amounts of power and torque was variable camshaft timing, with the four overhead camshafts being chain driven. Permanent four-wheel drive ensured that such prodigious power and torque could be relayed to the road surface while massive 50.8cm (20in) wheels with ultra-low profile tyres heightened the Hunaudières' dramatic looks.

Power and traction alone do not give a sporty drive – low weight is also essential if the handling and balance are to be savoured. To keep the weight as low as possible, the bodyshell of the Hunaudières was made of aluminium and carbon fibre, and the frontal area was minimized – thanks to the use of tiny headlights – to reduce drag as much as possible.

Also helping in this aim was the adoption of cameras behind the front wheels in place of conventional door-mounted mirrors.

Luxury interior

Another essential in any Bentley is a luxurious interior, and the Hunaudières did not disappoint, with its cabin swathed in Nubuck and Connolly leather. An engine-turned aluminium dash gave a taste of the pre-war cars that inspired the concept, and the dark green that was to be found inside and out was reminiscent of the fabulous 'blower' Bentleys of the 1920s.

All in all, the Bentley Hunaudières was an amazing concept, but probably something that was too daring for the typical Bentley buyer. And with both Lamborghini and Bugatti in its portfolio, the VW/Audi Group decided that these marques were more deserving of such dramatic lines.

Previous Bentley two-door cars had very graceful lines. The Hunaudières changed all that, with a very aggressive stance thanks to the mid-mounted engine: Bentley's first.

Bugatti Veyron

The Bugatti Veyron's two-tone paint scheme was unusual for such a modern car, but it worked well and evoked the glory days of Bugatti's most successful period in the 1920s and 1930s.

In order to transmit such a huge amount of power to the road, a strong four-wheel drive transmission was needed. This was originally based on the Lamborghini Diablo VT system.

Harking back to the 1930s, the Veyron's interior was wonderfully Art Deco. It was also quite harsh on the eye, featuring a lot of turned aluminium.

The engine was a 6.3l W18 unit, tucked away behind the car's two occupants. Inevitably, this meant it was massively powerful, developing 414kW (555bhp) – but bigger things were to come.

There were cooling slots and vents all over the Veyron's bodyshell – not only did the engine need huge amounts of air to breathe, but it needed to be cooled as well.

The Bugatti Veyron's interior was no budget cabin – only a very expensive car could have an interior such as this, with Alcantara, leather and aluminium everywhere. But it was still very retro.

There can be few concept cars that have had a more difficult gestation period than the Bugatti Veyron. Had the VW/Audi Group been less ambitious with its targets, the Veyron would have provided far fewer headaches than it did. However, the decision was made that the Veyron would not only offer 1001PS (987bhp/725kW), but would also have to be able to top (402km/h) 250mph. All very well, except that trying to design running gear that can cope with those numbers cannot be done easily – in fact, it can hardly be done at all.

Automotive evolution

Surprisingly, the original concept for the Veyron (or EB 18/4 Veyron to give it its full title) was much less powerful than the monster it became in production. Revealed at the 1999 Tokyo motor show, the Veyron was an evolution of the EB 18/3 Chiron shown at the 1999 Frankfurt motor show. That concept had been

designed by Italdesign, but the Veyron featured an all-new interior as well as a new bodyshell.

Like the Chiron, the dimensions of the Veyron were dictated by the car upon which it was based – the Lamborghini Diablo VT. This particular model was chosen because it was the largest and most powerful car in the VW/Audi stable, both Bugatti and Lamborghini being owned by the German company. The Diablo VT also featured a four-wheel drive transmission system, which allowed the Veyron to put its power down with the minimum of fuss – by the time the power had nearly doubled for the production car, it would need all the help it could get to transmit such prodigious amounts of power to the road. Instead of the Diablo's weedy V12 powerplant under

Bugatti Veyron

Debut:	Tokyo 1999
Engine capacity:	6300cc (384ci)
Configuration:	Mid-mounted W18, petrol
Power:	414kW (555bhp)
Top speed:	299km/h (180mph)
Transmission:	5-speed manual, 4WD
Length:	4380mm (172in)
Width:	2000mm (79in)
Designer:	Hartmut Warkuss

the engine cover, there was a 6.3l W18 unit that generated 408kW (555bhp). This engine was a series of three banks of six cylinders, and although it was normally aspirated in the original concept, no fewer than four turbochargers were installed by the time it made it to production.

Classic lines

Because the Veyron carried the hallowed Bugatti name, there were naturally plenty of design references to the glory days of the marque. The horseshoe-shaped radiator grille was the most obvious link; however, there was also a central 'spine' running the length of the car – very subtle, but a reference to the Atlantic of the 1930s. Even the colour scheme evoked memories of the pre-war cars, with two shades of blue being used to give the car a less heavy look. The Veyron would continue to be shown at just about every major motor show after the original concept was displayed, although those later displays sometimes used a car that was painted red instead of blue.

The Veyron was touted as a serious production possibility from the outset, and it was to be positioned at the very top of the market – well beyond the level of the top Ferrari or Lamborghinis. This meant that something pretty special had to be done with the car's interior, and exclusive materials were used throughout: everything was either covered in Nubuck leather or aluminium, with Art Deco–style switchgear on the centre console.

A large central dial housing the tachometer and speedometer was flanked by a quartet of smaller gauges monitoring the oil pressure, coolant temperature, fuel and battery voltage.

On the outside, features were equally exclusive, with 50.8cm (20in) alloy wheels wrapped in ultra-low profile tyres – 335/30 at the rear and 265/30 at the front. But whether such tyres would be able to cope with a 0–96km/h (0–60mph) time of less than four seconds seems unlikely – never mind a top speed of well in excess of 322km (200mph).

Despite the huge amount of technology hidden underneath the surface, the exterior design of the Veyron was unusually unfussy – scoops, slats and spoilers were integrated very well.

Ford GT90

Where the original Ford GT – the GT40 – had been curvaceous and beautiful, the GT90 was brash and angular. And it has to be said that few people thought it was anywhere near as handsome.

Four turbochargers and a 6l V12 engine conspired to produce 537kW (720bhp) – which Ford claimed was enough to despatch the 0–96km/h (0–60mph) sprint in just 3.1 seconds, and top 378km/h (235mph).

The GT90 was the car that took Ford's 'New-Edge' styling to its extremes, but at least it did not have to carry the company's corporate look.

Three was the magic number as far as this concept was concerned: there were three-sided shapes all over it, from the wheel spinners to the exhausts.

Taking its 'New Edge' styling theme to extremes, the GT90 cashed in on an iconic Ford name, but had nothing of the beauty of its GT40 forebear. However, it more than made up for this in both drama and performance – here was a car that was as much go as it was show. When the GT90 was first shown at the 1995 Detroit motor show, the McLaren F1 was the performance car to beat – which meant that a speed of 386km/h (240mph) had to be possible, along with

Incredibly overdesigned, the dash of the GT90 was a mess of triangles and circles that just did not gel. This marked the start of Ford's 'New Edge' design.

neck-snapping acceleration. But while the GT90 could claim to have nearly 75kW (100bhp) more than the F1 (and could be tuned to produce 671kW/900bhp if wanted), it was also a lot heavier. And it just did not have the looks to take on the McLaren …

Huge power

The result of 537kW (720bhp), an aerodynamically efficient bodyshell and 90kg-m (650lb-ft) of torque was the ability to sprint from a standing start to 96km/h (60mph) in just 3.1 seconds, while 160km/h (100mph) was attainable in 6.2 seconds. It may not have been pretty, but nobody could claim that the GT90 was not fast. Such performance was helped by the fact that the 6.0l V12 was equipped with four Garrett T-2 turbochargers. But despite the huge power, the engine was still completely tractable – there was no need to keep 4000 revs on the dial just to prevent it stalling.

Such astonishing straight-line performance, though, meant little if the GT90 did not also handle well. To that end, it had an unusually long wheelbase – of 2946mm (116in) – with hardly any overhang at either

Ford GT90	
Debut:	Detroit 1995
Engine capacity:	5927cc (323ci), 4 turbos
Configuration:	Mid-mounted V12, petrol
Power:	537kW (720bhp)
Top speed:	378km/h (235mph)
Transmission:	5-speed manual
Length:	4470mm (176in)
Width:	1963mm (77in)
Designer:	N/A

end. By putting the wheels into the corners of the car, it could be placed very accurately when being driven at high speed. And in typical supercar fashion, there was a low roofline and a cab-forward stance to hint at the amazing performance on offer.

Strength and lightness

The Ford GT90's monocoque was constructed of honeycombed aluminium, for great strength with minimum weight, and, for the same reasons, the outer skin was made of carbon-fibre composites. To allow access to the engine, gearbox, brakes, steering and suspension, both the front and rear ends were completely removable. Like the monocoque, the suspension was largely based on the Jaguar XJ220. To create downforce at high speed, there was a rear spoiler which could be angled as necessary; for maximum aerodynamic efficiency, the drag factor was kept to just 0.32 – a figure which is about as low as it is possible to go with this type of body shape.

The five-speed manual gearbox was also borrowed from the Jaguar XJ220, while the wheels were 48.2cm (19in) units all round – which were fitted with ultra-low profile 335/30 tyres made specially for the project by Goodyear. The concept as shown was fitted with rear-wheel drive, although the possibility of four-wheel drive was not ruled out altogether.

Inside were rather more creature comforts than buyers in this sector expected. A 10-speaker audio system was fitted alongside air conditioning and a phone system. Because comfort is as much about space as it is about equipment, there was also plenty of room inside the GT90's cabin, although the two seats were built to hold the occupants in place when the car was being

Taking the triangular theme to extremes, even the exhaust pipes of the GT90 emerged into a three-sided box which poked out of the back of the car.

cornered at very high speeds. The infrared sensors hidden in the B-pillars were a nice touch – they alerted the driver to other vehicles in the GT90's blind spots either side of the car.

When the GT90 was unveiled, there was much talk from Ford about the possibilities of it reaching production, as long as just 500 examples could be built, at a cost of between $100,000 and $150,000 each. Indeed, much of the work had been done for low-volume production to be a real possibility. However, as is so often the way, there simply was not enough positive feedback for the concept to make the transition to production car.

Where the GT40 had been graceful – although somehow quite brutal at the same time – the GT90 looked ungainly from just about every angle, especially this one.

Ford Indigo

Open wheels would be illegal on a road car, so tyre-hugging wheelarches were provided for the Ford Indigo instead, which not only turned with the wheels, but also moved up and down with them.

Housing the headlights on such a radical concept proved a bit of a nightmare – the solution was to make use of the wing mirrors and front aerofoil.

The Indigo was about performance above all else, which is why it was fitted with a 6l V12 engine. It was mid-mounted to give the best possible handling.

Practicality was low on the Indigo's agenda: there was no weather protection provided, nowhere to stow luggage and seating for just two people.

Rather than opt for doors that opened in the conventional way, Ford opted for scissor-action units, which made the car look more glamorous on the show stand.

The great thing about concept cars is that they rarely have to give more than a token nod to practicality or usability. And this was never more than apparent than with the Ford Indigo, which was closer to a single-seater racing car than it was to any road car. There was no weather protection, nowhere to stow any luggage, and a 6.0l V12 sitting behind the occupants' heads made the purpose of the Indigo abundantly clear: to go as fast as possible. But the tragedy of the Indigo is that it was never built – something which could have been a real possibility if enough support had been shown for the project.

The Indigo came about thanks to Jacques Villeneuve winning the Indy 500 in a Reynard-Ford. Earlier, Michael Schumacher had won the 1994 F1 World Championship in a Benetton-Ford, but Ford had failed to capitalize on its success, and now the company was adamant that it would not make the same mistake again. Once Villeneuve had claimed victory, Ford set about designing a concept that captured the spirit of Indycar racing, but which had the potential to go into very limited production.

Reynard was heavily involved in the development of the two Indigo concepts – one was produced with testing and development in mind, while the other was a show car. The development car was extensively tested at Silverstone, and Reynard's involvement meant that the aerodynamics, suspension and composites could be honed to perfection. The adoption of the 6.0l engine and Indycar semi-automatic gearbox dictated the car's lines to an extent, and to keep the Indigo as close as possible in

Ford Indigo	
Debut:	Detroit 1996
Engine capacity:	5972cc (364ci)
Configuration:	Mid-mounted V12, petrol
Power:	324kW (435bhp)
Top speed:	290km/h (180mph)
Transmission:	6-speed sequential manual
Length:	4453mm (175in)
Width:	2051mm (81in)
Designers:	Mark Adams/John Hartnell

concept to an Indycar the wheelbase was identical at 2895mm (114in).

No compromises

The Indigo was engineered to weigh as little as possible, but for some reason it featured a relatively complex door assembly on each side. This allowed entry and exit via a scissor-style door opening, and once inside there was very little space for the occupants – footwells were cramped, and there was not much room for anyone especially large. But practicality and comfort came low on the list of priorities – the Indigo was a car of few compromises. And that also explains why the front end features its bizarre-looking aerofoil – this keeps the front of the car down on the Tarmac and provides an area for the front lighting to be fitted. But because the fibre-optic lights

The Indigo looked uncompromising from any angle, but this view probably best shows the focus on aerodynamics and speed above all else. This wasn't a car for the family.

hidden within it are so directional, the main lighting had to be housed within the front of each wing mirror.

The interior was also stripped out, in a bid to save weight. There was no roof and not even a proper windscreen, although a minidisc player was fitted – this despite the fact that once the car was on the move, its occupants would be hard-pressed to hear anything over the roar of the engine sitting just inches from their ears. Four-point seatbelts kept the driver and passenger in place, and a starter button fired the V12 up, just as in a race car.

Race car engineering

The V12 engine was based on two V6s stitched together, and it was this engine which was later fitted to the Aston Martin DB7 Vantage. An all-aluminium unit with 48 valves and four overhead camshafts, this

Just like the exterior, the cabin of the Indigo was very focused. There were few creature comforts, and there was not even the provision of any weather equipment.

V12 was capable of producing more than 373kW (500bhp) if necessary. But even in standard form, with a mere 324kW (435bhp) on offer, the Indigo was allegedly capable of sprinting from 0–100km/h (0–62mph) in just under four seconds – probably fast enough for most buyers!

Following race car practice, the V12 was bolted directly to the back of the Indigo's monocoque, and this carried all the suspension loads. Attached directly to the back of the engine was the transaxle, with the gearchanges activated by buttons on the steering wheel – although there was still a conventionally operated clutch.

IAD Alien

Instead of having doors that opened independently of each other, the IAD Alien had a canopy which revealed the whole of the car's interior when raised.

The Alien was the car that was designed from the outset to look more amazing than the Lamborghini Countach. And from any angle it succeeded in spectacular fashion.

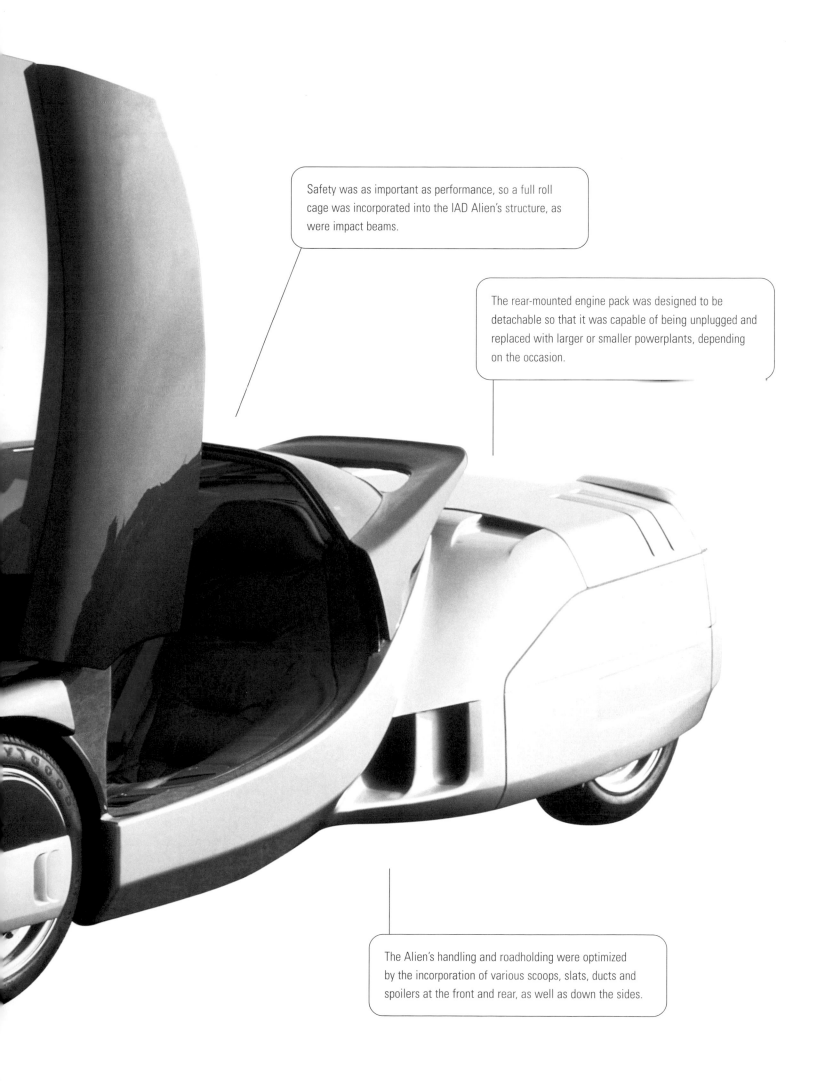

Safety was as important as performance, so a full roll cage was incorporated into the IAD Alien's structure, as were impact beams.

The rear-mounted engine pack was designed to be detachable so that it was capable of being unplugged and replaced with larger or smaller powerplants, depending on the occasion.

The Alien's handling and roadholding were optimized by the incorporation of various scoops, slats, ducts and spoilers at the front and rear, as well as down the sides.

mechanical components (engine, gearbox, cooling system) were kept separate from the passenger space. This gave the car its distinctive tapered body, which widened suddenly at the back. As the body widened, there were air intakes to feed the powerplant sitting behind the driver and passenger (it was strictly a two-seater).

Safety first

Although the Alien was never properly developed for production, it was designed with safety firmly in mind. To that end, there was roll-over and side-impact protection built into the structure, and the narrowed centre helped to improve the car's aerodynamics to levels well beyond what was normal for such a class of car. Not only that, but by paying close attention to detail with all the scoops, slats, ducts and spoilers, it was possible to increase the downforce to levels much greater than supercar drivers were used to as well.

The two most important aspects of the Alien were that it had to be the most dramatic car ever made and

When the brief for the design of the IAD Alien was set, it was to make a car that was even more spectacular than the Lamborghini Countach. Take a look at the photographs here, and you would have to agree that not only was the brief met, but it also produced a car so outrageous that there was no prospect of it ever going beyond the concept stage.

Making a mark

International Automotive Design, or IAD, was a British design consultancy that decided to make its mark. And this it did at the 1986 Turin motor show, unveiling a car that would not only be more eye-catching than anything produced by Ferrari or Lamborghini, but would also be more practical and even better to drive. If that sounds like a tall order, it is – so no one was surprised that the Alien took a whole two years to advance from initial thoughts to a non-running prototype on the IAD show stand.

Although the looks of the Alien were revolutionary, there was much more to the concept than mere aesthetics. The key advance was the way that the

IAD Alien	
Debut:	Turin 1986
Engine capacity:	Non-runner
Configuration:	Mid-mounted
Power:	N/A
Top speed:	N/A
Transmission:	N/A
Length:	3696mm (146in)
Width:	1600mm (63in)
Designer:	Martin Longmore

Great attention to detail was paid to the Alien's aerodynamics, with flush-fitting wheel covers playing their part in reducing turbulence at high speed. They did not help brake cooling, though ...

also offer a supreme driving experience. On the former count, it managed to avoid most of the usual supercar design clichés, although it still featured scissor-action doors, a cab-forward stance and a mid-mounted engine (the latter two being pretty much essential for a no-compromise hypercar). Even the door configuration was not what was initially planned – instead, the whole front end was to lift up in its entirety. But building this canopy would have led to glazing difficulties, so a more conventional solution was required.

Aerodynamic efficiency

The front and rear wheels were enclosed to improve aerodynamics, and, to make sure that the brakes did not overheat, there were ducts to channel away the hot air. There were 40.6cm (16in) wheels at each corner, and the Alien's height, at just 106cm (42in), gave the car a menacing look that was par for the course.

Inside, the Alien's two seats cosseted the driver and passenger, who travelled in a semi-reclining position. The initial plan had been for a circular steering wheel incorporating buttons to control the car's major functions, but by the time the concept was built there was a central handlebar onto which all the buttons were fitted.

The IAD Alien was never made into a running prototype. However, when it was shown, the plan was for it to be fitted with a flat-six or V6 powerplant, although potentially there could also have been a choice of V8 or V12 engines. It was even suggested that the car could be fitted with a 1.6l four-cylinder engine during the week, to be used for commuting – and at the weekend the whole unit could be swapped for a much larger powerplant with two or three times as many cylinders. Now that would certainly have proved revolutionary ...

The Alien's rear pod could be unplugged and something either more or less powerful could be substituted. In theory it made sense – but, of course, in practice it did not actually work.

Italdesign Aztec

More like two motorbikes attached to each other, the Aztec featured two separate cockpits for each of its occupants, each with its own set of instruments.

Down each side of the car was a service centre, for housing various pieces of equipment and monitoring such things as fluid levels.

The door arrangements were very messy: there was a separate canopy to be raised for each occupant, as well as a conventionally opening door.

The turbocharged five-cylinder engine in the Aztec was mid-mounted. Borrowed from Audi's 200 Turbo, it was further boosted to increase the available power to a maximum of 186kW (250bhp).

Four-wheel drive was becoming very fashionable when the Aztec was unveiled — and this car featured the company's famed quattro all-wheel drive transmission.

The amount of work that goes into producing a single concept can be astronomical, so it is rare to see a whole family of concepts unveiled at a motor show. At the 1988 Turin motor show, however, Italdesign was to do just that, with a trio of concepts all based on Audi mechanicals.

First there was the Asgard, which was a 6+2-seater people carrier that put the emphasis on practicality. Then there was the Aspid, a two-seater closed sports car which focused on performance and handling. And even more extreme was the open version of the Aspid, called the Aztec. This was exactly the same as the

All of the Aztec family of vehicles were built as fully running prototypes, but with no weather protection of any kind provided, the open-topped car was not one to be used in inclement conditions.

Aspid up to the waist, but instead of featuring a fixed roof, it had a pair of cockpits – one for each of the occupants. Each cockpit was enveloped by a canopy to keep the worst of the weather at bay, but there was no weather protection as such – this was a car to enjoy strictly when the sun was out.

Road racer

The profile set up by the windscreens was continued behind the seating area, as there were fairings over the rear deck to give that authentic road-racer feel. Protruding from the front of each fairing was a roll hoop, and discreetly incorporated into the rear flanks were the cooling ducts for the mid-mounted engine.

The five-cylinder powerplant of the Audi 200 Turbo was used for each of the concepts, but the power was boosted to 186kW (250bhp) – which equated to 37kW (50bhp) more than usual. Helping to put this power down was Audi's famed quattro four-wheel drive system, and there were ventilated disc brakes at each corner to help rein it in again once the car had reached the projected 240km/h (150mph) top speed. Both the Aspid and Aztec featured a five-speed manual gearbox, while the Asgard was equipped with a three-speed automatic.

Italdesign Aztec

Debut:	Turin 1988
Engine capacity:	2226cc (136ci) turbocharged
Configuration:	Mid-mounted in-line 5, petrol
Power:	186kW (250bhp)
Top speed:	240km/h (150mph)
Transmission:	5-speed manual, 4WD
Length:	4270mm (168in)
Width:	1970mm (78in)
Designer:	N/A

The Aztec was the perfect car to travel in if you did not get on with your passenger very much because each of the two occupants of the vehicle had their own separate compartments, complete with individual windscreen. The fighter plane canopies that each occupant was afforded was just the start of the aeronautical analogy, because not only did the driver get full instrumentation, but so did the passenger as well. Italdesign fell short of also giving the passenger a set of controls, but there was a handle which looked like half a steering wheel – the lengths to which Italdesign went to make the Aztec as symmetrical as possible were really quite odd.

Among the information available to the driver and passenger was a form of route guidance which also allowed for the provision of real-time data on traffic and weather conditions in the surrounding area. Without the benefit of GPS technology, it is not clear how reliable such a system would have been, but what was futuristic technology then is now becoming available in production cars.

In fact, the Aztec was pretty much like two single-seaters mated to each other, and the entry and exit arrangements were rather clumsy as a result. As with any normal car, there was a front-hinged door for each occupant, which opened in the conventional manner. Once that was opened, however, the canopy had to be tilted forwards before access was possible. Once the occupant was seated, the canopy was lowered again before the door was closed.

Information overkill

Outside, the design was just as overcomplicated, with 'service centres' being incorporated into the rear panels. On the right-hand side were digital gauges to monitor the levels of the coolant and brake fluid levels. There were also a removable thermometer, a 12-volt power outlet, a hydraulic lift and a gauge that showed how much filtering capacity was left for the engine's air filter. Quite why this information needed to be displayed so far from the driver's line of sight was never explained, but the service unit on the other side of the car was equally hidden from the driver. At least access to this was not generally needed with the car in motion, which is why the compartment also housed the fire extinguisher, a torch, a tyre compressor and the fuel filler.

The final twist in the tale came in 1990, when the design rights were sold to Italian company Compact, with a view to putting the car into limited production for the Japanese market only. A tiny number were built – at a cost of £300,000 each.

The Asgard was an eight-seater people carrier. When produced in 1988, this type of vehicle was still unusual – and that huge glass roof looked like the future for the genre.

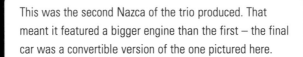

Italdesign Nazca

This was the second Nazca of the trio produced. That meant it featured a bigger engine than the first — the final car was a convertible version of the one pictured here.

Italdesign cranked up the power to 283kW (380bhp) with the Nazca C2, utilizing a mid-mounted 5.6l V12 engine from the BMW 8-Series. That was enough to give a top speed of almost 320km/h (200mph).

The Nazca's nose featured BMW's famous double-kidney grille — although this was not a commission on behalf of BMW, the Nazca was potentially a successor to the M1 supercar of the 1970s.

The entire cabin was topped off with a glass dome, which lifted to enable the doors below to be opened in the conventional way – a complicated solution.

To keep the weight down so that performance could be maximized, the bodyshell was made of carbon fibre – although this is light and strong, it is hugely expensive to manufacture.

The BMW M1 of the late 1970s had been quite a car — a powerhouse built in tiny numbers because it was so expensive, without really offering a true rival to more established supercars of the time. The Italdesign Nazca could have been the perfect encore to the first mid-engined supercar to have come out of BMW, but it was not to be. The Munich-based company had no official involvement with the Nazca, despite the twin-kidney grille being a strong clue of Italdesign's intention to build a BMW supercar for the 1990s. Things might have been different if the global recession had not hit just at that time, but it did, and the Nazca was relegated to museum exhibit status.

Three of a kind

The Nazca that was unveiled at the 1991 Geneva motor show was the first of three. First came the Nazca M12, which was followed by the Nazca C2, debuting later that same year at the Tokyo motor show. Finally, in 1993, came what was perhaps the most dramatic of

The wind-cheating lines of the Italdesign Nazca are most apparent in this overhead shot, where the teardrop shape of the car in plan view can be seen.

the trio — the Nazca C2 Spider. All were fantastic-looking supercars with amazing road presence and hugely powerful engines — but none of them made that leap to production status, as had originally been hoped.

The Italdesign Nazca may look very similar to the Aztec elsewhere in this book (see pages 98–101), but, apart from the basic layout of the two cars, there is little else in common. Yes, the engine sits in the middle of the car and there are seats for just a driver and passenger — but after that, the similarities end.

Power was provided by a BMW V12 engine, which had been breathed on by Alpina. Rated at 224kW (300bhp), it was claimed that the M12 would reach a top speed of at least 298km/h (185mph) while completing the 0–100km/h (0–62mph) dash in just 4.2 seconds. Nor did acceleration lessen once 100km/h (62mph) had been reached because the scorching

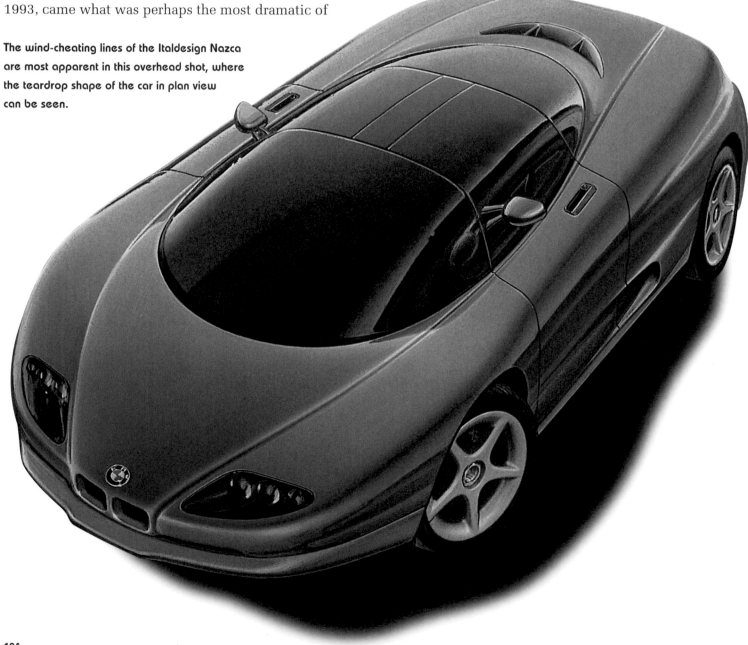

46kg-m (332lb-ft) of torque available meant the urge would have been relentless at pretty much any speed. By the time the C2 had been dreamed up, there was an even more powerful engine (261kW/350bhp), which was also lighter. And this time round, 322km/h (200mph) was claimed as being a real possibility.

Carbon-fibre structure

The first Nazca concept was highly developed when it first appeared – although whether it was ready for even limited production is doubtful. Nonetheless, Italdesign did look at the possibility of making 50 examples, which would have been hugely expensive because the Nazca's main structure was made of carbon fibre. In fact, this concept was the first vehicle

The most highly developed of the Nazca trio was the C2 Spider; if there had not been a global recession in the early 1990s, the car may well have gone into limited production.

made by the company to use carbon fibre in its construction, and after the Nazca was built, all of Italdesign's concepts were made of the composite.

Sitting on 45.7cm (18-inch wheels), the Nazca was fitted with ultra-low profile tyres (35-profile at the back and 40-profile at the front). Behind the spoked alloy wheels were 35.5cm (14in) Brembo ventilated disc brakes, and transmitting the power to the rear wheels was a five-speed manual gearbox.

The Nazca used all the classic supercar styling cues, with a cab-forward stance and an emphasized wedge shape. The low nose incorporated flush-fitting headlights and the whole of the passenger area was glass-topped. For some reason, the doors were split, with the lower half opening conventionally and gullwing upper halves – very fussy and also unnecessarily expensive to manufacture. Still, it made a change from the usual scissor-action units.

When Italdesign's Nazca C2 arrived, the differences over the M12 were relatively minor – a more powerful engine and small styling changes were about it. But the big news was the C2 Spider, which featured a sorted chassis and the 5575cc (340ci) V12 from the BMW 850CSi. With 283kW (380bhp) and the chance for pretty much fully open-topped motoring thanks to the removable door tops, the C2 Spider was the pick of the bunch. What a pity the global recession chose that particular moment to hit ...

Italdesign Nazca	
Debut:	Geneva 1991
Engine capacity:	4988cc (304ci)
Configuration:	Mid-mounted V12, petrol
Power:	224kW (300bhp)
Top speed:	298km/h (185mph)
Transmission:	5-speed manual, RWD
Length:	4365mm (172in)
Width:	1990mm (78in)
Designer:	N/A

MG E-XE

The whole of the MG E-XE's roof was made of darkened glass, which not only gave it a futuristic look, but also opened up the interior.

Inside was plenty of equipment, but this was only a mock-up because the technology did not yet exist for it to work. The design, though, worked beautifully …

Because of the engine's central location, the E-XE had a cab-forward design, which positioned the car's occupants towards the front of the car, behind a short bonnet.

The EX-E's 3l V6 engine was positioned behind the two occupants. It produced 186kW (250bhp) in this instance, but this could be easily tuned to make it capable of a reliable 298kW (400bhp).

From the rear, it is easy to see how the E-XE inspired much of the detailing of the MGF, which was to appear more than a decade later.

The British-owned motor industry has produced relatively few concept cars over the years, but, when one does get built, it tends to be worth waiting for. The MG E-XE was just such a concept – by the time it made its debut at the 1985 Frankfurt motor show, the MG marque seemed to be on its last legs.

The MGB had been axed years earlier, and the only presence MG had was due to cars such as the Metro, Maestro and Montego. What was needed was a hefty shot in the arm to show that there was still life in the company – and this is precisely what the stunning E-XE provided.

Virtual power

Although the E-XE was unveiled as a non-runner, it had been engineered to accept the 3.0l V6 engine that was normally found in the MG Metro 6R4. This was a compact unit closely related to the legendary Rover V8 powerplant, and it could be tuned to produce a reliable 298kW (400bhp) – a pretty good basis from which to start. In the EX-E, the quad-cam 24-valve

unit was detuned to produce 186kW (250bhp), and to help put the power down, the car was equipped with four-wheel drive. Transmitting this power to all four wheels was a five-speed manual gearbox, and there were all sorts of tricks up MG's sleeve to keep the car on the straight and narrow. As well as a central viscous control unit, there were limited slip diffs at the front and rear.

Adjustable ride height was also fitted, and an exceptionally low drag factor of 0.24 meant that the EX-E could in theory travel all the way up to 275km/h (171mph) before running out of steam. Located behind the car's two occupants, but just ahead of the rear axle, the 6R4 had the classic mid-engined layout of any supercar worth its salt – this was a car that would put driving enjoyment far ahead of such mundanities as luggage or passenger space.

More enveloping than those in most sports cars, the luxuriously trimmed cabin of the E-XE somehow managed to feel spacious while also acting like a snug cocoon for its two occupants.

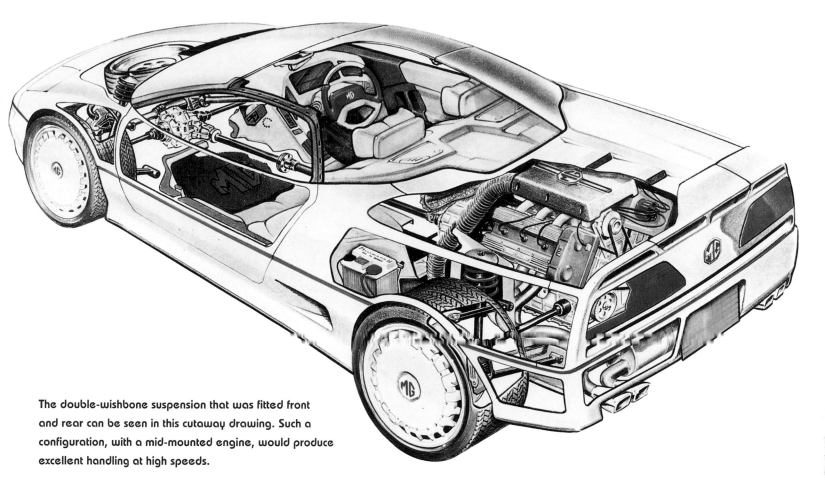

The double-wishbone suspension that was fitted front and rear can be seen in this cutaway drawing. Such a configuration, with a mid-mounted engine, would produce excellent handling at high speeds.

The car took its name from the fact that it was an EXperimental MG-E – although when MG released it onto the roads a decade later, the car was called the MGF. This was quite different from the concept shown at Frankfurt, but the essential premise was the same: it was a mid-engined sports car, if somewhat less potent. More importantly, though, the EX-E gave a good indication of what the MGF would look like when it finally appeared.

Equipment galore

One of the things that did not survive the translation to showroom car was the extensive use of darkened glass, which was all fitted flush to make it look more futuristic. A strong wedge shape with pop-up headlights was a classic sportscar styling cue. Also standard for the genre was an interior that did not have to worry too much about production constraints.

There were plenty of electronics, leather on just about every surface and theoretical equipment which could have been fitted, but which did not actually work in the concept. To that end, there was a partial head-up display (dubbed as the 'reflex information monitor'), which showed key information in the driver's line of vision, and also four-stage cruise control, climate control and automatic lights and windscreen wipers.

All these bits of equipment were only the start – a comprehensive entertainment and telephone system (incorporating satellite navigation) was also shoehorned into the MG's interior. As was a card-based ignition system which required a card to be inserted into a slot and a personal identity number to be entered before the car would start. Of course, none of this worked – at the time, electronics were still in their infancy. Yet today, many of these ideas are now a production reality in cheap and affordable cars.

MG E-XE

Debut:	Frankfurt 1985
Engine capacity:	2991cc (183ci)
Configuration:	Mid-mounted V6, petrol
Power:	186kW (250bhp)
Top speed:	275km/h (171mph)
Transmission:	5-speed manual, 4WD
Length:	N/A
Width:	N/A
Designers:	Roy Axe, Gordon Sked

Pininfarina Mythos

The powerplant was carried over wholesale, which meant it displaced 5l (305ci) and provided a healthy 291kW (390bhp). But the aerodynamics meant that the top speed was still only around 257km/h (160mph).

The height of the rear wing varied according to the speed of the car. With 30.4cm (12in) of adjustment available, it sat flush at rest, and rose with the speed.

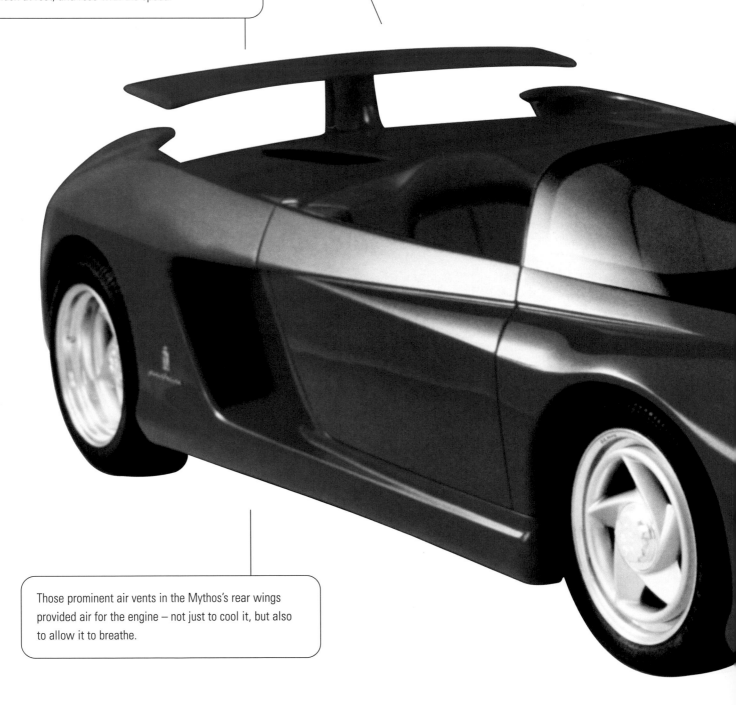

Those prominent air vents in the Mythos's rear wings provided air for the engine – not just to cool it, but also to allow it to breathe.

There was little in the way of decoration on the outside, and the inside was much the same. Leather abounded, but trim and instrumentation were minimal.

When you base a car on the Ferrari Testarossa, you cannot help but come up with something dramatic. Simply housing that flat-12 engine means that the result will be big and brutish.

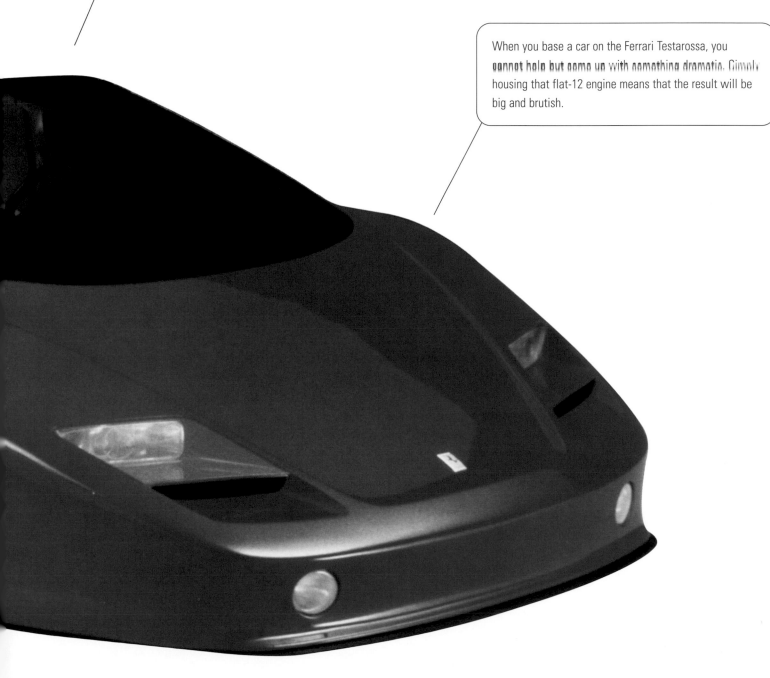

When you base a concept on a Ferrari Testarossa chassis, there can be only one outcome – a concept supercar which takes the best that the Ferrari has to offer and makes it even better. To that end, the 291KW (390bhp), 4942cc (302ci) flat-12 of the Testarossa was carried over, along with the Testarossa's transmission and suspension, steering and brakes.

The Ferrari, however, was not noted for its looks, which were dramatic but not beautiful; the Mythos was certainly a lot more pretty. And while it was claimed that the Mythos would never go into production in any form, certain elements of it were incorporated into future production Ferraris.

Flowing lines

Pininfarina began designing Ferraris in 1952, and, although other design houses have styled some Ferrari cars, it is Pininfarina that is synonymous with styling the cars bearing the hallowed prancing horse badge. But while previous Ferraris had been all about flowing lines – or as Pininfarina called it, 'linked panels' – the Mythos was about the relationship between volumes. Or, as Pininfarina explained, the fact that the engine and radiators of the car were at the back meant that the track of the car was much narrower at the front. And where the Testarossa hid this with its famous side strakes, which bridged the gap between the narrow front and the wide rear, the huge side scoops of the Mythos emphasized the difference.

The wheelbase of the Mythos was the same as the Testarossa's, but the length was around 170mm (6.7in)

The cab-forward balance of the Mythos is most apparent in profile, as is the pronounced wedge shape, which at the front of the car has been taken to extremes.

The Pininfarina Mythos was a fully functioning prototype, and here it can be seen being put through its paces. The ultra-wide track can also be seen from this angle.

shorter due to much less rear overhang. This emphasized the 'cab-forward' look of the car – a trend which became increasingly prominent during the 1990s. The side view was dominated by the layered construction (itself made necessary by the rear-mounted radiators), while the leading edge of the front spoiler moved forward by 2.5cm (1in) at high speed, to increase downforce. Echoing the Mythos's pronounced front spoiler were the side sills, and these then blended into those bulbous rear wings, which housed massive 43.1cm (17in) wheels wrapped in 335/25 ZR17 Pirelli PZero rubber.

Like the front spoiler, the rear fin moved according to how fast the Mythos was being driven. There was up to 30cm (12in) of vertical adjustment available – when the car was stationary, it looked as though a hoop spoiler were fitted, while at top speed, it looked

Pininfarina Mythos

Debut:	Tokyo 1989
Engine capacity:	4942cc (302ci)
Configuration:	Mid-mounted flat-12, petrol
Power:	291KW (390bhp)
Top speed:	257km/h (160mph) approx
Transmission:	5-speed manual, RWD
Length:	4308mm (170in)
Width:	2108mm (83in)
Designer:	Lorenzo Ramaciotti

Mythos, with the absolute bare minimum of trim or instrumentation to distract. Inspired by the sports racers of the 1960s, there was just a pair of wrap-around seats, few dials and minimalist trim panels. And, of course, there was no entertainment system necessary – there was a 12-cylinder engine just inches away to provide that. The same colour schemes were also in evidence – everything was either black or red, with leather being used to cover just about every surface.

Carbon-fibre construction

The Pininfarina Mythos was significantly lighter than the Testarossa, thanks to its carbon-fibre construction. A massive 255kg (562lb) was shed in the transformation from Testarossa to Mythos, which left the car with a kerb weight of 1252kg (2760lb). Despite this useful loss of weight, however, the top speed of the concept was rather lower than the donor car due to the rather inferior aerodynamics. Still, a top speed of 257km/h (160mph) should have been enough for most people who drove it – particularly bearing in mind how chaotic things can start to get at that sort of speed when there's no roof on offer!

more like an aircraft's tail fin. Somewhat bizarre, but nevertheless highly effective.

The key to the exterior design of the Mythos is that everything is integrated – the headlights, bumpers and spoilers all fit in seamlessly, rather than being used for decoration, and it works so much better for it. Even the wheels, which were made specially for the car by OZ, were fitted with centre caps that merely displayed the Ferrari emblem – there were no wheel nuts on show.

This clean design philosophy was continued inside the

Based on the Testarossa, the Pininfarina Mythos uses the same mid-engined layout and the mechanicals are also carried over. However, the lines of the Mythos concept were far cleaner.

Saab EV-1

The interior of the EV-1 was far more restrained than the outside. The cabin included seating for four people, although the rear seats were more of a token gesture, offering very little comfortable space.

Saab is renowned for its turbocharged engines, and the EV-1 was fitted with a boosted 1985cc (121ci) unit. This gave 213kW (285bhp) – enough to give a top speed of 270km/h (168mph).

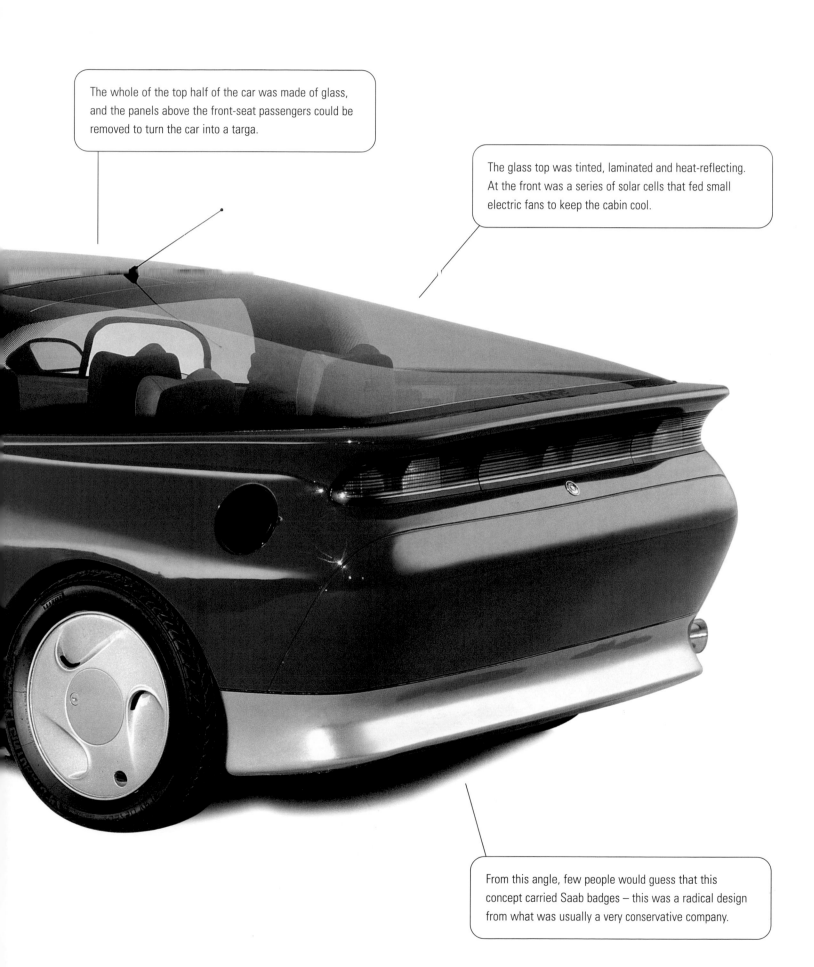

The whole of the top half of the car was made of glass, and the panels above the front-seat passengers could be removed to turn the car into a targa.

The glass top was tinted, laminated and heat-reflecting. At the front was a series of solar cells that fed small electric fans to keep the cabin cool.

From this angle, few people would guess that this concept carried Saab badges – this was a radical design from what was usually a very conservative company.

The only part of the EV-1 that was recognizably Saab was the nose, which featured the manufacturer's traditional grille. But it was flanked by a new, radical design of headlight.

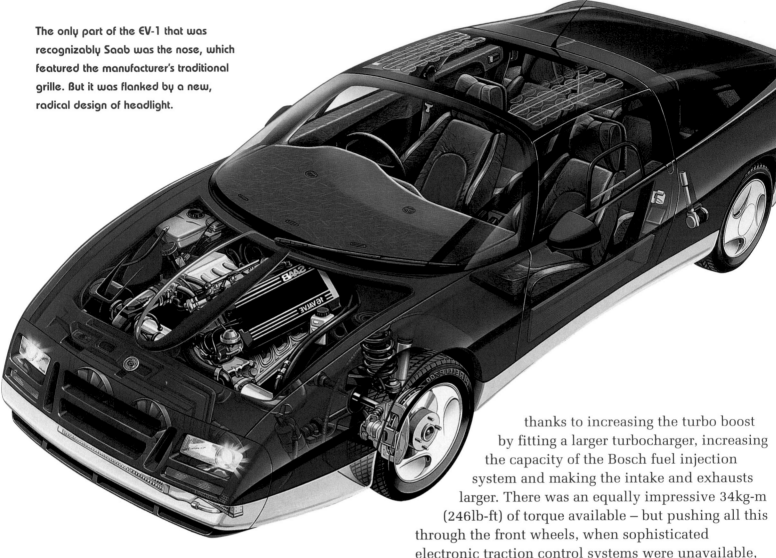

For a car maker as conservative as Saab, the EV-1 of 1985 was a real break with tradition. And had it gone into production, the EV-1 might have shaken off Saab's staid image of building dependable but dull cars. However, from the day the concept was unveiled at the 1986 Los Angeles Auto Expo, the Swedish manufacturer claimed that it was just an engine and styling test bed – and there were no plans for the EV-1 to reach the showroom.

Sports car or supercar?

The Saab EV-1 looked distinctly like a sports car – perhaps even a supercar – but it was no more than a sporting 2+2. Saab had dabbled with sportscar production with its Sonett series of the 1960s, but this had had minimal impact when set against its more traditional family cars – and Saab did not want to go down that route again.

Under the steel skin was a Saab 900 Turbo 16, which meant a twin-cam 16-valve 2.0l in-line four. But whereas the standard car pushed out 130kW (175bhp), the EV-1 had a much stronger 213kW (285bhp) on tap,

thanks to increasing the turbo boost by fitting a larger turbocharger, increasing the capacity of the Bosch fuel injection system and making the intake and exhausts larger. There was an equally impressive 34kg-m (246lb-ft) of torque available – but pushing all this through the front wheels, when sophisticated electronic traction control systems were unavailable, did seem rather foolhardy.

The EV-1's bodyshell was built of sheet steel in the main, but at each end plastic bumpers were fitted, which were designed to deform, then spring back into shape after a light impact. Headlights developed specially by Hella allowed light levels to be maintained despite far more compact dimensions, which in turn allowed a very low bonnet line. With a height of just 70mm (2.75in), these headlights opened the doors for much more adventurous frontal styling, as well as improved aerodynamics – the EV-1's drag factor was just 0.32, which went some way to giving the concept a top speed of 270km/h (168mph).

The doors featured layers of glassfibre and carbon fibre for reinforcement, to help in the event of a side impact. But the most striking thing about the EV-1 was the glazing – virtually the whole of the top half of the car was made of laminated glass, which was also tinted and heat reflecting. But even this technology could not prevent the interior from heating up to unbearable levels when the outside temperature rose, so Saab incorporated 66 solar cells into the removable

Saab EV-1

Debut:	Los Angeles Auto Expo 1985
Engine capacity:	1985cc (121ci)
Configuration:	Front-mounted in-line four, petrol
Power:	213kW (285bhp)
Top speed:	270km/h (168mph)
Transmission:	FWD
Length:	N/A
Width:	N/A
Designer:	Bjorn Envall

there was. The more sun there was, the more the fan was needed to keep the car's interior cool – which failed to take into account those subzero clear, sunny days that are all too frequent in winter …

Low-key interior

Unlike most concept car interiors, that of the EV-1 was very restrained. It was closely based on the fascia seen in the production 9000, which meant it reduced the amount of information displayed at night, to keep distractions as low as possible. To maintain visibility when things started to get humid, a heated windscreen was fitted. This is a feature that has very much become commonplace, but the tungsten wires were just 0.015mm in diameter, and that was innovative in 1986. Another feature which was not especially obvious was the use of ultra-light seats, each fitted with an injection-moulded chassis and back rest frame. All were fitted with leather trim, heating elements and electric adjustment.

glass targa top which sat above the front-seat occupants. These cells supplemented the standard 900 heating, air conditioning and ventilation system, to provide continuous ventilation. Although the idea was a neat one, it was not especially sophisticated – the cells were permanently connected to a fan, the speed of which was dictated by how much sunlight

Although the Saab EV-1's cabin was very sombre, the glass roof helped to reduce the feeling of claustrophobia. The design was also very sober, which was typical of the Swedish manufacturer.

Volkswagen W12

Helping to keep the weight of the W12 to a minimum, the bodyshell was made of Kevlar. That made it expensive, but it was also strong and light.

The power was transmitted to all four wheels, to help with traction. With 313kw (420bhp), the W12 needed to be as usable as possible, even in the wet.

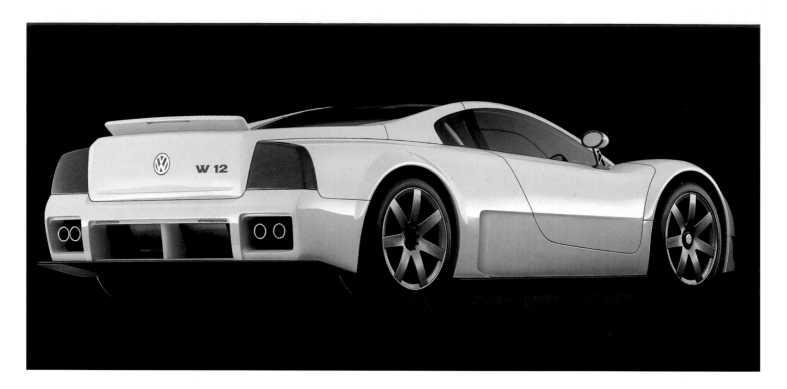

Had there not been a glut of supercars at the turn of the twenty-first century, the Volkswagen W12 may have become a production reality. But with so many all-new hypercars becoming available, most of them with already recognized prestigious badges, the Volkswagen probably did not stand much of a chance.

When the W12 made its debut at the 1997 Tokyo motor show, Volkswagen claimed it was just a one-off, but hinted that limited numbers might be made available if the reaction to it were favourable. Most commentators did indeed think the car was fantastic. However, the fact that it carried Volkswagen badges was not ideal and may have been enough to scupper the project ultimately. Not that it died very quickly because at the 1998 Geneva motor show a roadster

Compared with most contemporary supercars, the Volkswagen W12's lines were very neat. All the ducts and scoops were very well integrated into the vehicle's core shape, giving a smooth, seamless look to this high-performance machine.

version of the W12 was unveiled, and as recently as the 2002 Geneva motor show both Italdesign and Volkswagen were each parading a W12 coupé on their stands. But soon after that, the project was pronounced dead – the VW/Audi Group had enough supercars on its hands trying to make the Bugatti Veyron work, as well as getting two new Lamborghinis to market (Murciélago and Gallardo).

The reasoning behind the W12 was that it could be used by Volkswagen to take on the Mercedes-Benz CLK GTR at Le Mans – successfully racing in the GT1 class would give VW some much-needed credibility in the world of international motorsport. And with the engine fitted to the concept, there would be no problem tuning it to produce a reliable 522kW (700bhp) for endurance racing.

Compact engine

Under the skin of both the coupé and roadster, the mechanicals were largely the same, although the coupé was a non-runner and the roadster was fitted with a five-speed automatic gearbox. The W12 engine consisted of a pair of V6 engines mated to each other to produce a W12 unit – this consisted of four banks of three cylinders, which meant plenty of combustion chambers, but very compact dimensions. Thanks to its 5.6l capacity, there was a healthy 313kW (420bhp)

Volkswagen W12

Debut:	Tokyo 1997
Engine capacity:	5584cc (341ci)
Configuration:	Mid-mounted W12, petrol
Power:	313kW (420bhp)
Top speed:	160mph
Transmission:	6-speed manual, 4WD
Length:	4400mm (173in)
Width:	1920mm (76in)
Designer:	N/A

on tap, but Volkswagen claimed an extra 44kW (60bhp) would be easily attainable. This power was transmitted to all four wheels via a six-speed manual gearbox, with a viscous coupling ensuring the wheels with the greatest traction received the greatest amount of torque.

Lightweight

To keep weight down, the W12's monocoque was constructed of Kevlar, over which was draped a glassfibre skin. This kept the total weight down to around 1200kg (2646lb), which VW hoped would be low enough to get the car from a standing start to 96km/h (60mph) in not much more than four seconds.

The profile of the car incorporated the domed roof design that was by this stage a characteristic of Volkswagens, and the doors were hinged at the top front corner to swing upwards in true supercar fashion. Also following the supercar convention was the choice of wheels – monster 48.2cm (19in) alloys

were fitted, with 255/40 tyres on the front and 285/35 rubber at the rear.

To retain public interest in the W12, a slightly reclothed version was shown at the 2001 Tokyo motor show – which Volkswagen claimed was built to a production standard. The car was basically the same as the original coupé, but there was a different front end featuring reprofiled wings, while the front and rear lights were also updated. Meanwhile, the colour was changed to orange: the first coupé had been yellow and the roadster red. More significantly, the engine was uprated to 6.0l, enough to push power levels up to 447kW (600bhp). This in turn increased the top speed to 349km/h (217mph), while the 0–100km/h (0–62mph) time dropped to just 3.5 seconds. The W12 would have been quite a car, but it was not to be …

As was typical of a Volkswagen, the interior was a missed opportunity. It had all the visual excitement of a standard Polo or Golf, with a design that was far too timid.

Zagato Raptor

The interior of the Raptor was trimmed in leather and Alcantara. And instead of being stocked with equipment and instrumentation galore, it was an exercise in restraint.

Base a concept on the Lamborghini Diablo, and you cannot fail to produce something visually arresting. From every angle, this car looked a million dollars.

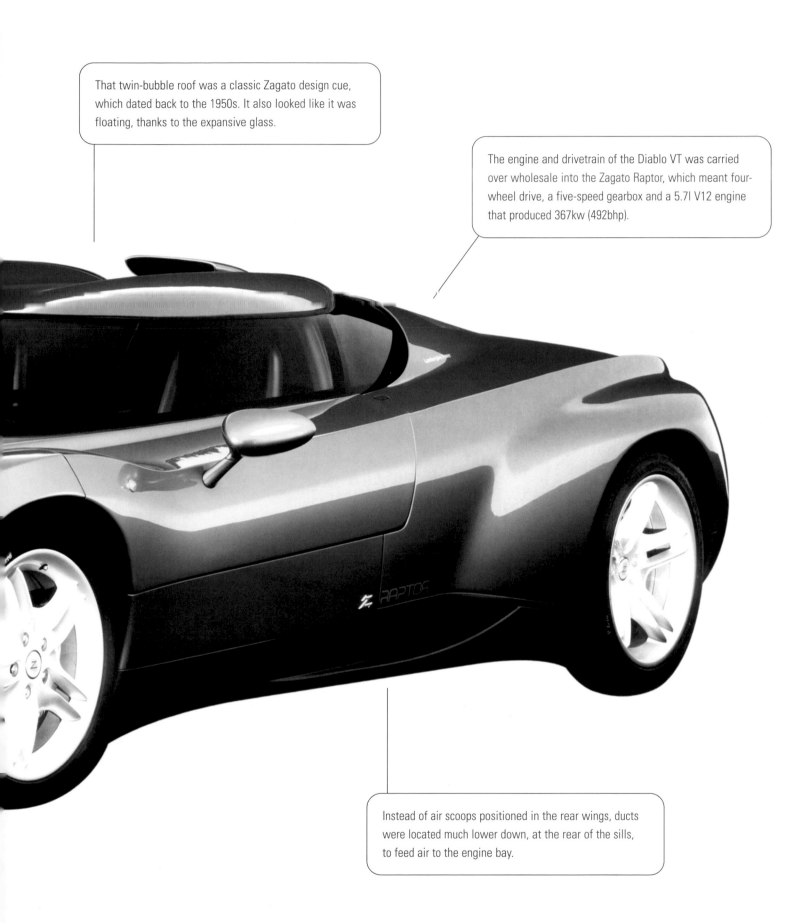

That twin-bubble roof was a classic Zagato design cue, which dated back to the 1950s. It also looked like it was floating, thanks to the expansive glass.

The engine and drivetrain of the Diablo VT was carried over wholesale into the Zagato Raptor, which meant four-wheel drive, a five-speed gearbox and a 5.7l V12 engine that produced 367kw (492bhp).

Instead of air scoops positioned in the rear wings, ducts were located much lower down, at the rear of the sills, to feed air to the engine bay.

You would think that it would be pretty difficult trying to build a car even more dramatic than the Lamborghini Diablo, but when Italian styling house Zagato was approached by bobsleigh champion Alain Wicki, that was exactly what it was asked to do. Wicki was used to travelling at 161km/h (100mph) just inches from the ground, so to find anything that could give such a sensation of speed on the road, it had to be Italian, very powerful – and, preferably, hand-built.

Lamborghini roots

The result was the Raptor, a concept based on the four-wheel drive Lamborghini Diablo VT, and which was also intended to help revive Zagato's flagging fortunes. If this car received the right response when it was unveiled at the 1996 Geneva motor show, Zagato planned to offer it in limited production form to a small number of wealthy enthusiasts. The aim was to use the Raptor as a showcase for Zagato's computer-aided design and manufacturing facilities, and to also provide Lamborghini with an extra model for its range – the assumption was that the latter

company would manufacture the car in its factory in Sant'Agata.

Considering the project began life only in the summer of 1995, it was an impressive feat to have a fully running prototype built by March 1996 – work on the chassis had begun only four months earlier. Having a working platform on which to build the car was a great help – the engine, transmission, suspension and steering were all used in their 'natural' form. That meant there was a healthy 367kW (492bhp) on tap, and, although no top speed performance testing was performed on the car, 322km/h (200mph) was reckoned to have been achievable.

Such performance was helped by a reduction in kerb weight over the Diablo, to just 1350kg (2976lb), although the fact that there was no roof would have done the Raptor no favours aerodynamically. However, because the Raptor was planned as a production-ready

Getting in and out of the Raptor meant raising that huge canopy that enveloped the occupants. Quite how the car would have fared in the event of a crash does not bear thinking about.

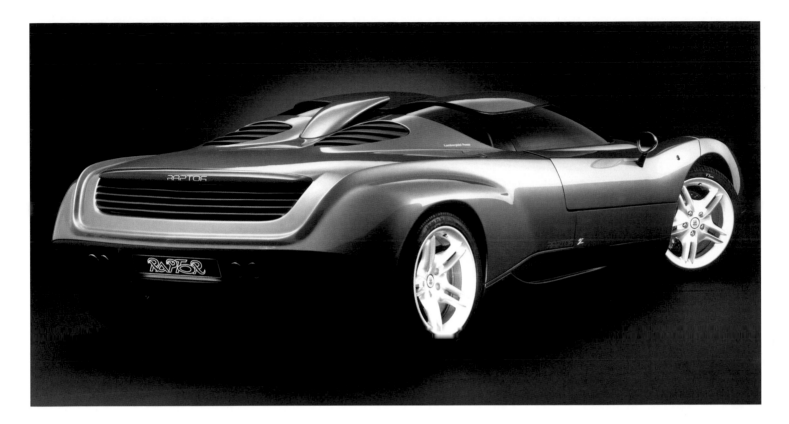

concept, a closed coupé version was also designed – although, sadly, this never got off the drawing board.

In true Italian supercar fashion, the wedge-shaped profile of the Raptor had a cab-forward stance – the occupants sat quite far forward so that the engine was closer to the middle of the car, to improve handling. To improve aerodynamics, there were no pop-up headlights – instead the lights were housed behind Plexiglass fairings. The double-bubble fairings behind the two occupants echoed the classic Zagato twin-bubble roof signature, while the rear was exceptionally clean thanks to the single wide light in place of the more usual pair of multi-coloured lamp clusters.

Rear visibility in the Raptor must have been a very difficult – even more so than for the typical 1990s supercar. But the Raptor's stylish Lamborghini-esque looks meant it certainly had presence.

The five-spoke alloy wheels for the Raptor were built specially, just like the brakes. Although the Diablo has pretty strong brakes, they were the one thing that the team at Zagato felt had not reached the required levels. As a result, a bespoke British Alcon racing system was fitted to make sure that the car could be hauled down from really high speeds, time and time again.

Simple cab

Inside the Raptor, everything was trimmed in Alcantara, a suedelike material that is as durable as leather – and also as expensive. With its beige colour, this material coated the wide centre console, seats and fascia, all of which were uncluttered. Apart from a digital display in front of the driver, there was no instrumentation on the dash, while the centre console featured only a single gauge – joined by a few switches grouped together. A thick Momo steering wheel carried the Zagato logo in its centre, and an aluminium-topped gearlever sat in an alloy H-gate – and that was it.

When the car made its debut, it was greeted enthusiastically by the press and public alike. By the time the show closed, 550 people had expressed an interest in buying one, but, as Lamborghini was going through major changes at the time, the project faltered. In the end, only one prototype was built.

Zagato Raptor

Debut:	Geneva 1996
Engine capacity:	5707cc (348ci)
Configuration:	Mid-mounted V12, petrol
Power:	367kW (492bhp)
Top speed:	322km/h (200mph)
Transmission:	5-speed manual, 4WD
Length:	4380mm (172in)
Width:	2020mm (80in)
Designer:	Norihiko Harada

Luxury Concepts

As production cars have become increasingly highly specified, their luxury concept counterparts have had to become ever more heavily laden with technology and equipment to be worthy of the name. Some of these cars have more gadgets fitted than any driver would ever use, yet the rate of development is showing no sign of slowing down as ever more luxury concepts appear.

The sky is always the limit when it comes to building a concept car that packs in the luxury features. After all, a concept has to look to the future, and thus to technologies that have yet to fully emerge. Taking this into consideration, the minds of some designers know no bounds when it comes to gadgetry and electronics, and the development of liquid crystal displays and microchips has let their imaginations run riot.

When describing a car, the word 'luxury' has always meant power, comfort, space and equipment, but such terms have also always been relative. Many of the luxury cars of just two decades ago would now be considered less luxurious than the run-of-the-mill offerings available today. And the luxury cars of tomorrow have to be something spectacular indeed to compete against the all-round capabilities of ordinary cars in the twenty-first century.

Considering this was Land Rover's first ever concept vehicle, it is impressive that the Range Stormer managed to incorporate most of the glamour that is essential in creating a true show-stopper for the demanding luxury market.

The result of this progress is a series of concepts which offer more than mere gadgets and power. They represent huge amounts of attention to detail, focusing on just about every aspect of car engineering. Transmissions have to shift that little bit more smoothly; engines have to be ever more refined; materials used within the cabin have to be more upmarket than offered elsewhere; equipment levels also have to rise without the dashboard or interior looking so complicated that potential buyers are put off.

Wanting for nothing

Cars such as the Audi Avantissimo and Cadillac Sixteen are the result, featuring high-quality materials throughout and equipment levels that leave the car's occupants wanting for nothing. But despite the amazing array of gadgets offered in cars such as these, their interiors are not intimidating, thanks to a deliberate understatement in the design. Huge reserves of power are also available, alongside impressive levels of safety features to prevent an accident. Despite this, they appear to be related to real-world cars that people can actually buy. Truly, the luxury cars of tomorrow.

Audi Avantissimo

Had the Audi Avantissimo made it to production, it would probably have been the world's most luxurious estate (station wagon) – it had huge reserves of performance, space and equipment.

With very conservative lines, the Avantissimo looked much like a grown-up A6 Avant – and all those Audi corporate design cues made it easily identifiable.

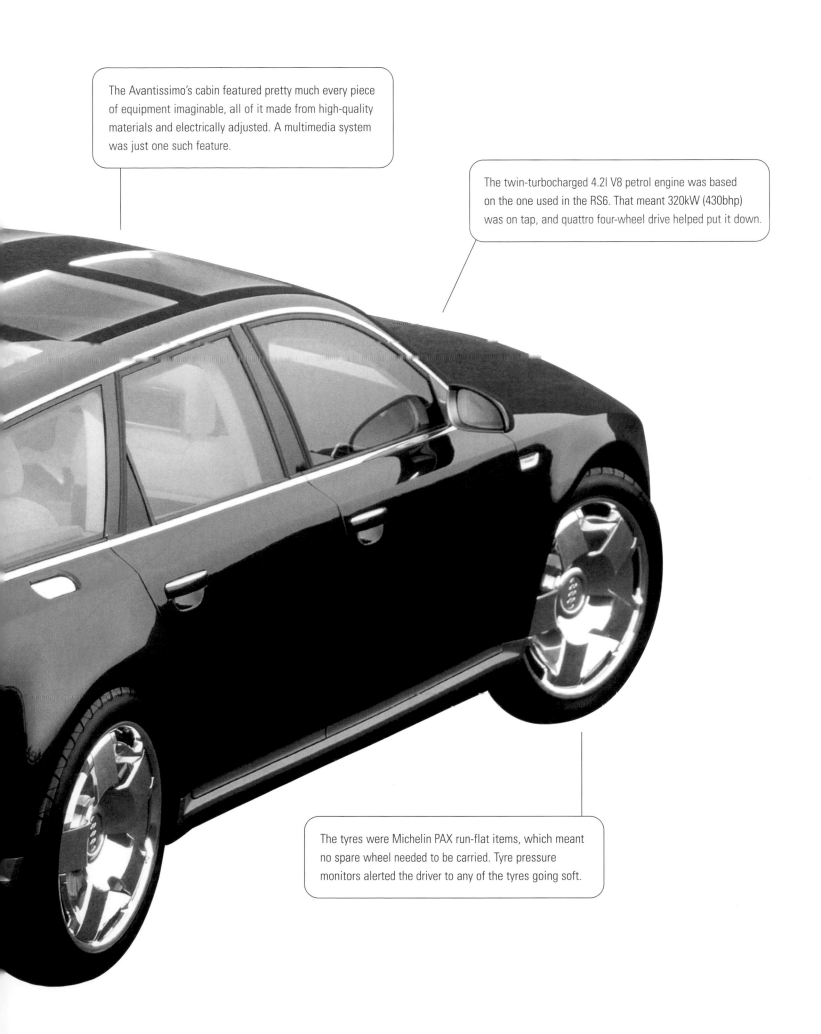

The Avantissimo's cabin featured pretty much every piece of equipment imaginable, all of it made from high-quality materials and electrically adjusted. A multimedia system was just one such feature.

The twin-turbocharged 4.2l V8 petrol engine was based on the one used in the RS6. That meant 320kW (430bhp) was on tap, and quattro four-wheel drive helped put it down.

The tyres were Michelin PAX run-flat items, which meant no spare wheel needed to be carried. Tyre pressure monitors alerted the driver to any of the tyres going soft.

Executive estates (station wagons) are commonplace, but true luxury load carriers are another matter. That was why Audi decided to see what an A8 estate might look like – nobody else was offering anything comparable, although there was no shortage of choice just one size down. Estate versions of cars such as the Audi A6, Mercedes E-class and BMW 5-series were popular – but what if somebody wanted more space, more luxury and probably even more performance? By taking the lines of the A6 Avant and blending them with those of the second-generation A8, the resulting load-carrier hid its bulk extremely well – although it certainly looked more butch than sleek.

The significant difference between the Avantissimo and both the A6 and all of Audi's luxury rivals is the method of construction. Whereas steel bodyshells are the order of the day for most car makers, the Avantissimo used the Aluminium Space Frame (ASF) construction of the A8 to keep weight to a minimum. And that is just as well because the finished shell was hardly lightweight with such equipment as permanent four-wheel drive, climate control and electric adjustment of everything from the windows to the steering wheel and seats.

Environmentally sound

Despite its aluminium construction, the Avantissimo could hardly claim to be ecologically sound – after all, a 4.2l V8 engine with a pair of turbochargers attached is not exactly the most fuel-efficient motive power. So to help the car achieve a more environmentally friendly status, solar panels were incorporated in the roof. The energy harnessed was then used to help keep the car's interior cool when ambient temperatures

Audi Avantissimo

Debut:	Frankfurt 2001
Engine capacity:	4200cc (256ci) twin-turbo
Configuration:	Front-mounted V8, petrol
Power:	321kW (430bhp)
Top speed:	250km/h (155mph) – electronically limited
Transmission:	6-speed auto/sequential manual, 4WD
Length:	5060mm (199in)
Width:	1910mm (75in)
Designer:	Peter Schreyer and Lutz Sauvant

started to climb. In keeping with its luxury status, every surface within the Avantissimo's interior was covered in either leather or Alcantara. Bright trim was everywhere, with chrome picking out details among the instrumentation, centre console, steering wheel and door trims. Such chrome and leather touches were nods to the past, but the rest of the interior was extremely modern. The Multi Media Interface (MMI), which would be fitted as standard to the second-generation A8, was first installed in the Avantissimo, and it was this system that let the driver control all the car's systems, from the satellite navigation and climate control to the stereo and telephone.

With those chromed wheels and liberally applied brightwork all over, it was clear that the Avantissimo was predominantly designed for the North American market.

Virtually all these features have now been incorporated into production Audis – but the most futuristic item that has progressed beyond the concept stage is that of fingerprint-based personalization. The Avantissimo used this to identify the driver so that the seating position, climate control settings and MMI configuration could be preset accordingly.

Although memory buttons are commonplace in production cars, the use of fingerprint recognition is the next step for luxury car makers, and Audi was the first with the A8.

Safety first

The Avantissimo naturally incorporated plenty of safety touches, not least of all a safe crash structure. To try to prevent an accident in the first place, the concept was fitted with electronic gadgetry galore: anti-lock brakes, electronic stability protection, traction control and electronic brake force distribution. If any of the tyres were punctured, they could be run

Everything about the Avantissimo had to shout luxury, and from this angle it most certainly did. Wood, leather – and just about everything was electrically operated.

flat at up to 80km/h (50mph), thanks to the fitment of Michelin Pax run-flat technology. Tyre pressure sensors monitored pressure loss, and the Pax system meant that the need for a spare wheel was eliminated. And if one of the tyres was flat, the ride would still be comfortable thanks to air suspension with three presets: Sport, Comfort and Automatic. Not only did this alter the firmness of the suspension, but the car's ride height could be adjusted as well, depending on how fast the car was travelling.

The Avantissimo was at first touted as a production possibility, the suggestion being that the forthcoming new A8 could be available as an estate as well as a saloon (sedan). But Audi got cold feet and pulled out of the project, despite few voices of dissent among those who reviewed it.

Buick LaCrosse

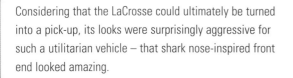

Considering that the LaCrosse could ultimately be turned into a pick-up, its looks were surprisingly aggressive for such a utilitarian vehicle – that shark nose-inspired front end looked amazing.

The sharp front end housed a 4.2l V8, which was tuned for torque, rather than power. And that, when combined with the automatic gearbox, guaranteed a relaxing, comfortable ride.

As well as potentially being a pick-up, the LaCrosse could be a five-seater luxury saloon (sedan), or even a convertible. In the latter mode, the prominent side rails did remain in place, though.

The interior felt very spacious, thanks to the pillarless construction, the use of light-coloured materials throughout and the glass roof that let in plenty of light.

Everything in the LaCrosse was electrically operated — the glass roof, pick-up bed, interior equipment and even all four doors, which opened at right angles for easier entry and exit.

Following the trend for building concepts with as much versatility as possible, the Buick LaCrosse was a five-seater saloon (sedan) and a pick-up all in one – with a bit of convertible thrown in for good measure. Or, as Buick put it, the LaCrosse was the 'master of metamorphosis'. Offering several bodystyles in one car meant that drivers would be able to do pretty much anything, without needing half a dozen vehicles. Whether or not anybody would buy a range-topping model which converted into a pick-up truck was, of course, open to debate – surely such a car would be too compromised to afford its occupants true luxury?

Opening up

The primary purpose of the LaCrosse was to offer stylish accommodation for up to five people. In true American fashion, there was power-operated everything, including all four doors – and to allow easy entry and exit, each of the doors opened a full 90°. The whole cabin was finished in very light colours (largely cream leather), to ensure it felt as spacious as possible, and a glass roof made the car feel even more light and airy. If the occupants still felt the interior of the LaCrosse was too claustrophobic, the roof could be opened up, along with all six side windows. That way, the LaCrosse became a five-seater luxury convertible –

Buick LaCrosse	
Debut:	Detroit 2000
Engine capacity:	4200cc (256ci)
Configuration:	Front-mounted V8, petrol
Power:	198kW (265bhp)
Top speed:	N/A
Transmission:	4-speed auto, FWD
Length:	5192mm (204in)
Width:	1952mm (77in)
Exterior designer:	Benjamin Jiminez
Interior designer:	Yuntae Kim

the roof measured a sizable 109 x 94cm (43 x 37in), so this really opened up the car's cabin. To stop things getting too noisy, there was an electrically adjustable wind deflector at the leading edge of the roof – although with all the side windows down and the glass roof opened, it could not have been especially tranquil travelling at speed.

Sometimes concepts feature design ideas that have no practical benefit, and the side-hinged bonnet of the LaCrosse was a perfect example of this. It was different just for the sake of it.

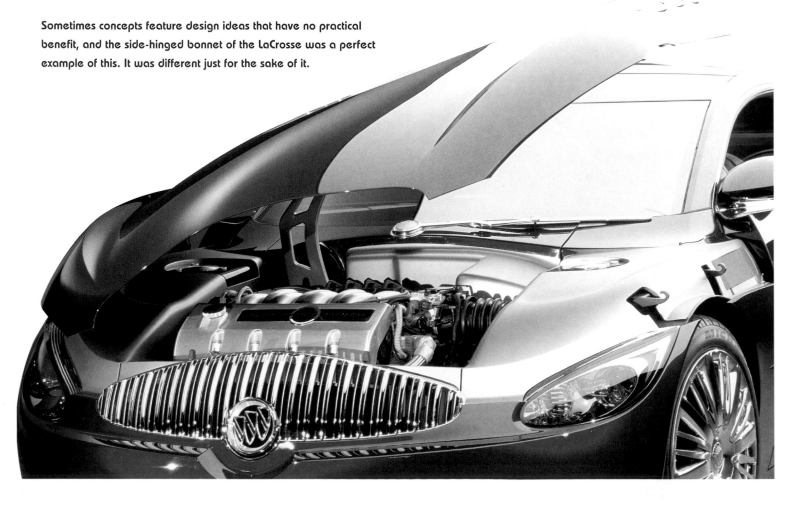

The pillarless design of the LaCrosse ensured that the cabin felt far roomier than more traditionally styled cars in the sector. This also allowed amazing flexibility for seating positions and storage.

The LaCrosse's cabin itself was uncluttered, with no instrumentation being visible at first, apart from an analogue clock in the middle of the fascia. Everyone was treated to first-class seating, and many of the car's functions were voice-activated. A joystick activated most of the rest, including the headlights, turn signals, wipers, gearbox, satellite navigation, climate control and on-board telephone.

A head-up display provided data for the driver, while an optional head-up display in front of the passenger could show either the same information or a constant view of the rear seats to make sure any unruly children could be monitored.

Voice command

Behind the adaptable cabin there was a split load bay, which allowed maximum space efficiency when carrying items that did not need the full height of the boot (trunk). But the really exciting part was the way the boot floor could be lowered to provide extra height so that especially bulky items could also fit in. And things did not stop there because a single voice command made it possible to transform the LaCrosse from a saloon into a pick-up.

First the sunroof dropped slightly before gliding along the arc of the roof. Then the whole assembly, including the rear window and boot lid, moved forward 94cm (37in) into the space vacated by the sunroof. Another glass panel then slid vertically from behind the rear seat to seal off the cabin area. While all this was happening, the middle section of the tail light display rotated down and out of the way and a hinged panel folded down to protect the upper surface of the bumper during loading.

This process produced a load bay that measured 258cm square (40in square), which was not especially large for a pick-up truck. If load space was more important than passenger space, however, the length of the LaCrosse's load bay could be more than doubled by folding forward the rear seat backs. A hinged panel bridged the gap between the boot floor and the seat back, creating a continuous, flat load bay that was more than 2.4m (8ft) long. Load lugging had never been so luxurious.

Cadillac Sixteen

Although the Cadillac Sixteen was big, its weight was well below that of many much smaller production cars. This was mainly thanks to the use of aluminium in the bodyshell's construction.

Everything about the Sixteen was extreme – only articulated trucks had wheels anything like as large as those fitted to this concept, which were some 60.9cm (24in) in diameter.

Although the interior initially looked spartan, it was actually equipped with everything anyone could ever need …or not – a drinks cabinet, computer terminals and even worktables.

Perhaps one of the most outrageous concept cars ever produced, the Cadillac Sixteen was so called because of its 13.6l V16 engine. And just like the engine, the whole car was huge.

The V16 engine was effectively two V8 engines mated together, and at full power it was capable of producing 735kW (1000bhp) and 138kg-m (1000lb-ft) of torque – without any turbochargers.

With Bugatti having unveiled for production a 736kW (987bhp) monster, and Maybach having put into production a super-luxury limousine, it was going to take something pretty special from Cadillac to really draw the crowds at the 2003 Detroit motor show. And the company certainly pulled out all the stops. The Cadillac Sixteen was a concept that combined the most outrageous aspects of both cars – a huge hyper-luxurious bodyshell and a massively powerful engine – in one crazy package.

Back in the 1930s, Cadillac had introduced the world's first production V16 engine, and with retro being immensely popular when the Sixteen was unveiled the company reckoned it was only fair to cash in on such a rich heritage. That's why the concept featured a new take on the V16 engine, with a pair of the company's V8s stitched together to produce a 13.6l powerhouse capable of generating up to 746kW (1000bhp) and an equally ridiculous 138kg-m (1000lb-ft) of torque. And all this was

Despite the huge dimensions of the Cadillac Sixteen, it hid its bulk very well, with smooth lines and subtle curves. The exterior styling was a design masterpiece, with close inspection needed to appreciate the finer details.

without the aid of turbochargers – Bugatti had resorted to a quartet of turbochargers to produce its 736kW (987bhp). But then the Americans always said that there's no substitute for cubic inches …

Burning Tarmac

All this power was transmitted to the rear wheels via a four-speed automatic gearbox. As the car was never going to go beyond concept stage in this form, it scarcely mattered that it would never manage to get 746kW (1000bhp) through just the rear wheels without lighting up the tyres each time the accelerator pedal was pressed. Four-wheel drive would have been needed for any production version of the Sixteen.

As a token gesture aimed purely at keeping the environmentalists happy, the electronics controlling the Sixteen's engine could shut down some of the cylinders so that the fuel consumption – and consequently the emissions – were not quite so frightening. This technology was called 'displacement on demand',and it allowed the Cadillac Sixteen to run on just eight – or even four – cylinders if the power requirements were not excessive.

At a time when 50.8cm (20in) wheels were more or less the limit on road cars – as well as concepts – the

Sixteen managed to go well beyond this. At each corner of the car were massive 60.9cm (24in) wheels housed in rubber band-profile tyres – a madly low-profile 265/40 R24 was used all round.

Lightweight structure

Despite the car's huge dimensions, weight was kept down to a surprisingly low 2270kg (5004lb), thanks to aluminium being used for much of the car's structure, as well as for the enormous engine. But all the high numbers relating to power, torque and cylinders were just an excuse to grab attention. The real reason for the

Cadillac Sixteen

Debut:	Detroit 2003
Engine capacity:	13,600cc (830ci)
Configuration:	Front-mounted V16, petrol
Power:	746kW (1000bhp)
Top speed:	N/A
Transmission:	4-speed automatic, RWD
Length:	5673mm (223in)
Width:	2058mm (81in)
Design leader:	Wayne Cherry

The Sixteen was intended to compete with the most luxurious cars available, so its interior was crammed full of wood, leather and aluminium. Equipment levels were also very high.

Sixteen was to show people the design direction that Cadillac was aiming to take – a 16-cylinder engine was just a red herring.

That exterior design was a work of pure genius: although the Sixteen was more than 5.5m (18ft) long, it did not look especially big and bulky. The use of a low waistline gave the car more dynamism, and subtle aluminium flashes along the flanks made it look even lower still. The long bonnet folded in two halves along the centre line of the car, just as Cadillac's pre-war cars had done, and in the rear over-riders, the four exhaust pipes were housed, so that they looked completely integrated with the rest of the car.

If the exterior was a work of art, the interior was even more so. The work of designer Eric Clough, it was a masterpiece of minimalism at first glance. Just about everything any occupant could ever need was in there – it just appeared when it was wanted. There were computer terminals available, along with a drinks bar and worktables. And it was also possible for the weary passenger to stretch out using the whole length of the interior, as the front passenger seat could be reclined to meet up with the rear seat, forming a full-length sleeping platform. This was a car for people who expected to be chauffeured.

Chrysler Atlantic

It is difficult to find a single straight line anywhere within the design of the Chrysler Atlantic – this mass of curves is simply out of this world.

Although there was a straight-eight engine under that V-shaped bonnet, it was merely a pair of 2l Neon powerplants joined together, a solution which was by no means special enough.

Inside was plenty of leather, but no wood. Carbon-fibre detailing brought the car completely up to date instead.

A four-speed automatic gearbox transmitted the 268kW (360bhp) available to the car's rear wheels; however, the Atlantic was never fast because the gear ratios were not set up properly.

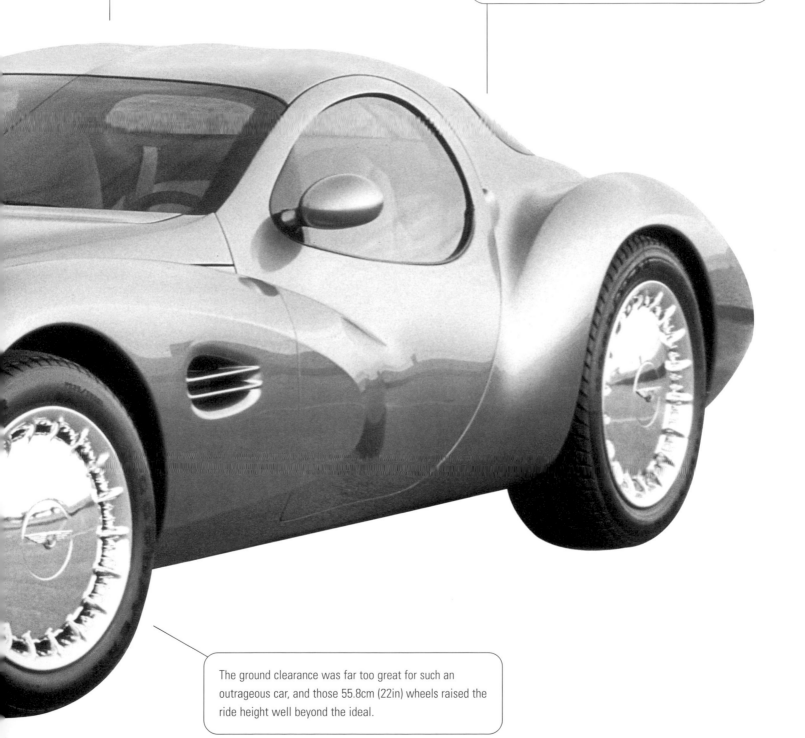

The ground clearance was far too great for such an outrageous car, and those 55.8cm (22in) wheels raised the ride height well beyond the ideal.

This is purely subjective, of course, but I reckon Chrysler's Atlantic is the best-looking concept car ever built. It has just the right mix of drama and realism to make it look as though it should be attainable – but only just. Its mass of swoops and curves means that from every angle there is something to tease the eye, and it has just the right of mix of retro and modern to look convincing without looking like a modern-day replica of something much older. Never mind the fact that the car must rate as one of the most poorly packaged and least practical cars ever – concepts do not have to worry about such things.

The Atlantic was never intended to be put into production, so it did not matter that it was so madly impractical. It was, however, built in steel, which does seem to suggest that Chrysler had perhaps thought about limited production, and the company had even gone so far as to see if the Viper's V10 engine would fit (it did). When you think that other loony Chrysler concepts such as the Viper and Prowler did make it into production, the Atlantic would have seemed quite restrained in comparison. Sadly, however, the concept was still destined to become nothing more than a museum piece.

The straight-eight was definitely the configuration of choice for luxury cars of the 1930s, which is why Chrysler created one specially for its Art Deco–style masterpiece, the 1995 Atlantic.

The Atlantic was inspired by (and took its name from) a Bugatti of the 1930s. This despite the fact that Chrysler had no connection with Bugatti, which at that time had made a failed attempt at a comeback with its EB110 supercar.

The original Atlantic's lines were similar to those of the 1995 concept, and, by creating a much smoother look than Bugatti's original, Chrysler had developed a concept which was guaranteed to wow showgoers at that year's Detroit motor show.

Smooth interior

Nor was it just the outside of the Atlantic that looked amazing – the interior featured just as many curves, even if it did look rather more understated. Wood trim would have been an obvious feature – which is why it was not chosen. Instead, the centre console featured a woven texture much like carbon fibre, while the seats and doors were trimmed in cream leather. Mimicking the central crease that ran the length of the outside of

Chrysler Atlantic

Debut:	Detroit 1995
Engine capacity:	4000cc (244ci)
Configuration:	Front-mounted straight 8, petrol
Power:	268kW (360bhp)
Top speed:	N/A
Transmission:	4-speed automatic, RWD
Length:	N/A
Width:	N/A
Designer:	Bob Hubbach

the car (a direct reference to the earlier Bugatti) was a similar crease along the interior.

As was becoming increasingly common by the 1990s, the Atlantic was engineered to be driveable. But it was not engineered to be production-ready – after all, the chances of something so outlandish making it to America's showrooms were far from good. To mimic the French original, the concept featured a straight-eight engine, with a capacity of 4.0l. This was achieved by joining a pair of Chrysler Neon 2.0l four-cylinder engines, which looked the part, but their

268kW (360bhp) were not enough to give the car particularly spritely performance. Nor did the engine make the right noises, as the exhausts were not tuned to give a particularly bassy sound; re-engineering such a minor fault would have been easy enough, though, if required. But ultimately, it was the performance which disappointed – something that looked as sensational as the Atlantic needed effortless power and huge reserves of torque. Part of the reason for the unimpressive performance was the fact that the gearbox was left unaltered after being taken from a showroom-ready Chrysler LH saloon (sedan). And that car did not feature the 55.8cm (22in) wheels of the concept – which had an enormous effect on the car's gearing.

Tubular chassis

Another problem was that the Atlantic was based on a tubular chassis that used suspension and steering from the Viper. The car was driveable, but it was so under-engineered that the slightest provocation resulted in the chassis flexing and the bodyshell twisting – getting this one ready for the showroom would have required some serious rethinking.

The Chrysler Atlantic looked completely outrageous from every angle. Everything was done to excess and yet it still looked beautiful, with a low centre of gravity and lines reminiscent of the classic sports cars of the 1950s and 1960s.

Citroën C6 Lignage

The cabin had to be packed with all the latest technology, which meant an Internet connection, multimedia system and voice-activated controls for the major functions.

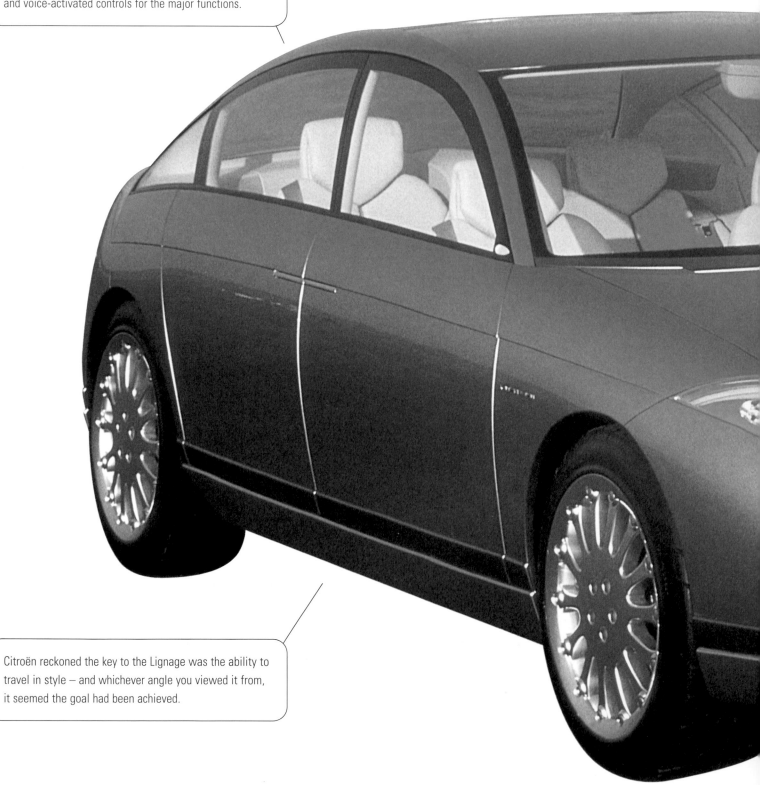

Citroën reckoned the key to the Lignage was the ability to travel in style — and whichever angle you viewed it from, it seemed the goal had been achieved.

It was the sheer size of the car that gave the C6 its presence – despite it looking quite bland from the front, those clean lines gave it class.

The C6 was not shown as a running prototype, but, as it was to head the Citroën range, this would have been powered by large petrol or turbodiesel engines.

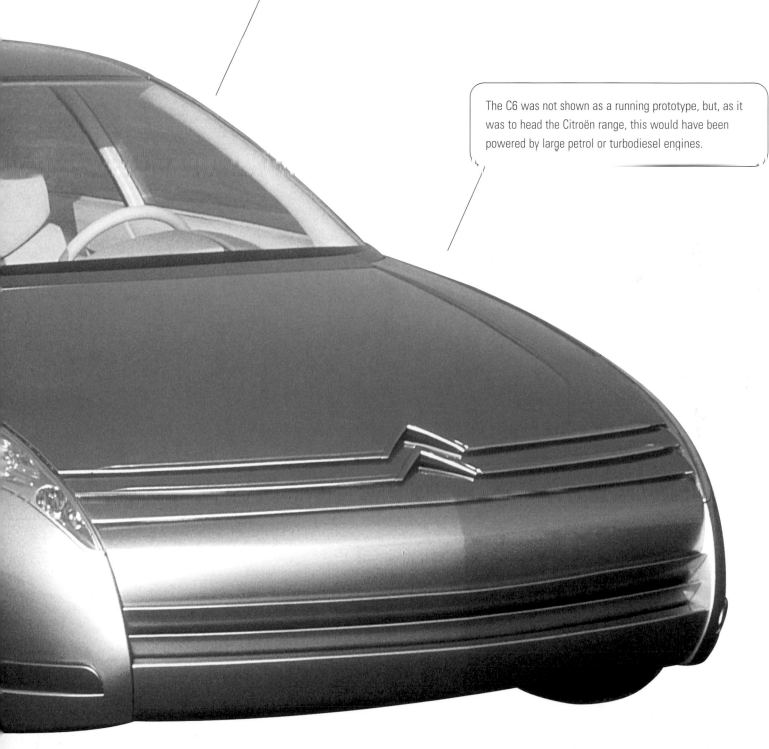

The slogans dreamed up for the Citroën C6 Lignage were 'The art of travel' and 'Travelling in style', which summed up the concept perfectly. Here was a car that went beyond mere transportation, and which also made an effort to return to Citroën's core philosophy of style and innovation. But the best part was the fact that there was a good chance the C6 Lignage, first seen at the 1999 Geneva motor show, would go into production in some form – and inject a bit of glamour and excitement into a range which had managed to become bland and unadventurous.

Integrated design

Although the C6 did not resort to having a retro look, it did utilize many familiar Citroën design cues – even the name was borrowed from the AC6 of 1928. To that end, it featured a long wheelbase with an accentuated front end and with flowing lines that ended with quite a short rear. The silhouette of the C6 suggested that it was a hatchback, but the car actually featured a boot (trunk) which was flanked by flying buttresses. The reason? A smooth profile was wanted, but buyers in

Flying buttresses were old-fashioned, but the C6 used them so that its saloon (sedan) bodystyle could be made to look more like a hatchback, which was a more popular shape for a car aimed at the luxury end of the family market.

Citroën C6 Lignage	
Debut:	Geneva 1999
Engine capacity:	N/A
Configuration:	Front-mounted
Power:	N/A
Top speed:	N/A
Transmission:	FWD
Length:	4920mm (194in)
Width:	1890mm (74in)
Design leader:	Mark Lloyd

this sector regarded a hatchback as downmarket. What was needed was a saloon (sedan) with the profile of a hatchback – hence the flying buttresses.

The roof line was quite low, although there was plenty of glass to ensure the cabin did not feel claustrophobic. A particularly neat design feature was the integration of chevron-shaped pieces of glass in the roof panel – which echoed the Citroën logo seen on the front and rear panels. This chevron logo was also replicated in more subtle ways around the car – look at

The C6 Lignage was to be Citroën's new range-topper, so its cabin was correspondingly opulent. High-quality materials and technology abounded, and there was plenty of space front and rear.

the rear lights and you will see that they look like boomerangs initially, but are really chevrons.

The exterior of the C6 was also designed for maximum aerodynamic efficiency. The door handles were completely flush with the body, and they popped out when a remote control was pressed. There were no exterior mirrors, with cameras monitoring the rear of the car instead – and there were no B-pillars either, which allowed a smoother profile while also opening up the C6's interior even more.

Spacious interior

The interior of the C6 was also designed to feel especially spacious, which is why the materials chosen were all lightly coloured. All the seats and trim panels were covered in magnolia leather, while all the wood inserts were made of light woods. Despite the C6 being a luxury car, the dash was not overburdened with switchgear and instrumentation. Instead, a minimalist look was chosen, and this kept the whole fascia clear and uncluttered. Exceptional passenger space was a key priority when it came to designing the C6's

interior, so there were four individual seats. In the rear was a centre console between the two individually sculpted seats, which was a continuation of the one seen between the two front seats.

The C6's gadget count was predictably high, despite the fact that it was largely hidden from view inside. As you would expect, the car's computer did rather more than just monitor the on-board systems. Much like a home PC, it was built to allow the four occupants to send and receive e-mails, while voice recognition software meant that it could also allow some of the functions to be activated without the need for the use of any switchgear. A keyboard operated by infrared allowed the two occupants in the rear seats to surf the Internet, and the package also included a state-of-the-art stereo system.

Under the C6's skin were plenty of technologies to make journeys as safe and comfortable as possible, including a hydraulically controlled suspension system at the forefront. Citroën said the C6 used Global Chassis Control technology, but the concept's specification also included a head-up display, swivelling headlights, a semi-automatic sequential gearbox and an intelligent speed regulation system, which helped to avoid collisions thanks to integrated obstacle detection. Pretty hi-tech, then!

Jaguar R-D6

Although Jaguar's expertise lay in building highly refined cars powered by petrol engines, the R-D6 packed a turbocharged V6 diesel unit up front, which was rated at 172kW (230bhp).

The grille would have been familiar to an S-type owner, but generally the designers resisted the temptation to throw in all the classic Jaguar styling cues.

Composites and aluminium were used extensively in the construction, but the final weight was still a hefty 1500kg (3307lb) because of all the equipment that was fitted.

It may look like a two-door coupé, but the Jaguar R-D6 is actually a five-door hatch. Unusually, the tailgate was side-hinged – just like the E-type.

Those gorgeous spoked wheels were 53.3cm (21in) in diameter, and they were wrapped in 72cm (30in) profile tyres – a much lower profile than most other show cars!

First there was the XK180, then came the F-type, and finally the R Coupé appeared – all of which supposedly illustrated the design direction in which Jaguar was heading. Then, at the 2003 Frankfurt motor show, the R-D6 was unveiled, and at a stroke the Coventry company was starting afresh with the way its cars looked. The problem was, this was the most

Jaguar R-D6

Debut:	Frankfurt 2003
Engine capacity:	2700cc (165ci), twin-turbo
Configuration:	Front-engined V6, diesel
Power:	172kW (230bhp)
Top speed:	249km/h (155mph)
Transmission:	5-speed auto
Length:	4330mm (170in)
Width:	2150mm (85in)
Exterior designer:	Matt Beaven
Interior designer:	Alister Whelan

True to Jaguar form, the R-D6 featured curves in every plane. But unlike before, this car was more aggressive – and it also packed a seriously powerful diesel engine.

daring concept yet from the company – and, for Jaguar, tradition had always held sway over radical change.

Take a look at the five-door silhouette of the R-D6 and you will probably think of the Mazda RX-8 – not least because of those rear-hinged back doors. Unlike the Mazda, however, the Jaguar featured a tailgate which was side-hinged – a reference to the classic E-type Jaguar. Perhaps the most surprising thing about the car, though, was its size – at 4330mm (170in) in length, it was 342mm (13in) shorter than Jaguar's smallest car (the X-type).

However, thanks to better packaging along with greater height and width (it was based on the floorpan of the range-topping XJ), there was plenty of space in the R-D6 for four to travel in comfort.

New design

Look for classic Jaguar styling cues, and you will not find many. The grille was similar to the one found on an S-type, and, from the point of view of looks, the twin headlights were not too dissimilar to the ones seen on generations of Jaguars. The technology was all new, with LEDs used at the front as well as the rear. The twin exhausts were integrated into the centre of the rear valance, and the door handles were all flush – they pivoted on their leading edge to activate an electrical actuator that opened the doors.

To maximize the interior space, the wheels were pushed to the very corners of the car – and the wheels chosen were monstrous 53.3cm (21in) spoked items wrapped in 255/30 R21 tyres at the front and 275/30 R21 items on the back. To keep weight down as much

Black leather with red backlighting provided a cocktail that was as radical as those external lines, and, although some details were questionable, it was certainly a breath of fresh air compared to many other luxury cruisers of the era.

as possible, the bodyshell was made of aluminium and composites, although at 1500kg (3307lb), the R-D6 was hardly a featherweight for a car so small.

The reason for the car's relatively high kerb weight considering its compact dimensions was the high equipment count. This was a true premium small car, which meant it had to be fitted with every gadget that buyers of much larger cars would be expecting. Satellite navigation, electric adjustment of just about everything that moved and a premium hi-fi were just the start of the equipment list. But the interior was less about all the toys fitted and more about the beautiful detail design that made the car feel really special.

Although there were wood and leather in the R-D6's cabin, this was not of the type that Jaguar buyers were used to. The timber was black-lacquered piano wood, while the dash, its surround, the seats and the trim panels were all finished in black leather. What set the car apart from Jaguar's production cars, however, was the amount of aluminium detailing spread around the cabin, making it look thoroughly contemporary and very classy. Rather less classy, though, was the starter button, which was hidden beneath a sliding cap in the gearknob, and said not 'start', but 'fire'. Tacky in the extreme!

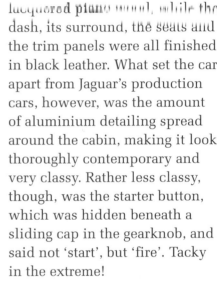

Diesel power

The five-door bodyshell design was only the start of the revolution for Jaguar: the fact that the R-D6 was powered by a diesel engine was just as radical. For a company which had only weeks before put its first ever oil-burning car on sale, it was quite unexpected to find a 2.7l twin-turbocharged diesel V6 under the bonnet. Tuned to produce 172kW (230bhp) and a delicious 51kg-m (369lb-ft) of torque, the concept was endowed with an electronically limited top speed of 249km/h (155mph) – and it would also sprint from a standing start to 100km/h (62mph) in under six seconds.

Lancia Dialogos

The Lancia Dialogos concept was intended to be as free as possible from extraneous details, which is why there are no windscreen wipers to be found.

The elegant nose on the Dialogos was incredibly simple, featuring just a grille and two headlights. An absence of scoops, slats, spoilers or extra lighting gave the car a rare simplicity.

Dialogos owners would get into the car using their Ego Card. This would set everything up for them, from the positioning of the seats to the setting of the car's climate control.

The Dialogos was one of the first concepts to feature rear-hinged back doors (harking back to earlier models), but they had become more conventional items when the car made production.

Other items that would usually be found adorning the rear of a car were largely eliminated on this vehicle. The Dialogos concept did not include door mirrors, door handles or an external radio aerial.

With the exception of innovators such as Renault and Citroën, there have been few mass-market car makers prepared to go their own way. So give thanks for Lancia and its concept, the Dialogos. At one point, the Lancia marque had lost some of its reputation for innovation, a fact that was noticed by its owner, Fiat, which was determined to reverse the situation. Hence the Lancia Dialogos.

The aim of the Dialogos was to bring something new to the luxury car market, with soft flowing lines, an innovative and spacious interior, and Italian engineering that would ensure the car was also a joy to drive. A fundamental part of the idea behind the car was that the occupants would meld with the car, in

From this angle, the Lancia Dialogos was reminiscent of the Lagonda Vignale of five years earlier – and it is certainly no worse off for that. It looked superbly graceful and unfussy.

effect having a dialogue with it – which explains the name of the concept.

Inspired heritage

The Dialogos offered the perfect fusion of past and future, with many of the design details inspired by cars from Lancia's rich heritage. The pillarless construction with rear-hinged back doors was a nod to the past; both the Aurelia and Appia of the 1950s had used the same layout. However, it was decided from the outset that the car would be no retro design, but instead classically elegant 'with the minimum of visual noise', as design chief Mike Robinson put it. That meant the exterior design had to be as clean as possible, so there were no door handles, wiper blades, aerials or exterior mirrors.

To get in, the owner of the car would carry an Ego Card, a personal control unit that was tailored to their preferences. As the car was approached by the owner, it would unlock and the interior settings would be adjusted automatically. This meant the seats would move to the correct position and the climate control would also set itself. Even more impressively, the suspension settings were also adjusted, along with the feel of the steering and even the gearchange shift programmes. Upon the doors opening (the rear doors were rear-hinged), the steering wheel would be in the

Lancia Dialogos

Debut:	Turin 1988
Engine capacity:	N/A
Configuration:	Front-mounted
Power:	N/A
Top speed:	N/A
Transmission:	FWD
Length:	4990mm (196.5in)
Width:	1950mm (76.8in)
Designer:	Mike Robinson

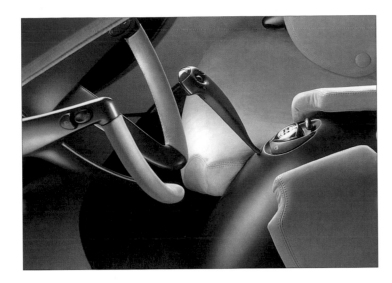

The steering wheel could be moved from one side to the other with the minimum of fuss, hinting at the long-distance grand touring capabilities of the Dialogos.

centre of the dash. It could be moved to the left or the right (electrically), depending on which country the car was to be driven in. And the instrumentation moved with it, as it was all displayed on a liquid crystal read-out. A pedal box was fitted on both sides, but only the one beneath the steering wheel would work – the other would become merely a foot rest.

The interior was a true work of art – minimalist, but impossibly classy at the same time. The seats were trimmed in chamois leather with cashmere upholstery, and even the wood was soft to the touch. The tops of the doors were trimmed with a copper and cloth weave, and the use of natural materials throughout made the cabin warm and inviting – a place to soothe away all of life's stresses.

There was also plenty of technology: adaptive cruise control, automatically adjusting headlights, lane holding assistance, and a gearbox that learned the driving style of the driver. This was a design with the technology to back it all up.

Sadly, despite the car looking amazing and journalists all around the world wanting desperately to drive the Dialogos, they could not. The car was a non-runner, and the interior and exterior design were really the only things on show: the boot was stuffed full of electronics and the engine bay was bare. This was one of those concepts that should really have been driveable – after all, it evolved into the Thesis production car – but it was not to be.

Possessing an interior which looked more like the sort of thing you would find in an expensively furnished apartment, the cabin of the Dialogos was trimmed throughout in soft leather and Alcantara.

Land Rover Range Stormer

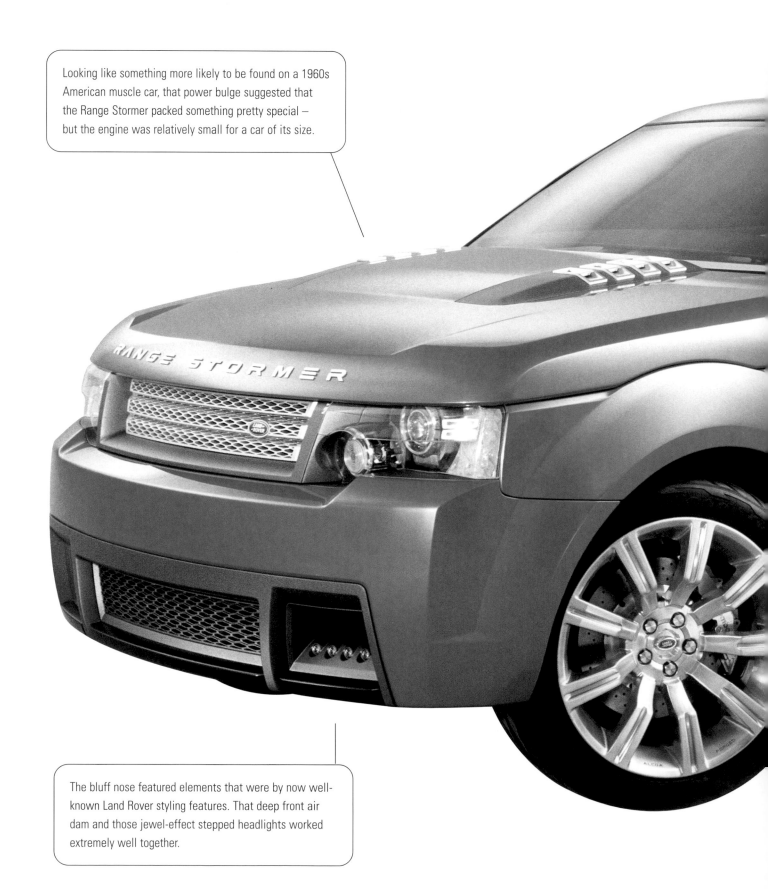

Looking like something more likely to be found on a 1960s American muscle car, that power bulge suggested that the Range Stormer packed something pretty special – but the engine was relatively small for a car of its size.

The bluff nose featured elements that were by now well-known Land Rover styling features. That deep front air dam and those jewel-effect stepped headlights worked extremely well together.

The 'floating roof' was a Range Rover trademark, first seen on the first cars that went on sale in 1970. It was achieved through a very simple technique – the pillars were blacked out.

The glass house was very narrow, which was emphasized even more by the unusually high waistline. It certainly gave the Range Stormer a very tough look, helped by the car's overall dimensions.

Whereas the original Range Rover had been a tough workhorse, this new car was about on-road driving pleasure. That is why it was fitted with 57cm (22-inch) low-profile tyres.

Despite Land Rover having launched its first car in 1948, it took until the 2004 Detroit motor show before it showed its first concept car, the Range Stormer. This offered a sneak preview of an all-new model that was to join the Land Rover range later that year, although – as was usual – the production car proved rather less radical than the concept.

Everything about the Range Stormer was glitzy and glamorous, and created largely for effect. From the bright orange paint to the scissor-action doors, Land Rover was determined to make sure that its first concept was not ignored. Nor was it.

Extreme aggression

Taking aggression to extremes, the square, boxy lines of the Land Rover Range Stormer used many of the design themes that had been so successfully introduced on the Range Rover a couple of years earlier. The glassed-in tail lights, with individual jewel lamps inside, were backed up by the four headlights featuring two pairs of stepped lamps.

Anyone following behind the Range Stormer would be left in no doubt regarding its sporting pretensions. The quartet of square tail pipes looked decidedly menacing without looking incongruous.

Land Rover Range Stormer	
Debut:	Detroit 2004
Engine capacity:	N/A
Configuration:	Front-mounted V8, petrol
Power:	N/A
Top speed:	N/A
Transmission:	6-speed semi-auto, 4WD
Length:	N/A
Width:	N/A
Designer:	Geoff Upex

However, unlike the units found on the Range Rover, those rear lights looked like they were filled with crushed ice – although in reality it was silicone that was packed in there. Substantial wheelarch blisters hinted at the power available from the supercharged V8 nestling at the front, and under those wheelarches were aluminium wheels that measured a substantial 55.8cm (22in) across. Deep bumpers at both ends with an unusually narrow

The scissor-action doors were impossibly complicated for a production car, although the sill that folded down to become a step up to the interior was a very neat touch not often seen on vehicles of this type.

glass house gave an especially muscular look, while four square exhaust pipes exiting from the rear valance lent sporty overtones. That this was a three-door car also enhanced its sporty credentials, though the production car was offered with five doors.

One of the reasons for just two side doors was the incorporation of fold-down sills, which could be lowered once each of the doors had been raised forward. As on the Range Rover, a 'floating roof' was fitted, which meant the pillars were all black. The effect was that the roof did not look as if it were connected directly to the car's main structure. The tailgate was classic Range Rover, which meant it was split horizontally – but with a difference. The top half opened conventionally, but the lower half slid down behind the rear bumper. Instead of a conventional wiper, the rear window was cleaned by high-pressure air jets, and inside the luggage bay was an adjustable boot (trunk) floor to make the most of available space.

Classic styling

Many of the styling cues incorporated into the Range Stormer harked back to the first Range Rover of 1970 – a car fitted with the classic Buick-derived Rover V8. Although that engine had long since departed by the time the Range Stormer was shown, it was a beautifully torquey and smooth powerplant. And the platform on which the concept was built – the second-generation Range Rover – meant that its reappearance in the Range Stormer was entirely appropriate,

especially in front of an American audience. Naturally the gearbox was an automatic, although it also offered a sequential manual option, as was customary by now.

Inside was equally avant garde, with twisted loops of thick saddle leather providing the seating, which was mounted on aluminium frames. The dash was surprisingly uncomplicated and, although the wood was kept to a minimum, there were some token slabs dotted around the cabin.

Equipment was largely predictable, with a satellite navigation system, climate control and high-performance hi-fi all controlled via a large screen. In the back were TV screens to show whatever was being played on the DVD player, and in place of the usual rear-view mirrors were TV cameras relaying images to the screen on the fascia. All this showed perfectly well what Land Rover was capable of when allowed to experiment, and people would have lapped up such a car. So it was a shame that the real thing was rather less appealing.

Aluminium abounded, but to go with it there were plenty of other materials used in the Range Stormer's cabin – and they all looked reassuringly expensive.

Lincoln Navicross

One of the styling aspects that gave the Navicross such a confident look was that sweeping swage line; it went from the car's nose to the bottom of the tail panel.

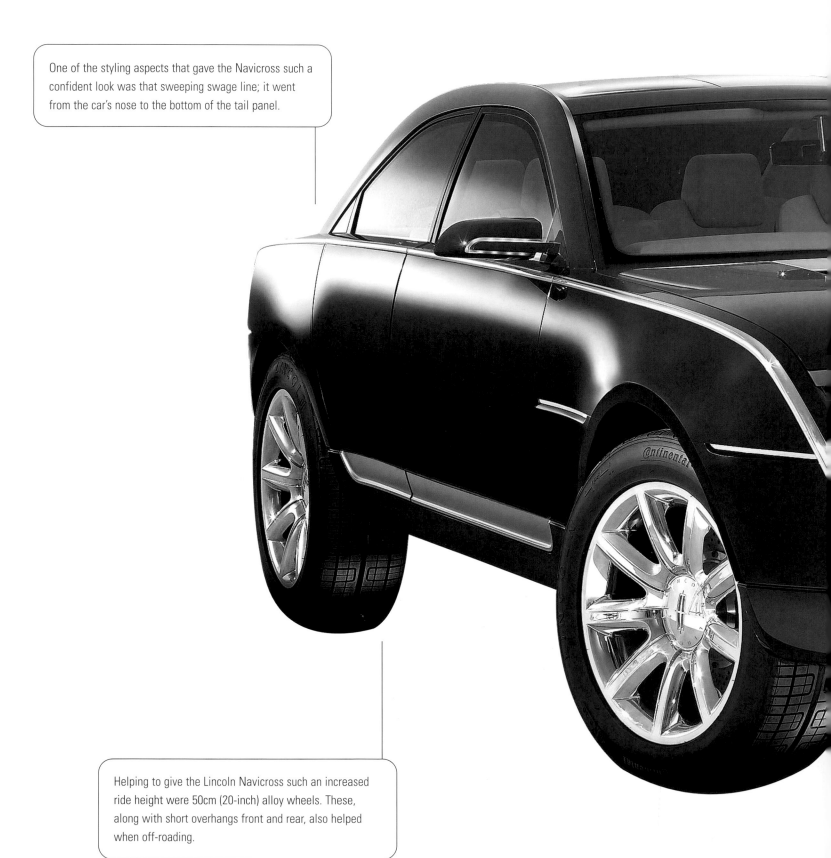

Helping to give the Lincoln Navicross such an increased ride height were 50cm (20-inch) alloy wheels. These, along with short overhangs front and rear, also helped when off-roading.

The raised ride height of the Navicross was supposed to give much improved off-roading capabilities. In reality, it would have merely compromised the on-road performance, thanks to the higher centre of gravity.

With a 4.2l all-alloy V8 engine under the bonnet, the Navicross would not have been wanting for power. It was also very torquey, which was perfect for off-roading.

American cars — especially luxury ones such as Lincolns — had long been well known for their exterior excesses. So it was a welcome relief for design enthusiasts to see such a clean frontal design.

The beautifully trimmed leather-lined cabin of the Navicross was fully opened up thanks to the adoption of rear-hinged back doors. There was seating for four passengers – in true luxurious proportions.

It may look like just a large, luxury saloon (sedan), but the Navicross is much more than that. Designed to be a sporty alternative to a full-blown sport-utility vehicle, this show-stopper was first seen on the Lincoln stand at the 2003 Detroit motor show, where it proved to be one of the most eye-catching exhibits.

After the appearance of the sinister-looking Lincoln Sentinel at the same event seven years earlier, it was clear that Ford's upmarket US division was set to take a new design direction. American cars had not been especially curvaceous since the 1950s, but these new cars were taking the hard edges to extremes – stand too close to either the Sentinel or the Navicross, and there was a good chance of cutting yourself. Still, it made a welcome change to the jelly-mould curves that so typified the 1980s and 1990s.

Polished all-rounder

Pigeonholing the Navicross is very difficult because Lincoln deliberately set out to produce a car that was capable of fulfilling a wide variety of needs. By taking

the best elements of the sport coupé, sport saloon and sport utility genres, this car was meant to be all things to quite a few people. Of course, the common theme running throughout this is the sport aspect, and it was this quality that the Lincoln Navicross was designed to encapsulate the best. It was to be a true driver's car, with a sharp, sorted chassis and plenty of power on tap.

Lincoln Navicross

Debut:	Detroit 2003
Engine capacity:	4.2l (256.3ci)
Configuration:	Front-mounted V8, supercharged
Power:	N/A
Top speed:	N/A
Transmission:	5-speed semi-auto, 4WD
Length:	4741mm (186.7in)
Width:	1862mm (73.3in)
Designer:	Gerry McGovern

Although the power output of the 4.2l, all-alloy, V8 engine was not disclosed, it would have been somewhere in the region of 298kW (400bhp) thanks to the adoption of a supercharger. This drove all four wheels via a five-speed automatic transmission, which was also fitted with a sequential manual gearchange option. That should have promised a pretty sporty drive, but the car's higher than usual centre of gravity would have reduced the car's ability to speed. This raised ride height, combined with short overhangs front and rear, helped to give the car some off-roading capabilities, but, of course, the reality is that if you try to be a jack of all trades, you end up being a master of none. And the sporty driving characteristics were compromised just as much as the off-roading ones. That raised ride height was helped partly by 50.8cm (20in) alloy wheels, which were wrapped in 366/60 R20 tyres, again offering a compromise between on-road sharpness and off-road durability.

Exterior lines

The exterior design of the Navicross was at best described as striking, although the words 'strong' and 'aggressive' also spring to mind. This was not a car to ignore. That heavily tapered, bluff front end flowed through to

an equally smooth rear end, with a continuous line of brightwork to help it along. The rear doors were hinged at the back to open up the cabin, and at the rear was a hatch instead of the more conventional boot (trunk); again, this made the link between a luxury car and a practical off-roader.

Although the exterior was perhaps something of an acquired taste, the cabin was much more inviting. Trimmed in terracotta and cream hide, it oozed luxury. Lincoln described it as having cleanliness and simplicity – a pleasant change from the minimalism with which many of its contemporaries were afflicted. There was plenty of instrumentation, which was all displayed on two large light-emitting diode viewing screens. These were reconfigurable, which meant that the information displayed on them could be changed to suit both the driver and the passenger. In the first instance, the driver would see the standard information (such as the speedometer, rev counter and fuel gauge), while the passenger would have Internet access and access to all the telematics along with any satellite navigation details. This just about summed up the Navicross: all things in excess.

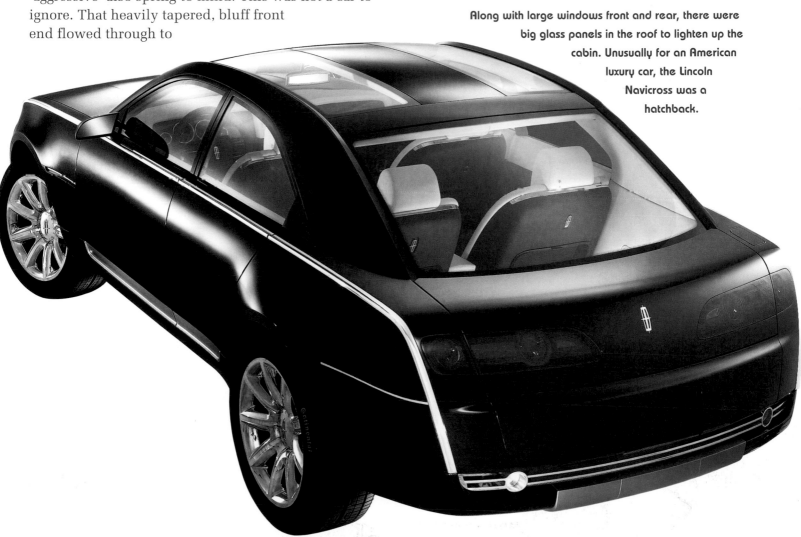

Along with large windows front and rear, there were big glass panels in the roof to lighten up the cabin. Unusually for an American luxury car, the Lincoln Navicross was a hatchback.

Subaru B11S

As was traditional for Subaru, the B11S was powered by a boxer engine, in this case a 3l, six-cylinder unit. With two turbochargers, the unit was good for 298kW (400bhp).

The design worked really well overall, but that nose was the fly in the ointment. Too much space given over to the various grilles made it look messy.

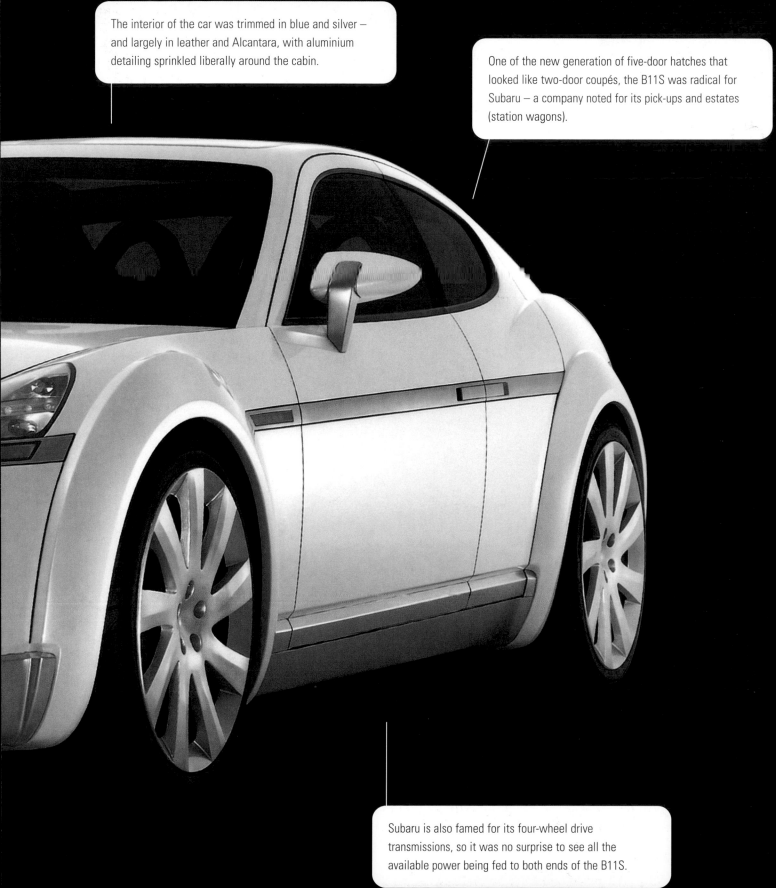

The interior of the car was trimmed in blue and silver — and largely in leather and Alcantara, with aluminium detailing sprinkled liberally around the cabin.

One of the new generation of five-door hatches that looked like two-door coupés, the B11S was radical for Subaru — a company noted for its pick-ups and estates (station wagons).

Subaru is also famed for its four-wheel drive transmissions, so it was no surprise to see all the available power being fed to both ends of the B11S.

For a company that was used to – and indeed synonymous with – building practical four-wheel drive saloons (sedans) and estates (station wagons), the B11S was a pretty radical departure from the norm for Subaru. Although it had a reputation for reliable and accessible performance – thanks largely to its Impreza Turbo – the company had always added a large dose of practicality to the mix. At first glance, the B11S (which was an abbreviation of Boxer 11 Sports) threw all that away, to focus instead on controversial design that put form before function. But look closely, and you will see that very little was sacrificed, even though the B11S still managed to be much more stylish than anything Subaru had previously offered for sale.

In profile the B11S looked plain, with overtones of the Renault Laguna. If it had not been beaten to it by the Mazda RX-Evolv, the design would have been considered original and innovative.

When it was unveiled at the 2003 Geneva motor show, the B11S was hailed by its maker as the first of a new generation of Gran Utility Turismos, which in theory made it a GUT. Rather unfortunate connotations aside, it did live up to the hype, offering a sporty driving experience combined with functionality and elegance – even if the latter did come in shorter supply than the other two.

Coupé-like saloon

The concept of the B11S was very much along the lines of the Mazda RX-8. That meant it featured rear-hinged back doors while the front doors opened conventionally. At the rear was a tailgate which also opened in the conventional way, but, despite this generally orthodox construction, the B11S still managed to look like a sporting coupé.

Perhaps the most radical aspect of the car's design – and the reason for it appearing to be rather less conventional than it really was – was the nose treatment. With a huge shield-shaped grille flanked by wide grilles either side, the front of the car was quite ungainly from some angles. Running along the length of the bonnet was a rib that was supposed to echo the

The Subaru B11S's grille was supposed to echo the layout of the flat-six engine that was tucked behind. The centre grille was the crankshaft with the pistons on either side.

Subaru B11S

Debut:	Geneva 2003
Engine capacity:	3l (183ci) twin-turbo
Configuration:	Front-mounted flat-six, petrol
Power:	299kW (400bhp)
Top speed:	N/A
Transmission:	5-speed auto, 4WD
Length:	4785mm (188in)
Width:	1935mm (76in)
Designer:	N/A

turbine of a small jet plane – a reference to the fact that Subaru's parent company, Fuji Heavy Industries, was also a manufacturer of aircraft.

The grille itself was a reference to Subaru's trademark boxer engines, which are basically powerplants with a 180° V angle between the banks of cylinders. The central grille represented the crankshaft with the combustion chambers being the grilles on either side.

BMW overtones

At the back, the tail treatment was reminiscent of the then recently launched BMW 7-series, with a deck that sat proud of the surrounding lights and wing tops. For BMW, this choice had proved massively controversial – the chances are that Subaru would have encountered just as much resistance to it had the

car seen production in the same form in which it was initially shown.

The lack of a B-pillar allowed much better visibility than in a conventionally engineered car, while also allowing easier entry and exit. The feeling of spaciousness within the cabin was both perceived and real, in the latter case thanks to a frosted-glass roof that allowed light to pour in and which was inspired by traditional Japanese umbrellas. Also helping were the space-efficient seating that was used and the unfussy design of the fascia. Everything was trimmed in blue or silver, with plenty of leather and Alcantara to heighten the sense of luxury. Added to this was a healthy dose of aluminium detailing, very tastefully used to pick out some of the car's switchgear and instrumentation.

Powering the Subaru B11S was a six-cylinder boxer engine – a powerplant configuration for which the Japanese company was famous. This 3.0l unit was capable of generating up to 299kW (400bhp) and 56kg-m (405lb-ft) of torque with the aid of a pair of turbochargers. To help transmit this to the road, there was a permanent four-wheel drive system which incorporated an electronic torque distribution system. This constantly monitored the traction levels at each of the four wheels and allowed those with the best levels of grip to be sent the highest levels of torque – in normal use, though, the B11S's rear wheels were fed two-thirds of the available power.

From this angle, the B11S looked as though it had come out of Chris Bangle's BMW design studio, although it remains slightly more attractive than most modern BMWs.

Technological Innovators

Cars are blamed for damaging the environment as well as killing and maiming thousands of people every year. By investing in new technologies that aim to reduce the negative impacts of private transport, these concept cars have introduced technologies that are already starting to filter into the production cars of today, improving cars both in image and in actuality.

Around the world, cars have a huge impact on societies, affecting economies, cultures and environments. Sometimes that impact is good, but sometimes that impact is bad, which is why it is vitally important that the car evolves as quickly and as far as possible. Manufacturers may focus on making cars safer in an accident or on reducing their negative effect on the environment. Producing more cheaply can also be beneficial, so that companies can boost their profits or simply so that more people can afford to get mobile.

All of the cars in this chapter focus on advancing car technology, usually by experimenting with new types of motive power, such as fuel cells or hybrid energy. But any environmentally focused car will also look very closely at the use of lightweight materials and computer-designed crash structures to make them both safer and lighter.

Returning to the pre-war school of thought regarding car construction, the General Motors Hy-Wire featured a separate platform onto which any form of bodyshell could be fitted. This made it an extremely adaptable concept, which opened up all sorts of possibilities.

Concept cars have also innovated safety-related technology. By the 1990s, concepts were being fitted with all manner of sensors and electronics to help reduce the likelihood of a crash. Many critics were initially sceptical that such technology would ever become commonplace in the production car, but now traction control, electronic stability protection and electronic brake force distribution are all features expected on showroom cars.

Car of the future

Despite all this, the most significant concept here is the GM Hy-Wire, which effectively throws away the rulebook and starts again. This really could represent the closest we have yet seen to the car of the future. Not only does it run as cleanly as possible (with a hydrogen fuel cell that produces just water), but also it is stuffed full of drive-by-wire systems that allow a clean-sheet approach to car construction as well as interior design. That in turn means anything goes when it comes to exterior design, in terms of both aesthetics and bodystyles. Never let anybody tell you that the word 'technology' is boring.

BMW E1

The BMW E1 tried to bridge the gap between city car and mid-sized hatchback, so it offered seating for four, but in a bodyshell with very compact dimensions.

Three versions of this E1 were built — one electric, one petrol and one petrol-electric hybrid. All versions featured aluminium bodyshells to keep weight down.

The interior of each car featured little in the way of equipment or instrumentation, but quality materials gave class to what there was.

This is the later of the two E1 concepts to be built by BMW. The double-kidney grille and kinked rear pillar make its origins instantly obvious.

Building such a small car meant BMW had to be pretty clever when it came to crash safety – but the car still featured small crumple zones front and rear.

There were two incarnations of the BMW E1, the first of which made its debut at the 1991 Frankfurt motor show, with the second following two years later. They were both electrically powered and, as the second one was not much of an advancement on the first, they both suffered from the same fundamental problem – battery technology simply had not been developed far enough to make the electric car a viable proposition as a main car for many drivers. And the cost of buying a full-sized car to use just for commuting was not economically viable for many people.

The first E1 featured a compact bodyshell with an unusually high roof line and just three doors. There was virtually no overhang at either end and its compact dimensions helped to keep weight down, as did its aluminium frame, onto which was hung a plastic outer skin. While all this did serve to reduce weight, the aerodynamics also had to be optimized to get the best possible range out of the batteries – the E1 achieved a drag coefficient of just 0.32.

Compact cruiser

Unfortunately, such diminutive dimensions also mean that crash safety is easily compromised – with virtually no space front or rear for crumple zones, some very clever engineering was required to make the car crashworthy. Areas which would normally be designed to crumple had to be reinforced, while the

BMW E1	
Debut:	Frankfurt 1991
Engine capacity:	Electric motor
Configuration:	Rear-mounted
Power:	34kW (45bhp)
Top speed:	120km/h (75mph)
Transmission:	Direct drive, RWD
Length:	3460mm (136in)
Width:	1648mm (65in)
Designer:	N/A

E1's main structure was more rigid than usual and had lots of lateral reinforcement. The inside of the E1 was kept very simple, all the controls being kept together in the centre of the fascia, and the three dials that made up the instrumentation being grouped together directly in front of the driver. Despite the short length of the E1, it was a four-seater, with the luggage

Compact dimensions and lightweight materials such as aluminium and plastics helped to keep the weight of the E1 as low as possible. But it still fared well in crash tests.

space unusually accommodating thanks to a low floor – the batteries were stored under the rear seat and the compact motor was under the boot (trunk) floor. But the weight and capacity of these batteries were the limiting factor – not only did they account for a quarter of the car's 880kg (1940lb) kerb weight, but they provided a range of just 96–145km (60–90 miles) as well. This was despite the fact that they were the most efficient batteries available at the time – the sodium-sulphur units were up to four times more efficient than conventional lead-acid types. Even so, it was not enough.

A successor arrives

The second E1, which was unveiled at the 1993 Frankfurt motor show, was available in three versions: petrol, electric and a petrol-electric hybrid. This concept was a result of the marriage of the technology used in the first E1 with the bodyshell of the Z13, a concept which BMW had originally revealed at the 1991 Geneva motor show.

There was also a new body design (changed from the first E1, and also different from the Z13). It used

Although the E1's interior was simple, it was typical BMW in that it was ergonomically sound and everything was of a much higher quality than most potential rivals offered.

aluminium for the main structure, which kept the car's weight down as much as possible. The look and structure of all three derivatives was identical – the differences were to be found purely in the motive power. As far as the electric version was concerned, the second-generation E1 was little more than a reskin of the earlier car.

The electric E1 was powered by a 34kW (45bhp) motor which sat between the rear wheels. This gave the car a top speed of 126km/h (78mph) and a range of up to 266km (165 miles), while the petrol-powered car was equipped with a 60kW (81bhp) 1100cc BMW motorbike engine. This engine was fitted between the front wheels, and this made it very easy to build the hybrid, which retained the rear-mounted electric motor and the front-mounted internal combustion powerplant. To save space and reduce weight, the hybrid E1 featured a battery pack just half the size of that used in the electric version.

Dodge ESX3

A bodyshell made of plastic helped to keep the weight down to just over a ton, assisting the ESX3 in making the most of the 70kW (94bhp available).

Mild hybrid – or mybrid – technology was to be found under the skin of the Dodge ESX3. This put the internal combustion engine first, but used battery power to supplement it.

Despite a high percentage of composites being used in its manufacture, it was still possible to recycle 80 per cent of the ESX3 – which was impressive.

Unusually for an American car, the ESX3 had a diesel engine with a displacement of just 1.5l (91ci). This drove the front wheels via an automatic transmission.

On the outside the ESX3 did not look especially radical, with that bluff nose incorporating oversized headlights and an understated grille. But it was certainly modern – Dodge called it 'faceted design'.

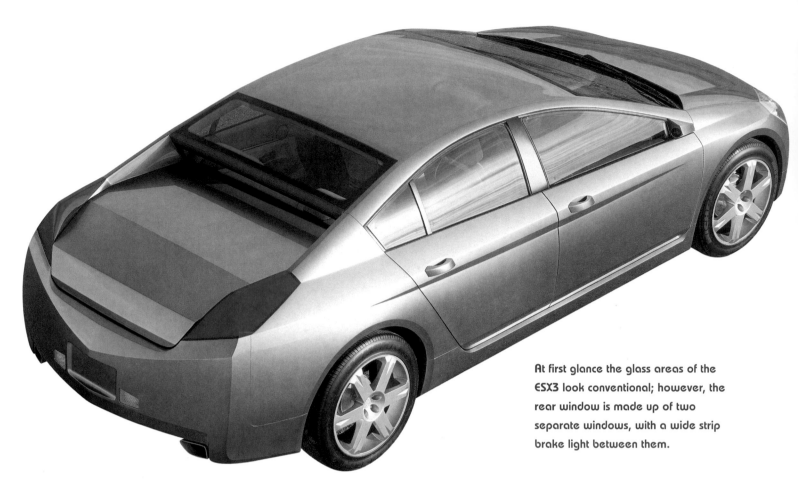

At first glance the glass areas of the ESX3 look conventional; however, the rear window is made up of two separate windows, with a wide strip brake light between them.

The fact that Dodge chose the 2000 Geneva motor show to first display its ESX3 concept was an indication of the company's intention to take on the Europeans at their own game. Traditionally, it is the Detroit motor show that is the American car industry's showcase for new cars and concepts, and so the fact that the ESX3 burst onto the scene at the first (and arguably most important) European motor show of the year was a bid to show that Dodge could compete on equal terms with marques such as BMW and Mercedes-Benz.

As the name suggested, the Dodge ESX3 was the third in a series of show cars – the first ESX had been unveiled in 1996 and the follow-up car in 1998. The series looked at how a hybrid car might be packaged, and these were developed as part of a collaboration of US government and industry called the Partnership for a New Generation of Vehicles (PNGV). The aim of the project was to develop affordable transport that would also be more environmentally friendly than what the US car makers had previously manufactured. Considering that the difference between the first Dodge ESX concept and its then-current production counterpart was a production cost of $60,000, while the difference between the ESX3 and the equivalent showroom car was just $7500, this third concept certainly showed promise.

The key to the whole concept was the hybrid technology beneath the skin. Dodge actually referred to it as 'mybrid' technology – short for 'mild hybrid' – as this still put the internal combustion engine first. But to help conserve fuel, this small diesel engine was backed up by an electric motor powered by a state-of-the-art lithium-ion battery. An electro-mechanical automatic transmission (dubbed EMAT) transmitted the power to the front wheels, and weight was reduced

Dodge ESX3

Debut:	Geneva 2000
Engine capacity:	1500cc (92ci) engine plus electric motor
Configuration:	Front-mounted in-line 4-cylinder diesel. Rear-mounted electric motor
Power:	55kW (74bhp) (diesel) + 15kW (20bhp) (electric)
Top speed:	N/A
Transmission:	Automatic
Length:	4897mm (193in)
Width:	1885mm (74in)
Designer:	N/A

to a minimum, so fuel consumption was reduced as far as possible. The PNGV goal had been set at 80mpg (129km) while the ESX3 managed to get to within 8mpg (13km) of this – further development would probably see the goal being achieved.

Advanced materials

By reducing weight as much as possible, performance could also be maximized. No top speed was quoted for the car, but the acceleration time of 11 seconds to get from standing still to 96km/h (60mph) was pretty good, as just 69kW (94bhp) was available with both the electric motor and the 1.5l diesel engine on song. The bodyshell was made of injection-moulded thermoplastic, and, by the time the car was finished, it weighed just 1020kg (2249lb) – which was pretty good going for a full-sized saloon (sedan) capable of housing a family and its luggage.

A car such as the ESX3 would also have to be fully equipped, so it featured a high-performance video and audio system along with climate control. There was also a multimedia display, which reduced the need for masses of switches throughout the cabin – instead,

everything could be controlled by a touch screen. It also meant that everything could be personalized far more easily, according to what the driver and passenger wanted. By rethinking how these were built and integrated into the car, it was possible to reduce weight even further.

The problem with using advanced materials to keep weight down is that it is not very easy to recycle them – Dodge aimed to tackle that comprehensively with the ESX3, and the result was a vehicle that achieved 80 per cent recyclability. Clothing all this technology was a sharp suit, which Dodge referred to as having 'faceted design'. This was a look becoming popular globally – sheared surfaces and faceted angles gave a clean look without being bland. The tail lights gave a three-dimensional effect while also recalling the fins of Chrysler's cars from the late 1950s, and the rear window sloped sharply before being abruptly truncated – something that was striking, if bizarre.

Practical and functional were the key words when it came to the interior of the ESX3 – this was supposed to be an affordable car rather than a luxury express.

GM Hy-Wire

The abolition of the steering column and conventional pedal box meant that the cabin could be given over to its occupants, contributing to spaciousness. Swapping from left- to right-hand drive was also a simple matter.

The fuel cell provided energy for an electric motor which was capable of developing 94kW (126bhp) when running continuously. For overtaking, it could produce a peak of 129kW (173bhp) in short bursts.

A key technology that allowed new ways of thinking was the use of drive-by-wire electronics. By eradicating mechanical linkages, the whole cabin could be opened up.

A hydrogen fuel cell provided the motive power – an innovation that helped create an uncluttered cabin design along with a complete new method of car construction.

It may seem a bit obscure initially, but the name of the GM Hy-Wire gives a big clue to the technologies that it showcased – namely hydrogen fuel cell power and drive-by-wire electronics. And these are two of the most important technologies to enter the automotive field at the start of the twenty-first century.

The Hy-Wire was GM's attempt at showing how both could be used in a practical, usable family car – even if there was no chance of the concept making it into production very soon after its debut at the 2003 Detroit motor show.

Production ready

The Hy-Wire was a development of the Autonomy that General Motors had shown a year earlier – the latter concept was showcasing the technology, while the former one showed how it could all be packaged into a car that could actually be used from day to day. And to really drive the point home, this was no non-running show special – the Hy-Wire was capable of being driven just like any production car.

The reason for the importance of the hydrogen fuel cell part of the GM Hy-Wire was that this was considered the way forward for road cars when the concept was unveiled. Petrol and diesel engines were highly developed, but were more polluting than the fuel cell, and hydrogen is also one of the Earth's most abundant elements, while fossil fuels are a finite resource that is dwindling. The hydrogen-powered

The registration plate seen hear reads 'Autonomy' – that was the name of the Hy-Wire's predecessor which originally showcased the fuel-cell technology. The Hy-Wire designers took this innovation and put it into a practical family car.

fuel cell stack, which was effectively the Hy-Wire's engine, supplied electricity for the three-phase electric motor – running continuously, it generated 94kW (126bhp), but was capable of peaking at 129kW (173bhp).

The drive-by-wire technology was just as important as the use of a fuel cell – if everything continued to be controlled by levers, pulleys and other mechanical actuators, no real progress could be made in terms of packaging, reductions in production costs or, to a degree, safety. By introducing solenoids and cables to take care of the activation of controls such as brakes, clutch, steering and engine speed, however, all sorts of benefits could be realized, some of which were not initially obvious.

Removing the conventional pedal box would mean more footwell space, and also less hardware in the cabin to cause injuries in the event of a collision. The Hy-Wire could also be converted from left-hand drive to right-hand drive in just 10 seconds, with the steering 'wheel' moving electrically. Drive-by-wire also allowed easy tuning of components so that the level of output achieved for any given input could be tailored to an individual driver's requirements.

GM Hy-Wire

Debut:	Detroit 2003
Engine capacity:	200 single fuel cells, connected in series
Configuration:	Rear-mounted fuel stack
Power:	129kW (173bhp)
Top speed:	160km/h (100mph) approx
Transmission:	FWD
Length:	4953mm (195in)
Width:	1870mm (74in)
Designer:	N/A

See-through interior

Inside the Hy-Wire was space for five occupants with plenty of room left over for luggage, and, to emphasize just how uncluttered the cabin was, plenty of glass was used in the construction. By using glazed units for the front and rear panels, it was possible to see right through the car, and the lack of a B-pillar allowed it to be even more open. Even the backs of the seats featured window-like recesses, and, because there was no engine in front, there was no need for a grille. Consequently, the front of the Hy-Wire was also fitted with a glass panel, so that the driver could see the road ahead – literally.

The key to the Hy-Wire's potentially low production costs was the 'skateboard' construction of the main platform, on which the concept was based. This was a chassis 27.9cm (11in) thick, which housed everything that was needed to make it go, stop and steer. The initial concept was fitted with a single motor that was located between the front wheels – the aim was for smaller motors to be fitted to each wheel to distribute the workload.

Between the rear wheels was the fuel cell stack, while in the centre of the car were three hydrogen tanks. To all this the bodyshell was bolted – which meant that it would be no problem to offer several different bodystyles for any given model range.

By getting rid of all the fixed linkages, the cabin of the Hy-Wire could be opened right up. This was all made possible by the adoption of drive-by-wire technology.

Honda Dualnote

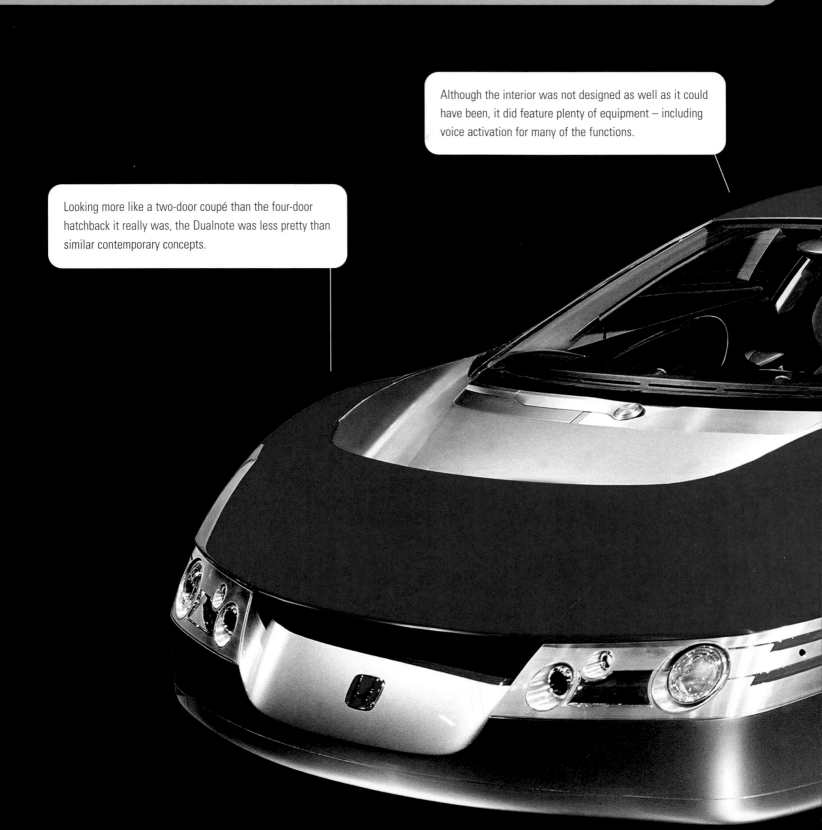

Although the interior was not designed as well as it could have been, it did feature plenty of equipment – including voice activation for many of the functions.

Looking more like a two-door coupé than the four-door hatchback it really was, the Dualnote was less pretty than similar contemporary concepts.

The Dualnote's 3.5l V6 petrol engine was positioned behind the rear-seat passengers, which helped to produce exceptional handling for the class of car – but, on the downside, it ate into the cabin space.

Helping the petrol engine to provide motive power were three electric motors – which meant that there was 294kW (394bhp) at the driver's disposal.

Safety was important to Honda, so the Dualnote was built with four-wheel drive. It also featured a six-speed clutchless manual gearbox with fully automatic mode.

The two-tone paint scheme of the Honda Dualnote was effective in its simplicity – although it was an old idea, it made a refreshing change to see it on a 21st-century concept.

How would you like a car that offers nearly 298kW (400bhp) yet can still travel more than 80km (50 miles) on a gallon of fuel? It's a tempting prospect, and one that Honda offered in the Dualnote which was first shown at the 2001 Tokyo motor show. But despite the fact that the car looked like it came from the future, and some of the technology that it packed also appeared to be similarly out of this world, the reality was that everything under the skin of the Dualnote was possible to put into production there and then. The only drawback to the car was that it would have proved to be far too expensive for the average family to afford …

Positioned in the middle of the Dualnote was a 3.5l V6 petrol engine, and this, when combined with the three electric motors that were also fitted, was capable of developing a rather tasty 294kW (394bhp), which was channelled to all four wheels. Transmitting this power was a six-speed clutchless manual gearbox, which also incorporated a fully automatic mode.

Wedge shape

The Honda Dualnote was a full four seater, despite the fact that the engine sat behind the back-seat passengers, which reduced the available space considerably. As was becoming increasingly popular at the time, the fact that there were four doors was masked by the design, which suggested that the car was really a two-door coupé.

The use of a two-tone paint scheme was an interesting way of trying to emphasize the wedge-shaped profile of the car, especially as the red and silver-grey colour scheme contrasted so heavily with each other. Sadly, the design was rather too clumsy – there was no way the paintwork on its own could make it look any more graceful. The droopy nose with its small inset headlights presented something of a missed opportunity – it would have looked so much more attractive had the proportions been right.

At least the overall shape of the Dualnote was appealing, and its spoked alloy wheels made it look really quite sporty – at the front, they were 45.7cm (18in) in diameter, while the rear ones were 2.5cm (1in) larger. Wrapped in 45-profile tyres, the car also looked utterly contemporary – compared with other concepts of the time, the tyres were actually quite high profile.

Honda Dualnote

Debut:	Tokyo 2001
Engine capacity:	3.5l (214ci)
Configuration:	Mid-mounted V6, petrol
Power:	294kW (394bhp)
Top speed:	N/A
Transmission:	RWD
Length:	4385mm (173in)
Width:	1725mm (68in)
Designer:	N/A

Inside the Dualnote was a colour scheme which echoed that of the bodywork – unfortunately, the cabin also continued some of the clumsiness seen on the outside. A prominent centre console ran the length of the interior, and the dash was trimmed in black and silver – which was lifted by plenty of aluminium detailing. The seats, however, were trimmed in red, which did not tie in with any highlights elsewhere in the cabin. As with the exterior design, the Dualnote's cabin was something of a missed opportunity.

Gadget overload

To compensate, the gadget count was high, with voice activation for most of the functions. The instrument panel was designed to deliver only the necessary information when needed. Divided into three optimally positioned display units, the first showed speed, engine rpm and other basic information. The display also notified the driver of incoming telephone and e-mail messages. The centre display, located at the bottom of the windscreen to minimize driver distraction, incorporated an arrow navigation display to indicate branches in the road ahead, and night vision, which used an infrared camera to detect pedestrians. The image was then processed and displayed to the driver. The final display was the information monitor, which used a multi-function display that automatically changed both the settings and the display mode as necessary to show e-mail, Internet, telephone information and vehicle information such as the navigation screen.

In March 2002, the concept was shown at the New York auto show, as the Acura DN-X. This was exactly the same car, but, as Honda had relaunched itself in the United States using the Acura brand, it made sense to rebadge the concept using this identity.

At a time when most concepts featured light cabins and a sense of space, the Dualnote went the other way. Its interior felt quite claustrophobic, as it was finished in dark colours.

Mitsubishi ESR

The Mitsubishi ESR's petrol engine ran at a constant speed, merely charging the batteries rather than actually driving the car. Dual spark plugs and a catalyst helped it to run very cleanly.

The beauty of the ESR was to derive the best possible efficiency from a petrol engine by boosting it with a battery-driven powerpack, which was kept charged by the engine.

Advances in electric motor technology made the ESR a viable proposition – but at a price. New materials and better manufacturing tolerances made the motor more efficient than usual.

Perhaps one of the ugliest concept cars ever, the Mitsubishi ESR looked especially awkward from the rear three-quarters. At least the front featured slightly less unusual proportions.

Regenerative braking was also used in the ESR to keep the battery pack topped up. This turned the motor into a generator whenever the brakes were applied or if engine braking was used.

How many abbreviations and acronyms can you fit into one car? In the case of the Mitsubishi ESR, plenty! Even the car's name is an abbreviation, short for Ecological Science Research, but thrown in for good measure were MVV, IGBT, EHC and SHEV, among others – but more of that later.

Electric motor, turbo engine

The point of the ESR was to test the viability of series hybrid personal transport, in which an electric motor and an internal combustion engine worked in harmony to reduce fuel consumption, and hence emissions. To that end, the ESR housed an electric motor at the front, and a turbocharged 1.5l petrol engine in the rear. The electric motor powered the car, but, where necessary, the batteries powering the motor would be charged by the internal combustion engine. Considering the electric motor could not run at 100 per cent efficiency, the laws of physics would normally dictate that there would be thermal losses from both the petrol engine and the electric motor. But Mitsubishi claimed that this system was more efficient than simply using either the motor on its own or the internal combustion engine. If the car was being used in an urban environment, it would run on battery power alone, this means of propulsion being called battery-operated mode. But if a boost was needed because the speed was increasing, or the journey was a

Mitsubishi ESR	
Debut:	Frankfurt 1993
Engine capacity:	AC induction motor
Configuration:	Front-mounted
Power:	70kW (94bhp)
Top speed:	200km/h (124mph)
Transmission:	3-speed automatic, FWD
Length:	4535mm (181in)
Width:	1725mm (679in)
Designer:	N/A

long one, the petrol engine would cut in to charge up the batteries – this was named hybrid mode.

The key to the extra efficiency of the ESR's electric motors was the development of a new type of AC motor, which was not fitted with a commutator. Increased manufacturing precision also helped to reduce power losses, and the ability for the motor to spin up to

The rear doors of the ESR were designed for optimum practicality – they made entry and exit much easier than conventional units. But the ESR's front doors were designed for show and were less practical.

The shape of the ESR was certainly effective at high speeds, making it the consummate sports car. It was a pity that the shape had not been designed to be easier on the eye!

15,000rpm thanks to the adoption of ceramic bearings was also important. Use of all this technology allowed Mitsubishi to go overboard on the abbreviations – Japanese manufacturers tend to like cramming as many of these into their concepts as possible, whereas American and European makers are less inclined to do so. Therefore, the motors incorporated Insulate Gate Bipolar Transistors (IGBTs), while the petrol engine was dubbed the Mitsubishi Vertical Vortex (MMV) engine. All of which sounds impressive, but is for most consumers ultimately meaningless.

Smooth running

Of more interest was the fact that the petrol engine ran at a constant speed, to reduce emissions by running as efficiently as possible – after all, it was merely charging the batteries rather than powering the car directly. Each of the four cylinders was equipped with two spark plugs to ensure the most thorough combustion possible, and, to clean the emissions even further, there was also an electrically heated catalyst (EHC). And it was not just the petrol engine that charged up the batteries, as the ESR was also equipped with regenerative braking. This turned the motor into a

generator when the brakes were applied. So rather than the motor driving the car, it charged up the batteries by harnessing the car's kinetic energy and converting it back into electricity.

To make the car run as efficiently as possible, an aerodynamic and light bodyshell was designed. With a drag co-efficient of just 0.25, the ESR used lightweight materials to keep the weight down – the use of computer-aided engineering also helped to keep the car's structure as efficiently designed as possible.

The ESR's interior was designed to be as simple as possible, although it was still pretty futuristic. Liquid crystal displays dominated the dashboard, with all read-outs being presented electronically. The rear-view mirror was replaced by a camera mounted in the back of the car – this relayed pictures to a monitor on the dash. Most of the switchgear for the ESR's equipment was placed around the steering column, and all four occupants were protected by airbags in the event of a collision.

Volvo ECC

If the ECC has a shape that seems vaguely familiar, this is because it went into production as the S80 several years after being shown in concept form.

To reduce rolling resistance as far as possible, and thus help maintain economy at low speeds, the car was fitted with low rolling resistance tyres. These ran at double the normal pressure.

To deliver on the promises, the ECC's bodyshell was made of aluminium, which reduced weight and aided recyclability. Low wind resistance also helped to reduce fuel consumption.

Powering the ECC was a gas turbine engine combined with an electric motor. The former was for high-speed use, while the latter was for urban driving.

The ECC included a hybrid powertrain engine consisting of a gas turbine and electric motor combination. The electric motor was used for low-speed, urban driving, while the gas turbine was saved for use at higher speeds.

Looking suspiciously like the S80 launched in 1998, the Environmental Concept Car (ECC) was first seen as far back as September 1992. The brief for this concept was to design a car which offered quality, safety, comfort and performance, but which would also be environmentally friendly. The car's design would allow a drag coefficient of just 0.25, although in the event, the final result was a Cd of 0.23 – quite remarkable for a four-door saloon (sedan). The ECC also needed to be identifiably a Volvo, so it had to draw on styling themes from previous cars built by the company – the Amazon's sides, the broad shoulders of the 144 and the V-shape of the bonnet (which had been a Volvo characteristic since the PV444) were all incorporated into the design.

Lightweight efficiency

With a bodyshell made of aluminium, intended to be fully recyclable, the ECC's light weight also aided fuel economy and performance. By opting for aluminium, the all-in weight of the finished car was 1580kg (3483lb), which was equivalent to a 12 per cent reduction (or 215kg/474lb) if the same car been built

Soft materials and flowing curves marked the start of a new era in Volvo design – both inside and out. It was the perfect blend of safety and luxury that Volvo fans had come to love.

in steel. But although aerodynamics and weight both have a part to play when it comes to saving fuel, the key to fuel efficiency at low speeds is to reduce the rolling resistance of the tyres as far as possible. To that end, the ECC sat on custom-made Goodyear 205/60 R15 E-matic rubber, inflated to a massive 4.6kg/sq cm (66psi) – which is about double the pressure of a conventional tyre.

Something which proved to be rather a blind alley was the choice of a hybrid powertrain – or, more specifically, a gas turbine and electric motor combination. Driving through a two-speed automatic transmission was an electric motor which generated 40kW (53bhp) during continuous running, but which could be called upon to produce up to 71kW (95bhp) in short bursts.

This power source was to be used in urban driving, while the 42kW (56bhp) gas turbine was saved for driving at higher speeds. By pooling these two sources

Volvo ECC

Debut:	Paris 1992
Engine capacity:	N/A
Configuration:	Front-mounted
Power:	42kW/56bhp (gas turbine) + 71kW/95bhp (electric)
Top speed:	175km/h (109mph)
Transmission:	2-speed auto, FWD
Length:	4487mm (177in)
Width:	1804mm (71in)
Designer:	N/A

The problem was that gas turbines may be more efficient than conventional internal combustion engines, but they are also not very well suited to driving wheels via transmissions. Because it is closely related to the turboprop aircraft engine, the gas turbine is good at producing thrust, but not directly to driving wheels. Similarly, the electric motor has never been a viable means of propulsion in the passenger car because of limited range and the inherent heavy weight of the associated battery packs. So, in a way, the ECC combined the worst of both worlds in that both of its power supplies were inappropriate for passenger-car use.

Regenerative braking

Perhaps the best thing about using electric power to propel a car is that a motor can become a generator when braking. The ECC utilized this technology, so that, when the brakes were applied, the batteries were topped up using regenerative braking – this could provide up to 45kW (60bhp). The result of all this was a car which could run for nearly 805km (500 miles) between refuelling stops, and when used in electric mode, was capable of meeting the Zero Emissions laws that California was due to bring in shortly after the ECC made its debut.

Despite the cutting-edge technology used throughout the ECC, its interior was pretty conventional – Volvo, thankfully, did not fall into the trap of making it look like something out of Dan Dare.

of motive power, the ECC could reach 100km/h (62mph) in 13 seconds and achieve a top speed of 175km/h (109mph), while burning up less fuel in gas turbine mode than a conventionally powered car. Carrying the HSG (High Speed Generator) tag, this means of propulsion allowed the car to drive as similarly as possible to a conventional car, but to have far less of an impact on the environment.

There was a lot of technology packed into the ECC, and Volvo would have been quite naïve to think such a complex car could realistically go into production.

Family and Fun

The term 'family car' may conjure up images of a boring saloon (sedan) that just melts into the background, but it does not need to be that way. All the cars included here suggested a way of providing practical transport for the future, but they also had one other thing in common: they did it with a combination of design flair and technological innovation.

If there is one segment of the concept car world where something resembling sanity should prevail at least some of the time, this is it. Designers cannot throw caution to the wind and let yet another whimsical concept emerge from their studios. Instead these cars have to be able to carry people and their luggage while also being totally usable every day of the week.

At one time, these restrictions would also have meant cars with little in the way of design flair – either inside or out. Take a look at the earliest concept in this chapter, the Ford Eltec, and this is all too apparent. It was not intended to be anything special in terms of its levels of luxury or sportiness, and the result was a box on wheels. Sure, it offered a glimpse of future technologies, including variable-length inlet manifolds and lean-burn fuel injection, but it excited no one.

The aim of the Nissan Yanya was to bring multipurpose ability to the ever-growing and commercially crucial city-car market. The Yanya was firmly aimed at those fashion-conscious young buyers who put style above all else.

Old and new

Compare the Ford Eltec with more recent concepts, and the differences are stark. The SEAT Salsa or Saab 9-X are perhaps the best examples of this, but the Rover TCV and Renault Fiftie cannot be ignored. While offering affordable transport for families, they also have some design flair inside and out. Their cabins are inviting, with materials throughout that look expensive even if they are not. Attention to detail means that they are eminently usable, and equipment levels have also been ramped up.

But it is not always about the things that the buyer can see – under the skin there have been huge advances that are not immediately obvious. In fact, those strides have been so large that, in many cases, what was previously cutting-edge is now taken for granted. For example, none of the cars in this section is now seen as especially revolutionary when it comes to engines or transmissions. Some of them have better packaging than others and some are better looking than others. But they are all different in their own way and, if these concepts represent the future of motoring, it's a very bright future that we can look forward to.

Chevrolet Nomad

Although the Chevrolet Nomad as a whole is reminiscent of the original production car that bore the same name, it is the rear end styling that most closely captures the spirit of the production model.

For such a small car, those 50cm (20in) wheels were ridiculously oversized. Somehow, however, they managed to look in proportion when wrapped in the Nomad's ultra-low profile tyres.

The production Nomad of the 1950s and the later concept of the same name had both been built to typical American dimensions. But the new car was far smaller, reflecting the compact economics of today.

For such a small car, the 2.2l turbocharged engine offered a lot of power, with a rear-wheel drive configuration that should have made it superb to drive.

Transmitting the 186kW (250bhp) to the back was a five-speed gearbox that offered a fully automatic mode or the opportunity to shift ratios manually, in sequence.

When a concept carrying Chevy Nomad badges was unveiled at the 2003 Detroit motor show, it was not the first time the name had been revived for a show car. A concept had been produced for the 1999 Detroit motor show that used the same name. And it was not only the name that was taken from Chevrolet's classic 1950s estate (station wagon); the lines also paid homage to the original production car. But whereas the previous cars were (very) full-sized cars, this new one was nearly as small as the new production BMW Mini.

Small is beautiful

The reason for the Chevrolet Nomad's size was the unexpected success of the Mini in the United States. More than 56,000 examples were sold after it was named the North American Car of the Year 2003, suggesting that small no longer meant an automatic sales handicap. The new Nomad concept offered the first hint that America's car makers were searching for an answer to that under-sized automobile from across the pond. It was also a truly international effort, being

The Chevrolet Nomad's simple dashboard layout worked effectively. Even if many of the details were not very original, they still managed to combine practicality and a strong sense of design.

Chevrolet Nomad	
Debut:	Detroit 2004
Engine capacity:	2200cc (134.2ci) turbocharged
Configuration:	Front-mounted, in-line four, petrol
Power:	186kW (250bhp)
Top speed:	N/A
Transmission:	5-speed semi-auto, RWD
Length:	3950mm (155.5in)
Width:	1700mm (66.9in)
Designer:	Simon Cox

the creation of a British designer leading a team based in the West Midlands, with the car being assembled by Pininfarina, in Italy.

Simon Cox, Director of the GM Advanced Design UK studio in Coventry, was the man behind the Nomad. He claimed not to be targeting the Mini specifically, but there were certain similarities. The greatest of these was a strong personality; a car that had character

The glass house on the Nomad was extremely narrow – it looked as though the pillars had been shortened, or the roof 'chopped', in true hot-rod style.

and plenty of soul. The Nomad's appeal needed to cross generations; the idea was that anybody, of any age, should be happy to drive it.

The Nomad was very compact, and also lower, wider and much more flexible than its size would have suggested. That meant it could be used by business people, families, or even the sort of driver who would want to paint a great big white stripe down the middle of it and take it to a track. It really was a case of anything going!

The concept was based on a tubular steel chassis with independent suspension and disc brakes all round – something that was considered a relatively sophisticated combination in the United States. Again, against conventions, GM managed to resist squeezing in a monster V8 (such as the 6l, 'small block' unit from the new Corvette that was introduced at the same time), instead preferring to use a lightweight turbo-charged 2.2l, four-cylinder engine with variable-valve timing, which was also to power the Solstice – the

new small, lightweight sports car in the mould of the Lotus Elise. In the Nomad concept, this powerplant sent 186kw (250bhp) to the rear wheels, via a five-speed automatic gearbox. There was also a very handy 33kg-m (240lb-ft) of torque available, and the choice of a sequential manual mode within the gearbox made the driving experience more enjoyable, offering the driver full control of whichever ratio was selected at any time.

Giving the car its purposeful stance were 50.8cm (20in) alloy wheels, which were clothed in 245/40 tyres. Considering the relatively small dimensions of the car, this could be deemed to be either overkill or the height of cool, depending on your view. But one thing was certain – it looked utterly contemporary as a result. Despite the long wheelbase, huge wheels and powerful engine, the driving experience offered by the Nomad was not the most important thing. Instead, it was the combination of dynamics and practicality that were the key: there was plenty of space inside for really tall drivers. Even better, the car was a proper four-seater, where the seats were not just suited to small children. In addition, both back seats could fold independently, while the armrest separating them flipped forward to reveal a gap for long loads to be slid through. Then the boot (trunk) floor could slide out, and the rear window could be lowered into the tailgate and the back section of the roof fully detached. If this still would not accommodate your load, you probably needed a truck.

Practicality was a part of the new Nomad mix, with all sorts of interior configurations possible. The result was a flexible carrying ability that belied the compact dimensions.

Citroën C-Airdream

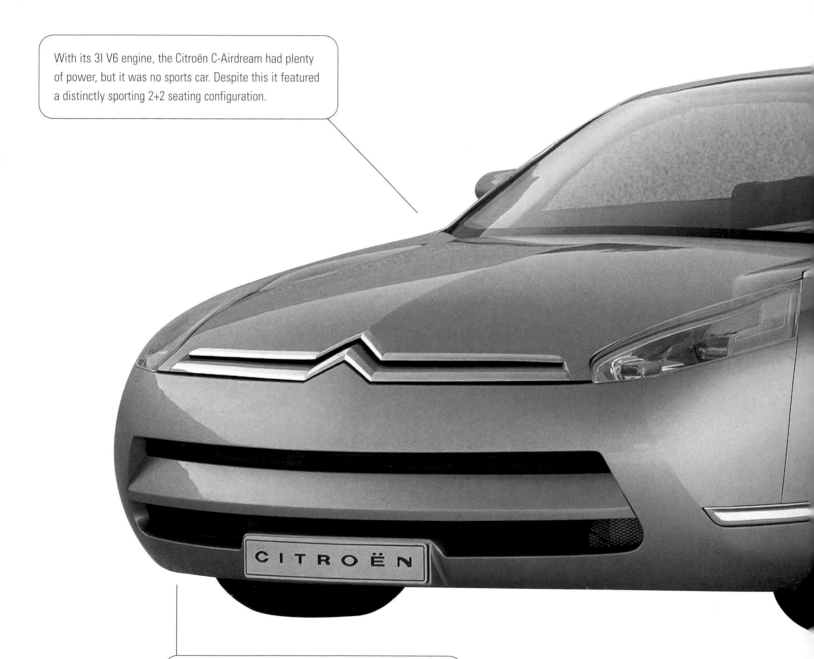

With its 3l V6 engine, the Citroën C-Airdream had plenty of power, but it was no sports car. Despite this it featured a distinctly sporting 2+2 seating configuration.

Offering a glimpse of Citroën's future design direction, the nose of the C-Airdream featured a slim grille which incorporating the trademark chevron logo, along with large, narrow headlights.

The C-Airdream's steering operated on a by-wire system, which meant that there was no mechanical link between the road wheels and the steering wheel. This allowed a variable steering ratio.

From this angle the C-Airdream looks like a sporting estate (station wagon), but it was actually more of a coupé – although its cabin was considerably more airy than usual, thanks all that glass.

More than most car manufacturers, Citroën recognized the value of fluid-controlled suspension. That is why the C-Airdream was fitted with a computer-controlled system known as Hydractive3.

The C-Airdream was Citroën's distinctive twist on the 2+2 coupé format, and, in a bid to regain its title as one of the most innovative car makers around, the company finally managed with this concept to come up with something that captured the beauty of its cars from the 1970s. Truly original it could not claim to be, but, where Citroën's production cars had become derivative, the C-Airdream looked bold, sporty and full of class. Even better, it was rumoured that this was the start of a reappraisal of Citroën's whole ethos, suggesting that a new design direction was just around the corner.

Classic glamour

Capturing the glamorous look of Citroëns from some three decades earlier, the C-Airdream featured a long bonnet and a cabin set relatively far back. There was a long front overhang, but the one at the back was much shorter. All this added up to a dynamic, sporty look that had just the right balance between aggression and sleekness. Naturally it looked utterly modern, with those large headlights much of the way up the front wings. Between them was a very subtle air intake, which incorporated the Citroën double-chevron logo, and in the lower portion of the nose was a gaping air dam, to feed air to the V6 powerplant.

This exterior design was executed by British designer Mark Lloyd, and thanks to those sleek lines it was not just about form – there was function, too. A drag coefficient of 0.28 meant it was slippery enough to be fuel-efficient and quiet. The brief was to come up with a car that featured sports styling with

a light, bright and spacious interior, and this latter quality was achieved by fitting a glass roof that more or less opened up the cabin completely.

But the styling of the C-Airdream was not the important part – although it did suggest the direction in which Citroën was to head over the coming years with a new range of production cars. What it heralded was a move to highly advanced technology, to produce some of the best driving machines available. The greatest innovation, which was used to activate several systems, was by-wire technology. This allowed systems such as the braking and steering to be activated by solenoids rather than mechanical linkages, freeing up space in the cabin, improving safety and reducing weight. It also meant that the steering could have a ratio – and assistance – that varied radically depending on the steering input and the speed at which the car was travelling. At parking speeds, it could be very highly geared, so that a small movement of the steering wheel would turn the front wheels a lot, while at higher speeds this would be reversed so that the car felt more stable.

The pedal assembly was also eliminated; however, whereas most other concepts replaced conventional mechanical linkages with pedals that activated electronics, the C-Airdream was fitted with no pedals at all. Instead there were buttons on the steering wheel, which allowed the car to brake and accelerate.

The Citroën C-Airdream probably looks the most sporting from the rear, although the oddly-shaped expanses of glass are also more evident when it is viewed this way.

The adoption of drive-by-wire technology allowed the interior of the C-Airdream to be fully opened up – space-consuming mechanical linkages were no longer required.

Not only that, but also all the gearchanges were executed by pressing buttons on the multi-function steering wheel – this was a return to the true innovation of Citroën's earlier years.

Under the bonnet was a 3l, V6 engine developing 157kw (210bhp), which was mated to a sequential auto-adaptive automatic gearbox. But perhaps the best thing about the C-Airdream was the suspension – something for which Citroën had always been noted in the 1960s and 1970s. Back then, the company had fitted its cars with fluid suspension, giving them a balance between ride and handling that other car makers could only envy. However, such complexity inevitably led to perceptions of poor reliability, whether or not it was deserved, so conventional steel systems filtered into the range. This concept aimed to revert to something more innovative, with its Hydractive3 system that was electronically controlled.

Even better, Citroën claimed that key elements of the C-Airdream would be introduced into its production car range soon after. As this book went to press, the first signs that this was true were becoming evident; it was long overdue.

Citroën C-Airdream

Debut:	Paris 2002
Engine capacity:	2946cc (180ci)
Configuration:	Front-mounted V6, petrol
Power:	157kW (210bhp)
Top speed:	N/A
Transmission:	Automatic, FWD
Length:	N/A
Width:	N/A
Designer:	Mark Lloyd

Ford Eltec

Hindsight makes it easy to see that the Ford Eltec was a thinly disguised foretaste of the Mk5 Escort – the nose, profile and rear were all very similar.

The Eltec's 1.3l lean-burn petrol engine offered adequate power while also being kind to the environment. It was simple, but featured several good touches, such as a variable-length manifold.

The Eltec featured an unusual amount of glass – the tailgate, side windows and windscreen gave superb all-round visibility, while the roof was also largely constructed of glass.

Details such as those high-mounted rear lights were deemed too radical for production, although they did become increasingly popular within about a decade of the Eltec being shown.

Active ride meant the Eltec's suspension was controlled by an on-board computer to ensure it was composed when cornering, while also offering a comfortable ride.

It may not look especially cutting edge in these photographs, but, when the Ford Eltec made its first appearance at the 1985 Frankfurt motor show, this represented a glimpse into Ford's future – and in hindsight it also looked remarkably like the Mk5 Escort of 1990. Just the name Eltec, which was short for Electronic Technology, hinted at the purpose of this concept – to showcase how electronics could be used to make a standard family car of the future safe, comfortable and clean.

Much of the technology incorporated into the Eltec has become commonplace in the time since the car was first shown, but the fascinating thing is the level at which much of the equipment is now fitted. Whereas the Eltec was a mid-range hatch, even cars two sizes smaller are now fitted with anti-lock brakes, continuously variable transmissions and electronic control of all of the engine's functions from the fuel injection to the ignition. And it was not just the

The Eltec was a fully working concept, and it served as a testbed for new technologies such as Ford's continuously variable transmission and electronic control of the major engine functions.

technology hidden under the skin that was important to the Eltec: the skin, designed by Ghia, was also of major importance. Not only was the glass flush, but also it was on just about every surface above waist height. Even the roof was glazed, and instead of having just a simple glass roof, there were five louvred panels which could be angled upwards to provide ventilation.

Alternatively, it was possible to slide the whole lot back to open the car right up. But if that made the interior too breezy (or noisy), they could be kept shut, and the cabin would not become too hot because all of the glass was tinted.

Window lights

The overall lines may not appear to be particularly adventurous, but there are some nice touches. Perhaps the most useful is the rear light positioning. Years before Volvo started to stack its upper rear lights either side of the rear window on the V70, Ford did it on the Eltec. The lower rear lights incorporated multiple bulbs for safety, and to improve aerodynamics the nose-mounted grille was dispensed with – although it has to be said that this gave the car a bland front end.

At the design stage the Eltec looked like a bigger car, as it was much sleeker. In this shot it looks more like one of the Probe series that spawned one of Britain's best-selling cars, the Ford Sierra.

Making the most of all that computing power was active ride, which meant the suspension was computer-controlled to provide the best possible balance between ride and handling. Conventional wisdom dictates that if a car has a soft and comfortable ride, it will roll like a barge in a gale when it comes to the corners. But using active ride makes it possible for a car to have compliant suspension on the straights, which then stiffens up on the bends to corner more flatly.

Alongside the electronic anti-lock brakes fitted to the Eltec was traction control. This electronic form of wheelspin avoidance technology is now fitted to just about all cars, but when the Eltec was revealed the only form of traction control was mechanical, in the shape of limited-slip differentials.

Pioneering engine technology

The all-alloy 1.3l engine was produced specially for the Eltec, and produced 60kW (80bhp). It was a lean-burn unit, which meant less fuel was injected into it and it therefore ran more cleanly. It also featured three valves per cylinder to help reduce emissions, and just one overhead camshaft. While all these specifications have now become standard – or even exceeded – on most cars, the variable-length inlet manifold was truly pioneering. The idea has now made it to production (BMW uses it), but it is still far from normal to find it fitted to a production car. Also designed to cut emissions, by reducing any sudden throttle inputs, was drive-by-wire. This replaced the more usual throttle cable with a potentiometer, which signalled to the car's electronic control unit (ECU) exactly how much fuel and air to inject into the combustion chambers. Again, this may be usual now, but in 1985 there was nothing on the road using such technology.

Ford Eltec

Debut:	Frankfurt 1985
Engine capacity:	1300cc (79ci)
Configuration:	Front-mounted in-line four, petrol
Power:	60kW (80bhp)
Top speed:	169km/h (105mph)
Transmission:	Continuously variable transmission, FWD
Length:	4122mm (162in)
Width:	not known
Designer:	N/A

Ford Model U

At the front of the Model U was the world's first hydrogen-fuelled internal combustion engine; a 2.3l supercharged four-cylinder unit that developed 88kW (118bhp) while being nearly 100 per cent clean.

The transmission was as revolutionary as the powerplant. An electric motor and a pair of clutches allowed power from the engine, the motor or both.

In a bid to save weight the Model U was constructed from lightweight materials as much as possible. That meant the use of aluminium and composites.

It was significant that the Model U concept for the masses looked more like something from the battlefields of World War II; it indicated the enormous rise in popularity of the off-roader among modern drivers.

To help make the Model U run as efficiently as possible, there was a regenerative braking system. This reclaimed energy that would otherwise be lost during braking.

When your best-selling car to date is called the Model T, and you want to recall the good times, the obvious thing to do is pinch the name – or at least use something closely related. So it was the Model U, which aimed to offer transport for the masses, just as the Model T had done nearly a century before. But whereas the Model T had offered cheap, basic transport, the idea behind the Model U was that it would be a technological *tour de force* that used pioneering technology to solve some of the problems brought about by the car.

The internal combustion engine had by now been refined to the point where both petrol and diesel engines could be quiet, efficient and clean, but the problem of dwindling oil reserves remained. Indeed, alternative fuel sources were being widely explored at

The Model U's sparsely equipped cabin featured a very spartan dash design. Apart from a few instruments, everything was displayed on a central read-out – simplicity combined with practicality.

The Ford Model U followed the vogue for rear-hinged back doors. This allowed the easiest possible access to the cabin, which was sparsely equipped.

the time that the Model U made its debut at the 2003 Detroit motor show. Ford's competitors were looking into hydrogen fuel cells as the most viable means of propulsion, but this concept housed the world's first hydrogen internal combustion engine.

Big power

The Model U's powerplant was a 2.3l, supercharged, four-cylinder unit, which was coupled to a hybrid electric transmission. While offering a 480km (300-mile) range, it could return around 45 miles per gallon, yet its emissions were virtually zero – which represented something like a 99 per cent reduction in carbon dioxide output.

Within the hybrid transmission, the torque converter from a conventional transmission was replaced by a high-voltage electric motor and two hydraulic clutches that permitted the motor to operate independently of, or in concert with, the engine. The electric motor simultaneously fulfilled the role of flywheel, starter, alternator and hybrid traction motor.

The use of this system meant that the Model U could operate on either the hydrogen-powered engine or the electric motor, or both for extra power. A regenerative braking function reclaimed energy that would otherwise be lost as heat, storing it in the 300-volt, air-cooled battery pack for the next time the accelerator was floored. The innovations did not stop with the mechanicals: the Model U also featured both an interior and an exterior which were reconfigurable. This meant that the car could be adapted to suit any owner's individuality. Thanks to its modular construction, an owner could upgrade both the inside and the outside as their tastes or budget changed. There was a series of slots in the floor, door panels and instrument panel, into which different components could be mounted, moved around or added later. The slots were designed to provide power and access to the vehicle's electronic network, allowing true personalization of the cabin.

The inside featured the world's most advanced speech recognition system, allowing the occupants to communicate with the car. Voice commands activated all the major functions, including the climate control system, satellite navigation, cellular telephone and entertainment console. Outside, the three-box profile had a tough modular look, with body panels that were visually separated through different finishes and which were made of different materials. The sides of the body had a glossy appearance, while the doors featured a matt finish. They were also grooved for both design appearance and structural integrity. To save weight, the bodyshell was constructed of aluminum and the front side panels were made of composites.

Ford Model U

Debut:	Detroit 2003
Engine capacity:	2.3l (140.3ci)
Configuration:	Front-mounted
Power:	88kW (118bhp)
Top speed:	N/A
Transmission:	Hybrid electric
Length:	4230mm (166.5in)
Width:	1810mm (71.3in)
Designer:	Lauren van den Acker

One of the key things about the Model U was its adaptability – it was claimed to be as capable of performing rugged jobs as it was of driving to an evening out. Further, the Model U could be converted from completely closed to completely open; in the latter guise, it looked like a pick-up and the rear seats could be removed to provide a longer loading floor. The roof was a power-retractable canvas soft top, which opened rearward to offer a nearly open-air motoring experience.

Looking as though it were little more than a full-scale Tonka toy, the Model U had a cloth roof which opened the car up to the elements.

Nissan Dunehawk

Flexibility and practicality were the priorities for the interior: there were multiple seat configurations and masses of space available behind the two front seats.

Unlike most modern off-roaders featuring monocoques, the Nissan Dunehawk was fitted with a separate chassis, which enabled it to venture into the wilds without fear of getting stuck.

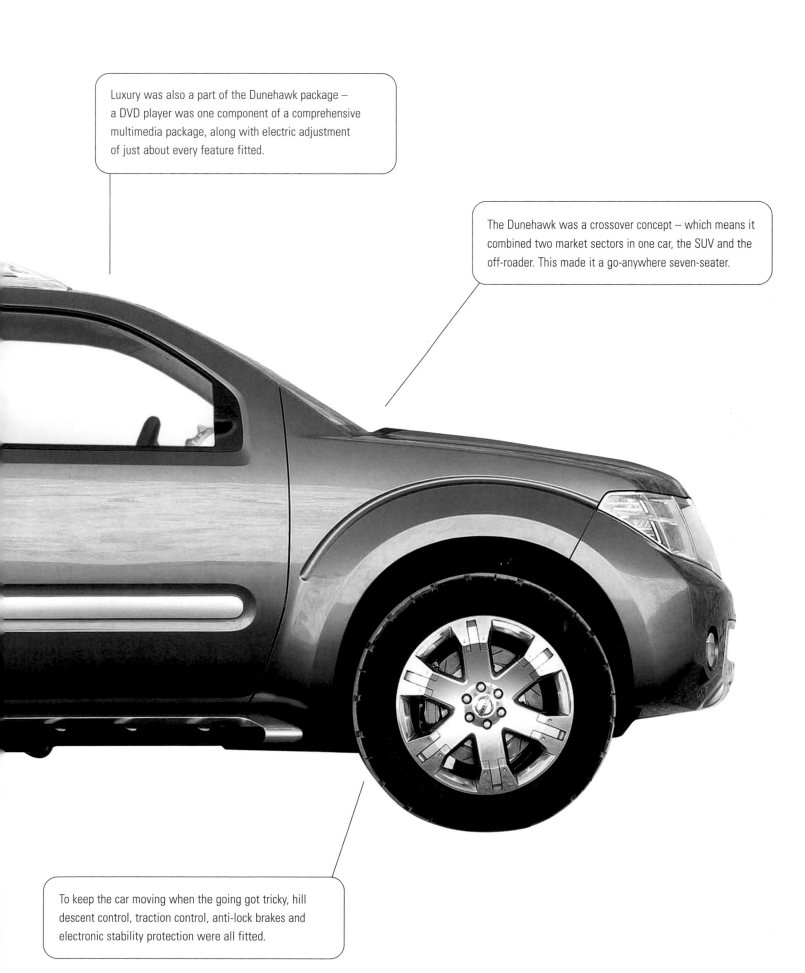

Luxury was also a part of the Dunehawk package –
a DVD player was one component of a comprehensive
multimedia package, along with electric adjustment
of just about every feature fitted.

The Dunehawk was a crossover concept – which means it
combined two market sectors in one car, the SUV and the
off-roader. This made it a go-anywhere seven-seater.

To keep the car moving when the going got tricky, hill
descent control, traction control, anti-lock brakes and
electronic stability protection were all fitted.

Until the arrival of the Volvo XC90, no sport utility vehicle (SUV) also offered proper seating for seven. There were plenty of off-roaders which had an occasional third row of seats, but it took Volvo to do the obvious thing, and introduce proper seats for third-row passengers. With a niche having been established with the XC90 – and one which was an overwhelming success – Nissan realized that there was a ready market for a people carrier crossed with an off-roader, and decided to exploit this with the Dunehawk, a crossover concept first shown at the 2003 Frankfurt motor show.

Whereas Volvo had chosen not to turn its contender into a proper off-roader, Nissan decided to go the whole

nine yards and create a machine that was as capable as anything to come out of the gates of Land Rover. More intriguingly, it also claimed that the Dunehawk pointed the way for the company's off-roaders of the future – the X-Trail had shown that Nissan was not afraid to style its off-roaders boldly and aggressively, and the new concept certainly held promise.

The Dunehawk featured a separate ladder frame chassis, which was effectively confirmation that this was intended to be a proper off-roader first and an on-road car second. If on-road manners and refinement had been the priority – as had become common with most SUVs – a full monocoque would have been chosen. This choice, though, meant that the car was best suited for tackling rough terrain and towing big and heavy trailers.

There were 50.8cm (20in) wheels all round, which also helped when the going got tough, and naturally there were plenty of electronics to help out if traction

In keeping with a 21st-century concept, the Nissan Dunehawk was designed with an interior that was packed full of electronics and multimedia systems. This screen was effectively an in-car PC situated above the gear system.

Key to the Nissan Dunehawk's off-roading abilities were very short overhangs front and rear, thus allowing the car to tackle really rough terrain far more effectively.

became an issue. Alongside electronically controlled differential locks were traction control and electronic brake force distribution. Anti-lock brakes were also included, and hill descent control made sure that the car did not run away with its occupants if a steep hill was being tackled when traction levels were low.

Bold and angular

So far, all this technology has been fitted to production off-roaders for several years – what distinguished the Dunehawk from all these was its bold, angular design. Although Nissan declared that a cylindrical design theme had been adopted when styling the Dunehawk, this is not immediately obvious. But look closely, and you will see that beyond the mass of straight lines the body sides are quite rounded, with the waistline being significantly wider than the roof and chassis. This theme continues on the tailgate, as well as on the wheelarch blisters and in some of the interior fittings.

Inside was generally much more angular, with the cabin bisected by a very prominent central console. Within the instrumentation was a liquid crystal display that showed in real time the amount of traction available at each wheel – there were sensors on all four wheels as well as within the four-wheel drive transmission. There was also a TV screen linked

to a camera within the rear panelwork, to make sure that the car was not reversed into anything while off-roading or parking in town.

Rear-seat passengers also got a taste of luxury, being provided with DVD players and headrest-mounted TV screens. They also benefited – as did the front-seat occupants – from the glass roof that kept the interior light. But if luggage were the priority rather than passengers, it was possible to fold the second and third row of seats away, which provided enough room to carry a pair of bikes, standing upright during transit. Sadly, if the Dunehawk ever reaches production, the chances are that all this will be scaled down.

Nissan Dunehawk

Debut:	Frankfurt 2003
Engine capacity:	N/A
Configuration:	Front-engined
Power:	N/A
Top speed:	N/A
Transmission:	4WD
Length:	4795mm (189in)
Width:	1900mm (75in)
Designer:	N/A

Nissan Yanya

The interior of the Nissan Yanya was as flexible as the exterior, with the seating being configurable in several different ways. An Internet connection was also provided for each of the occupants.

In normal driving conditions, the front wheels were driven by the petrol engine. But when grip levels reduced, the rear wheels were driven by an electric motor.

When two seemingly opposing sectors of the market take off, there is a school of thought that says combining the two in one car will mean that a company cannot fail to take customers from each segment. So when the global market saw rises in supermini and sport utility vehicle (SUV) sales in the early twenty-first century, Nissan decided to put the two sectors together to create a new kind of car – the off-roading supermini. But just in case attracting two sectors was not enough, Nissan threw in a third and fourth: when the Yanya was unveiled at the 2002 Geneva motor show, it was capable of being turned into a full convertible or even a pick-up truck!

Stylish solutions

The reasoning behind the Yanya was that it offered 'a practical, hi-tech, stylish yet affordable solution for the daily and weekend lives of the young, sophisticated and active global city-dwellers of the future'. In other words, it would be able to do everything that was asked of it, regardless of whether it was commuting, load lugging or just enjoying a weekend drive.

The amazing flexibility offered by the Yanya was down to the variety of ways that the body panels could be arranged. With everything in place, it was a four-door SUV, but by removing the four panels that made up the roof assembly, and storing them inside the tailgate, the Yanya became a convertible. The tailgate itself was a neat design, as it could be used in very cramped spaces. Instead of being hinged at the side or bottom, an alloy frame moved the tailgate slightly backwards and away from the car, and it was then lowered vertically.

The interior of the Yanya was equally clever, as it was capable of being converted into a mobile living room. A storage module between the rear seats could be moved forward and its side panels extended to form a table. Inside this module were the controls for the stereo and satellite navigation. And to mark a sign of the times, there was also the facility for all four occupants to link up their computerized personal organisers and the ability to hook up to the Internet.

In case the Yanya's occupants could not distinguish what was what inside the car, everything was colour-coded to make it easy. To that end, the function switches, such as the seat adjusters and column stalks,

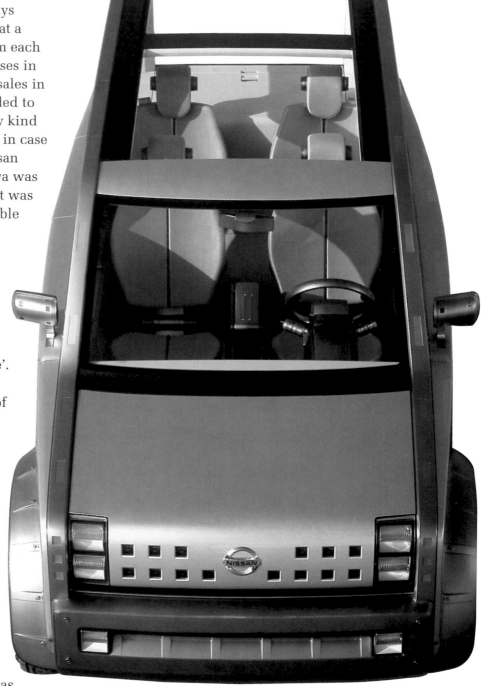

The least flattering angle from which to view the Yanya was the front, where it looked as though the car had been designed with a slide rule and square set.

were painted yellow. Meanwhile, blue acrylic marked out any protective surfaces and much of the cabin was finished in grained aluminium alloy. Channels in the floor, into which the seats and storage modules were set, allowed the interior furniture to be moved around to suit the occasion. The versatility of the Yanya's interior was perhaps its most important feature, as this was a car designed to suit just about any use to which it could be put. The rear seats were designed in the same way as theatre chairs – their base cushion was hinged at the rear to fold upwards, so that when stowed vertically behind the front seats they took up very little space. All the seats featured built-in speakers in the head restraints, which meant that music could be heard even if the roof was fully open, and also allowed each occupant to set the sound level at whatever was comfortable for them.

Lightweight transmission

Under the skin, the Yanya featured a part-time four-wheel drive system, which was both simple and lightweight. Capable of delivering economy for regular city driving, it also had sufficient four-wheel drive capabilities for doing a bit of off-roading at the weekend. The system consisted of a motor, clutch and reduction gear along with a generator that served as

Flexibility makes any car more enjoyable to own, and the Yanya could be geared for a number of tasks. By designing a car to be usable in just about any situation, instant popularity – so the manufacturers reason – should be guaranteed.

Nissan Yanya	
Debut:	Geneva 2002
Engine capacity:	N/A
Configuration:	Front-mounted
Power:	N/A
Top speed:	N/A
Transmission:	4WD
Length:	N/A
Width:	N/A
Designer:	N/A

the power source for driving the motor – and a control unit to manage the whole set-up. If the front wheels started to slip, the control unit activated the generator to produce electric power for operating the motor installed at the rear of the vehicle.

Opel Junior

The Opel Junior was all about frugal motoring – it was designed to take up as little road space and use as small an amount of fuel as possible.

Helping to boost performance and economy was the low drag coefficient. By using flush glazing and integrating the bumpers, headlights and door handles, the vehicle's aerodynamics were optimized.

GG-CT 932

Keeping weight to a minimum (it weighed just 650kg/ 1433lb) meant that the most could be made of the 41kW (55bhp) available. Top speed was 151km/h (94mph), but it could also achieve 110km per gallon (70mpg).

The interior put practicality above all else. There were cubby holes in every conceivable space and the bare minimum of instrumentation, although the model could be easily upgraded to include extras.

When it was unveiled at the 1983 Frankfurt motor show, the Opel Junior was touted as being Germany's sauciest car, which was certainly not the ideal word to describe what was actually a very intelligently designed small car concept.

The aim of the Junior was to provide transport in comfort for up to four people, while occupying as little road space as possible. This meant that not only did the car have to be as space efficient inside as possible, but also it had to sit rather taller than was normal for small cars at the time. Although cars have now become taller to allow greater interior space without having to be significantly longer or wider, the Junior was unveiled at a time when it was unusual – although far from unprecedented – to build upwards.

Ease of production

Compared with the Nova/Corsa of the time, the Junior was 90mm (3.5in) taller and 40mm (1.5in) wider – but it was 210mm (8.3in) shorter, which was very important when it came to making the car more manouevrable around town, where the Junior would predominantly be seen. Two-thirds of the car's overall length was given over to passenger space, with the interior incorporating some very clever design touches. The cabin was built so that it would be much easier than normal to build the car with either left- or right-hand drive, mainly helped by the use of a

For a car designed in the early 1980s, the lines of the Opel Junior were exceptionally clean and modern. That meant that the car was more aerodynamic, and so more frugal and environmentally friendly.

Opel Junior	
Debut:	Frankfurt 1983
Engine capacity:	1200cc (73ci)
Configuration:	Front-mounted
Power:	41kW (55bhp)
Top speed:	151km/h (94mph)
Transmission:	FWD
Length:	3410mm (134in)
Width:	1570mm (62in)
Designer:	N/A

symmetrical unit that included the pedal box, hand brake steering column and heating/ventilation system.

Scattered around the cabin were cubby holes galore, with consoles and lockers under the seats and beneath the dash. The dash itself featured a set of instruments of a modular design. The basic set of gauges consisted of the speedometer, fuel gauge and coolant temperature gauge, and pre-wiring the dash to accept extra dials meant that there was no need for any further wiring to be installed once the car had left the factory. These extra dials, which were cubic (like the standard set of instruments), would just slot into place to make contact with the wiring already in place.

With flexibility being the key to the Junior's cabin, it was no surprise that the radio could be removed easily to be used as a portable set. The two-piece plastic roof could easily be

swapped for a canvas item or even a see-through panoramic panel to open the interior altogether. As if this were not enough, the seat covers could be removed and used as sleeping bags, while the removable stowage cases in the doors could be used as shopping bags. Nor was that all – the dash-mounted clock could be removed and used as an alarm clock, and it was even envisaged that this stowage container concept would be expanded to include a travel set with razor and hair dryer.

Economy rules

Although the Junior's *raison d'être* was economy, it also had to be fun to drive. With its 41kW (55bhp) 1.2l engine, it could sprint from a standing start to 100km/h (62mph) in 15 seconds and go on to achieve a top speed of 151km/h (94mph) – not exactly breathtaking performance, but very respectable for a car that aimed to be as cheap to run as possible. Such

performance was possible with so little power because the Junior weighed just 650kg (1433lb), giving it a power-to-weight ratio of 63kW (85bhp/ton) that was on a par with production cars which were perceived to be rather more sprightly. And the fact that it was capable of travelling more than 112km (70 miles) on every gallon of petrol was also pretty impressive – at that time, there was nothing else on the market to equal the Junior's blend of performance and economy.

The concept's slippery shape was also key to achieving this balance – with a drag coefficient of just 0.31, it was amazingly aerodynamic for such a small car. This was achieved by paying great attention to detail, fitting bumpers, glazing, headlights and door handles to sit flush with the bodywork.

The Junior's cubic instruments could be changed simply by unplugging them and fitting new ones. Similarly, extra gauges could be added with the minimum of fuss as the wiring was already in place.

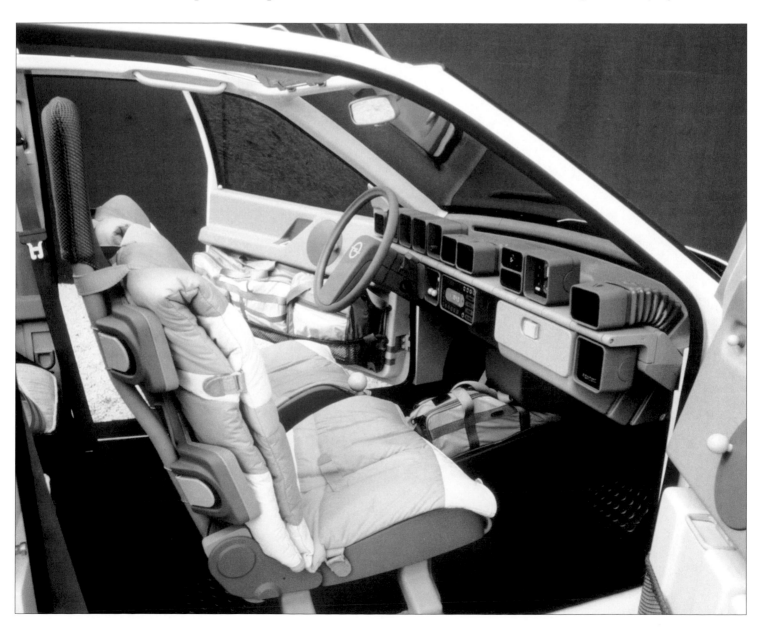

Opel MAXX

The steeply sloping front end made the Opel Maxx aerodynamic, thanks to its monobox design. The rear was sharply cut off to maximize the interior space available.

A three-cylinder, 1l engine gave the Maxx plenty of performance in urban driving, while a five-speed sequential gearbox with auto option made it very easy to drive.

This was an economy car, so the interior of the Maxx was straightforward, having little in the way of gadgetry – apart from a built-in telephone.

Lightweight materials, including aluminium and plastic, were used in the construction of the Maxx, to ensure that it was as fuel-efficient as possible.

Two versions of the Maxx concept were built – this is the short-wheelbase one. Its reduced length made it even more practical around town than the larger model.

As the twentieth century drew to a close, environmental concerns over the impact of cars on the planet were becoming increasingly prominent. Whereas most people aspired to own something bigger and more luxurious than what they already had, few could afford to keep upgrading to something more cosseting and with ever greater performance. And as roads became increasingly congested, it made sense to look carefully at how personal transport could be made more efficient without sacrificing comfort altogether. To that end, General Motors came up with a pair of Maxx concepts, which were first shown at the 1995 Geneva motor show and which showed General Motors' vision of the future of urban motoring.

There were short and long-wheelbase versions of the Maxx on display, both of which were powered by the then-new 973cc (59ci) cast-iron three-cylinder engine that would come to be the standard entry-level powerplant for the Corsa. In short-wheelbase form, the Maxx was 750mm (30in) shorter than the Corsa, and, by using aluminium extensively in its construction, the fuel efficiency and manouevrability of the car were superb. The car was even 75mm (3in) shorter than the original Mini, but, despite its compact dimensions, two rows of seats were installed – giving enough space to house four people because of the high roof line. Thanks to the slippery shape of the Maxx, the low rolling resistance of the tyres and the lightweight construction, the car could supposedly achieve up to 116km (72 miles) per gallon, although such figures are normally arrived at in a laboratory, rather than in the real world …

Smart concept

The concept of the Maxx was very similar to that of the Smart, in that its outer panels clipped onto a central monocoque, which was what gave the car its strength. But whereas the Smart's engine was mounted in the rear, the Maxx's was positioned more conventionally, at the front of the vehicle. The front wheels were driven via a five-speed electrically actuated sequential gearbox, the ratios being selected by a rocker switch located on the steering wheel. And if the driver did not want to change gears manually, there was also the option of moving the transmission to fully automatic mode.

The Opel Maxx may have been a microcar, but its cabin was very grown-up, if a little spartan. The lightweight materials used in its construction were shown off inside.

Perhaps the most important aspect of the Maxx was its modular design – GM envisaged being able to offer a whole family of cars without having to invest in new tooling for each one. To that end, the theory was that it would be possible to turn the two-door Maxx (the smaller one of the two) into a saloon (sedan), convertible, pick-up, off-roader or sports car. Meanwhile, the four-door version would be the space-efficient people carrier or load lugger, capable of carrying up to six people and up to 500l (5797ci) of

This short-wheelbase Maxx was comparable with the MCC Smart, but Opel did not feel its project could economically enter production. It would have cost as much to buy as a Corsa.

cargo. While the project was still on the drawing board, there were even thoughts of Maxx-based taxis and ice cream vans being built on a bespoke basis.

Inside the Maxx, things were equally space-efficient, with very thinly padded seats and a completely flat floor to minimize cabin intrusions. The simple dash featured a large digital display for most of the instrumentation (which was basically the rev counter and speedometer, and little else), and the small amount of switchgear fitted was grouped together in the centre of the fascia. Unusually for such a small economy car, there was also a telephone integrated into the dashboard, but, otherwise, few gadgets were fitted – lightness and simplicity were key to this concept.

Interestingly, the literature given away to promote the Maxx at the time of its launch stated quite categorically that the concept was 'a technology study only' and that there were 'no production plans for the Maxx, nor is it proposed as a replacement for any current Vauxhall/Opel product'. Perhaps the company was merely trying to maintain interest in its then-current product range, or maybe it really did believe that the Maxx was not the way forward.

Opel Maxx

Debut:	Geneva 1995
Engine capacity:	973cc (59ci)
Configuration:	Front-mounted 3-cylinder petrol
Power:	37kW (50bhp)
Top speed:	153km/h (95mph)
Transmission:	5-speed sequential, FWD
Length:	2975mm (117in)
Width:	1575mm (62in)
Designer:	N/A

Pontiac Aztek

The bonnet of the Pontiac Aztek seems to have been designed to fit an altogether different car. So ungainly is it that the car is said to resemble a rhinoceros.

Up front was a 3.4l V6 petrol engine, the power from which was fed to the front wheels via a four-speed automatic gearbox.

The Aztek's cabin was quite a relief after the outside. It was tastefully trimmed in sombre colours, which were lifted by yellow highlighting.

Although the car was supposedly an off-roader, its monocoque construction and minimal ground clearance meant that it was really set up best for on-road driving.

Crossover vehicles were becoming increasingly popular by the end of the twentieth century, which was no surprise as these were the cars that combined two or more sectors to provide the best of all. Or perhaps the worst if things failed to go according to plan. With the Aztek, Pontiac tried to combine the best attributes of a mid-sized saloon (sedan), van and sport utility vehicle – the latter being the type of car which was becoming increasingly popular in the United States at the time. So what a shame that Phil Kucera, who designed the Aztek, produced such a hideous car that few people could take it seriously. What was even more tragic was that the Aztek went into production not long after being shown – with barely anything in terms of exterior design being changed in the meantime.

Fussy design

Perhaps the reason for the Pontiac Aztek's aesthetics being so questionable was the fussy design, although it may have simply been the rather odd proportions. Although the nose of the car had to be recognizably Pontiac, nonetheless the design language used could have been rather more cohesive without the car losing its corporate look. The split grille, Ram Air bonnet

and cat's eye headlights marked the concept out as a Pontiac, but the bulbous, nose-heavy look made it look positively prehistoric. The mass of slashes and blisters along the Aztek's flanks also did little to hide its bulk – instead, they just made it look very messy and overdesigned. Pontiac itself, however, reckoned that the Aztek featured ribs standing out at the side that 'hinted at the solid, resilient strength of a lean, well-contoured athlete'. While marketing departments are very good at coming up with meaningless phrases and hype, this one takes the biscuit for being completely unbelievable!

True to 21st-century form, the Aztek was an off-roader that did not really have the ground clearance to do any proper off-roading – which was just as well, because few owners would ever take the car anywhere near anything as demanding as a dirt track, never mind a full-blown assault course. Also, in common with most other modern off-roaders, the Aztek's monocoque construction was slanted in favour of on-road driving

The Aztek was basically ugly whatever way you looked at it, but at least from the rear its chief saving grace is apparent: the practicality that it offered, with plenty of easily accessed storage space.

rather than any rough stuff. The ladder frame underbody construction, as Pontiac called it, meant that the Aztek would be less capable when tackling rock-strewn tracks – but at least it would be much more refined when cruising along metalled roads.

Front-wheel drive

The Aztek looked as though it was fitted with four-wheel drive, but only the front wheels were driven. Powering these via a four-speed automatic gearbox was a 150kW (200bhp), 3.4l V6 engine, which also provided 31kg-m (225lb-ft) of torque. Naturally, there were disc brakes all round, equipped with anti-lock circuitry, while traction control ensured that, if things got a bit slippery in the harbour while reversing the boat into the sea, all would not be lost.

As the exterior was so ugly, it was something of a relief that the interior was rather more palatable. The silver, black, grey and yellow colour scheme worked very well, with the yellow being used to lift things a bit. There was space for four occupants, although the rear seats could be folded up or removed with the minimum of fuss – versatility was the order of the day where the Aztek was concerned.

The dash was largely conventional, and it worked all the better for it, although at night a three-dimensional look was assumed, which started to complicate things

The yellow, silver and grey interior colour scheme of the Aztek provided a welcome contrast to the car's exterior, although some of the detail design, such as the instrumentation, was overly fussy.

a bit. The circular gauges were joined by a liquid crystal display along with a dot matrix digital display – and in case this did not give the driver enough to think about, there was also a head-up display that allowed the major functions to be monitored much more easily.

Pontiac Aztek

Debut:	Detroit 1999
Engine capacity:	3400cc (207ci)
Configuration:	Front-mounted V6, petrol
Power:	150kW (200bhp)
Top speed:	180km/h (112mph)
Transmission:	4-speed auto, FWD
Length:	4546mm (179in)
Width:	1956mm (77in)
Designer:	Phil Kucera

Renault Fiftie

The Fiftie's roof featured a series of slats, to open up the interior. By folding the rear window flat, the cabin could be opened up even further.

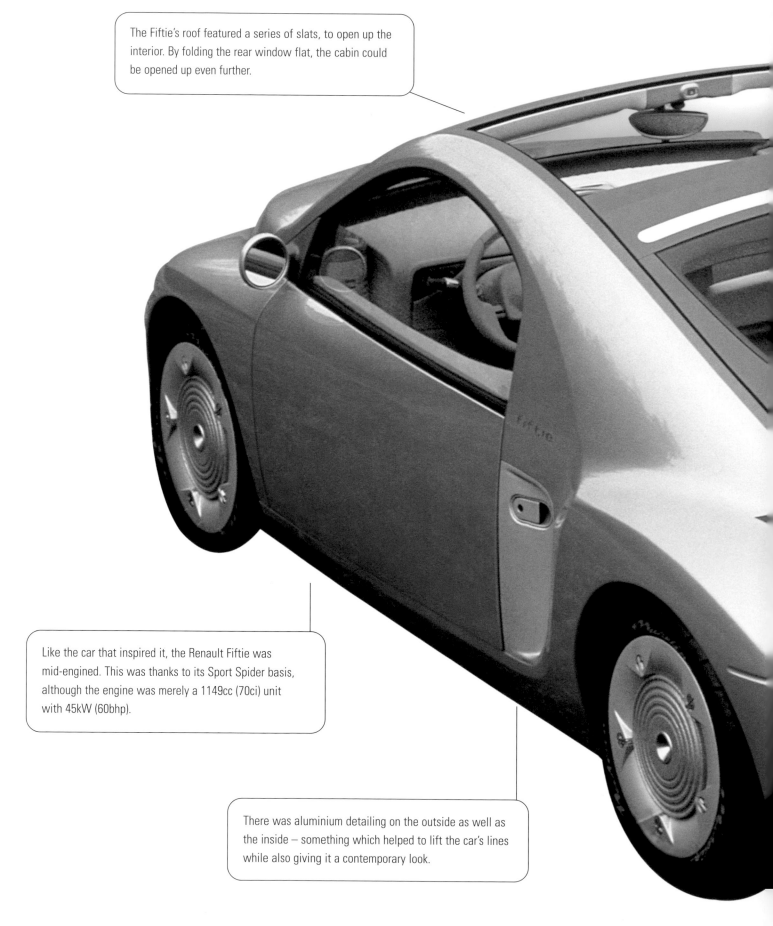

Like the car that inspired it, the Renault Fiftie was mid-engined. This was thanks to its Sport Spider basis, although the engine was merely a 1149cc (70ci) unit with 45kW (60bhp).

There was aluminium detailing on the outside as well as the inside – something which helped to lift the car's lines while also giving it a contemporary look.

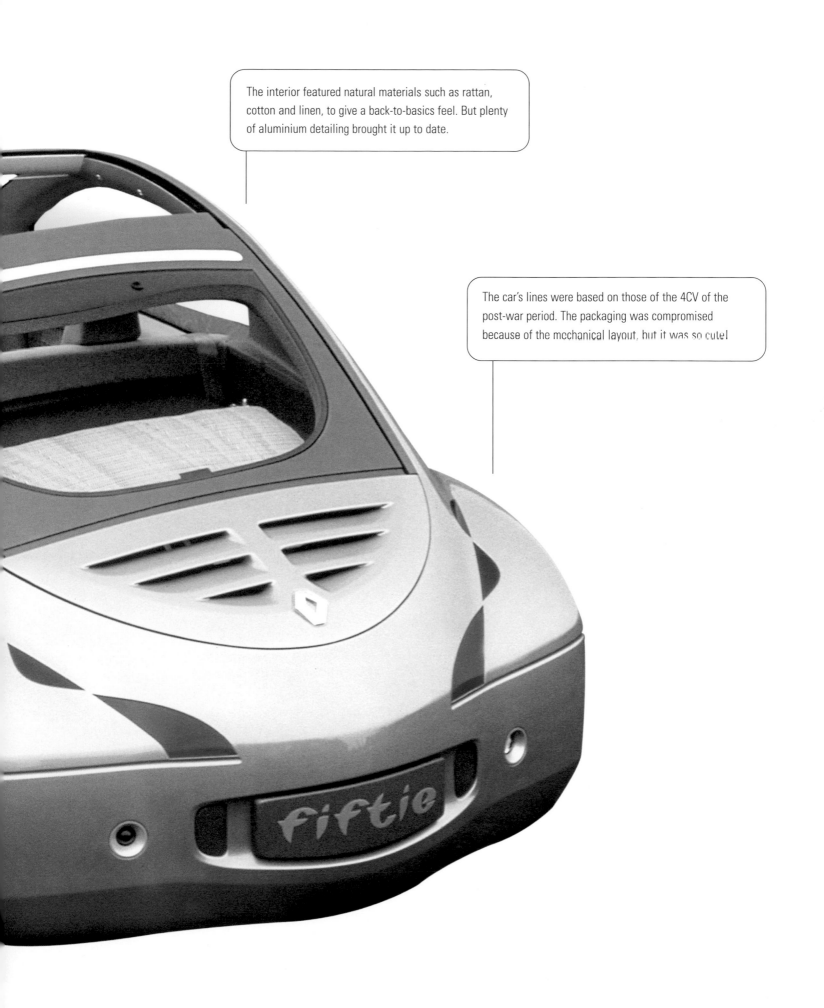

The interior featured natural materials such as rattan, cotton and linen, to give a back-to-basics feel. But plenty of aluminium detailing brought it up to date.

The car's lines were based on those of the 4CV of the post-war period. The packaging was compromised because of the mechanical layout, but it was so cute!

The Renault Fiftie was produced to mark half a century since the introduction of the Renault 4CV, the car of choice for the middle classes in post-war France. For this reason, the concept was heavily inspired by the production car of 50 years earlier, although there were a lot of neat touches which ensured the 1996 car was rather more contemporary.

The greatest tragedy about the Renault Fiftie was that it was never put into production. It would surely have been popular enough for it to be built at a profit, even if produced in only small numbers. It might even have become the European equivalent of the retro-styled Figaro, built by Nissan on the Micra platform.

Whereas the Nissan Figaro was based on a humdrum supermini, the Fiftie's origins were rather more

The rear lights on the Fiftie were truly inspirational; Renault also used them on the Avantime when this went into production. They were meant to resemble kites fluttering in the wind.

inviting – underneath the 1940s-style carbon fibre bodywork was the chassis of the Renault Sport Spider. Unfortunately, the Fiftie did not also borrow the Spider's 112kW (150bhp), 2.0l powerplant – instead, it was chosen as the vehicle to introduce an all-new engine. This was the E-series in 1149cc (70ci) form, which pushed out 45kW (60bhp), and which would go on to power the Clio and Twingo. It was mated to a five-speed manual gearbox with an automatic clutch, so, although the gears were changed conventionally, there were only two pedals in the footwell.

Renault Fiftie	
Debut:	Geneva 1996
Engine capacity:	1149cc (70ci)
Configuration:	Mid-mounted in-line four, petrol
Power:	45kW (60bhp)
Top speed:	N/A
Transmission:	5-speed manual
Length:	N/A
Width:	N/A
Designer:	Benoit Jacob

The Sport Spider may have seemed like an odd choice on which to base what was essentially a completely different type of car, but it made sense because of the engine position. The 4CV had been fitted with a rear-mounted powerplant, and the Sport Spider's aluminium chassis could easily be adapted for a one-off car.

Back to basics

The reasoning behind the Renault Fiftie was that it was intended as a leisure vehicle, for two people to escape the city. It was built for economy rather than outright performance, and included as standard in the car's equipment list was a rattan picnic hamper, stowed in the front-mounted luggage area. The use of rattan was deliberate – this natural material seemed contemporary yet also suggested a 'back-to-basics' feel. As a result, there were also rattan inserts in the interior, alongside aluminium detailing. The seats were trimmed in cotton and linen – once again giving the cabin a very natural look – and to keep it all light and airy, the materials chosen were all very light in colour. The dashboard could be moved backwards and forwards, complete with steering wheel and pedals, so that the seats could remain fixed – something which required far more ingenuity than might at first be appreciated.

Helping to keep the interior well lit was a sunroof made of slats, which folded back to stow inside the rear window – which, in turn, could then be stowed away flat. This feature was also directly inspired by the 1946 4CV, which could be ordered with a soft top which allowed the whole of the passenger space to be exposed to the elements. The outside of the Fiftie also used aluminium trim to break up the expanses of

yellow, although the mass of curves and the car's relatively diminutive proportions meant that it could hardly be called slab-sided. There was no grille at the front because of the engine's location; however, alloy strips hinted at one to ensure the car's nose did not seem bland. Other aluminium detailing included the air intakes just ahead of each rear wheelarch, and the Fiftie's slatted roof was coloured grey, to contrast with the rest of the paintwork.

The tiny apostrophe-shaped headlights looked especially neat, and were the opposite of the overlarge headlights that became popular not long after the Fiftie made its debut. At the rear, the series of small lights scattered across the rear wings were intended to resemble kites fluttering in the wind – they may have looked a little odd, but no one can possibly claim that they were derivative.

From the mid-1990s, most concepts used at least some alloy detailing in their cabins, but few used it on the outside. Not so the Fiftie, where it was used to great effect, as can be seen on this door locking panel.

Renault Zoom

Inside the Renault Zoom was a bench seat with plenty of space for two. Gadgetry was kept to a minimum, and the colours were funky to inject some youth appeal.

Perhaps the reason why the Zoom failed to reach production was its motive power source – electricity. To this day, nobody has been able to overcome the shortcomings of the electric car.

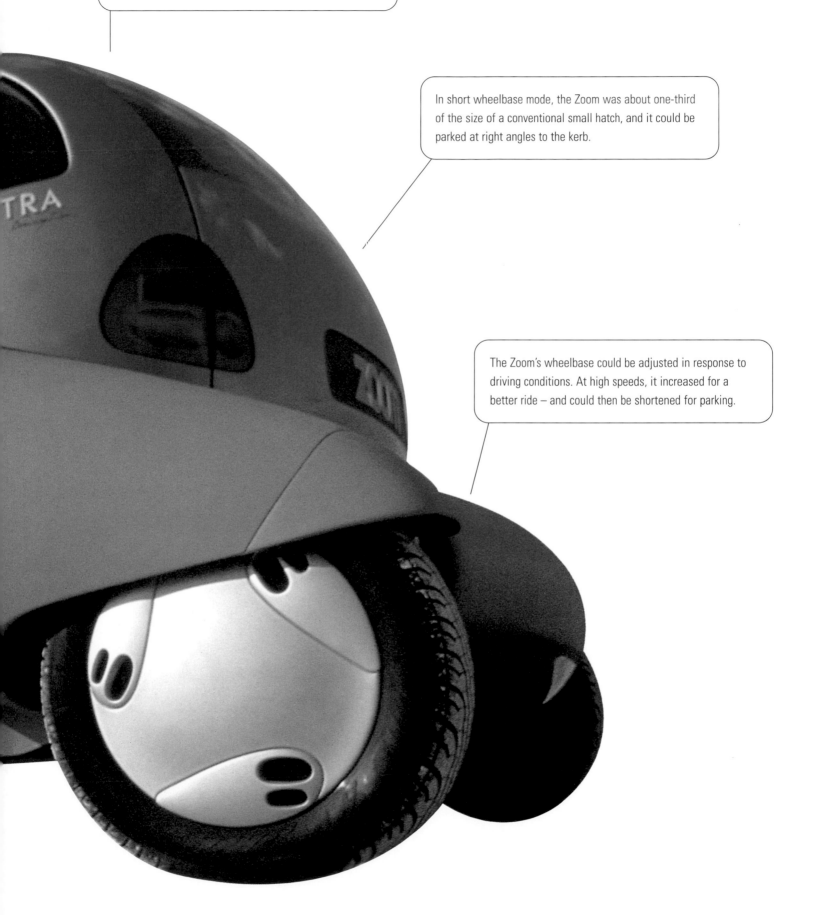

To reduce weight, the Zoom's bodywork was made largely of composites. This also meant that the car did not need to be painted and that it was self-healing after a scrape.

In short wheelbase mode, the Zoom was about one-third of the size of a conventional small hatch, and it could be parked at right angles to the kerb.

The Zoom's wheelbase could be adjusted in response to driving conditions. At high speeds, it increased for a better ride – and could then be shortened for parking.

Once in a while, car makers come over all economically aware and release a concept aimed at minimalist motoring – and the Renault Zoom is just the sort of thing they come up with. Developed and built in conjunction with Matra, this microcar was perhaps one of the cleverest of the city cars released during the 1990s because it could be shortened and lengthened at will, depending on the type of use it was going to get. During normal use, it was at its longest, with an extended wheelbase that made it more comfortable over badly surfaced or undulating roads.

But when the Zoom needed to be parked, the rear section could fold in on itself to reduce the car's length and thus make it easier to park. Indeed, it was so short in this state that it was possible to park at right angles to the kerb, the car being barely longer than most cars were wide. It was even reckoned that three Zooms

For some reason, Renault assumed that at some unspecified time in the future everyone would be dressing in silver Lycra suits. It hasn't happened yet, and neither has the Zoom.

could fit into the space needed by just one Renault 19 hatchback. And as if that were not enough, the ingenious design of the doors meant that even when the car was parked in the tightest spaces, the occupants could get in and out. Dubbed Elytron doors, these roll-over mechanisms opened outwards by 120mm (4.7in) before rotating about an axis inclined at 9° off the horizontal. It may sound complicated, but the important thing was that the Zoom's occupants could enter or leave without problems.

Armchair on wheels

As one writer commented, the Zoom was no bigger than a good armchair – and every bit as comfortable. Nor was it much more polluting because the Zoom's motive power was provided by an electric motor. (Of course, all this did in reality was to shift the pollution to wherever that electricity was generated.) But perhaps the most important thing about the Zoom was that at the time of its launch in 1992, at the Paris motor show, the hope was that within three years

Renault hoped that the Zoom could be built economically, and running prototypes were built to show that idea was realistic; those who drove them said the car worked excellently.

many of France's cities would have the necessary infrastructure for electric cars to become viable. The French government and EDF, the French utility company, aimed to have a network of charging points installed to allow electrically powered cars to become a genuinely practical proposition for many of the country's residents.

At a time when annual new car sales in France totalled around one million, it was envisaged that up to 100,000 Zooms could be sold. The reasoning behind this was that a range of 150km (93 miles), and the fact that most people tend to travel solo, meant that the Zoom would suit most commuters, even if only as a second car. And it was not spartan; the equipment included satellite navigation, a stereo system and a hands-free telephone.

Recycled racer

Initially, it seemed that few of the technologies incorporated in the concept could be retained in production. But once the car was costed out, Renault claimed that, for the same sort of price as a mid-range Clio, the Zoom could be built complete with the composite bodywork and adjustable wheelbase. These composite panels were self-coloured, so there was no need to paint the car – something which helped to boost its environmentally friendly credentials. As did the fact that some of the Zoom's components, such as its chassis, door structures and some of the suspension components, were produced from recycled materials. Incredibly, the waistline of the Zoom's body shell was covered in a self-sealing skin that was capable of rebuilding itself by molecular assembly. It may sound like the stuff of science fiction, but it was a reality – self-healing paintwork for when the car was scratched!

Renault Zoom	
Debut:	Paris 1992
Engine capacity:	Electric
Configuration:	Front-mounted, transverse
Power:	25KW (33bhp)
Top speed:	121km/h (75mph)
Transmission:	Continuously variable transmission, FWD
Length:	2650mm (104in)
Width:	1520mm (60in)
Designer:	N/A

Rover TCV

The tapering roof line aided aerodynamics and made the car look very stylish. The boot (trunk) floor could be lowered so that luggage bay space was greater than usual.

Aiming to offer the optimum combination of practicality, adaptability, luxury and style, the Tourer Concept Vehicle, or TCV, signalled a new design direction for MG-Rover. It certainly looked modern.

All sorts of seating configurations were possible in the TCV, to give the optimum balance between carrying passengers and hauling luggage – loads up to 3m (10ft) long could be carried.

This view of the front end was probably the least flattering of all the car's angles. Those large headlights are vying for prominence with the oversized grille.

Although the TCV was a non-runner, it was expected that a 2.5l V6 engine would be fitted, and there was the possibility of four-wheel drive. The car was based on a Rover 75 platform.

The first Rover-badged concept since the CCV of 1986, the TCV of 2002 was Rover's demonstration that it was on the way back up after a prolonged period of uncertainty about the company. Ever since Rover had been sold by BMW for a token £10, few had much faith in Rover's chances of survival – the TCV was meant to prove that the company had at last found a way to replace its ancient range.

Luxurious and adaptable

Rover claimed that the rather unimaginatively named Tourer Concept Vehicle (TCV) was a vehicle combining luxury style and driving enjoyment with exceptional practicality and adaptability. It certainly managed that because its interior was built to be so flexible that it could carry just about anything that was smaller than the load bay, whatever the shape. When the car made its debut at the 2002 Geneva motor show, it had a washing machine stuffed into the load bay, sitting upright. It may have been an odd accessory to put into a car for such a glamorous event, but it showed just how usable this new car would be if it made production – assuming such characteristics were not lost in the move from concept to production car.

The key to the great flexibility was a load bay floor which could be lowered several inches until it was

The TCV's heavily sloping windowline at the back of the car was a neat touch – it made the vehicle look sleek while offering masses of luggage carrying capacity.

Rover TCV	
Debut:	Geneva 2002
Engine capacity:	2497cc (152ci)
Configuration:	Front-mounted V6, petrol
Power:	130kW (174bhp)
Top speed:	N/A
Transmission:	5-speed manual/auto, FWD
Length:	4500mm (177in)
Width:	N/A
Designer:	Peter Stevens

nearly level with the bottom of the bumper. Doing away with the spare wheel meant that it was possible to use the space that would otherwise be taken up with an accessory which was rarely used in the car's lifetime – and, in case the worst did happen, the fitment of run-flat tyres meant the car would not be left stranded.

The rear seats could be folded flat (level with the floor), as could the front passenger seat, and the result was that loads of more than 3m (10ft) could be fitted in – very impressive for a car so compact on the outside. For even greater flexibility, it was possible to replace the centre rear seat with various slot-in

The high roofline coupled with a boot (trunk) floor
that could be lowered meant that the Rover TCV
was capable of carrying all sorts of things that a
normal estate car (station wagon) could not.

30mm (1.1in) higher than was typical
for the genre suggested it was built to go
off-roading. A Rover 75 platform could
accommodate four-wheel drive running
gear, but the official line was that such
a move would be highly unlikely – and,
anyway, the company was not allowed
to build an off-roader under the terms
of the deal signed when Land Rover was
hived off from Rover and sold to Ford.

The plunging windowline towards
the rear, despite the fact that the
roofline was more or less level, gave the
car a much sleeker look, thanks to the
clever use of contrasting colours. At the
front was a very bold grille, and the
headlights were equally prominent –
which was why the look did not quite
work. Everything was vying for
prominence, and the overall effect was
far too busy, but there was no doubt
that the TCV certainly moved Rover's
design language forward.

The problem was whether or not it
moved it too far forward, alienating the
company's traditionally conservative
buyers at the same time as the badge put off the
younger buyers that the TCV was supposed to attract.

modules, such as a child seat, entertainment centre,
refrigerator/food warmer or business desktop unit.

Although the TCV was shown at both the Paris
and Geneva motor shows of 2002, it was never
fitted with any running gear. The suggestion was
made that the engine and transmission might be
those of the range-topping 75, which meant a
2.5l V6 channelling its power to the front
wheels, while the concept itself was positioned
between Rover's 75 and 45.

Aggressive looks

On the outside, the car featured bold styling,
with plenty of sharp lines and a raised ride
height to make the car even more aggressive.
The TCV was not intended to be fitted with
four-wheel drive, but the fact that it sat around

From the front, the TCV's grille and headlights compete for
attention, making the design seem overly fussy and
congested.

Saab 9-3X

The heavily tapered window line of the 9-3X was like nothing else on the road. It gave an uninterrupted glass area round most of the car, ending only at the rear pillars.

Like most Saabs, the 9-3X was fitted with a full-time four-wheel drive system, and to transmit the power there was a five-speed gearbox with automatic or manual modes.

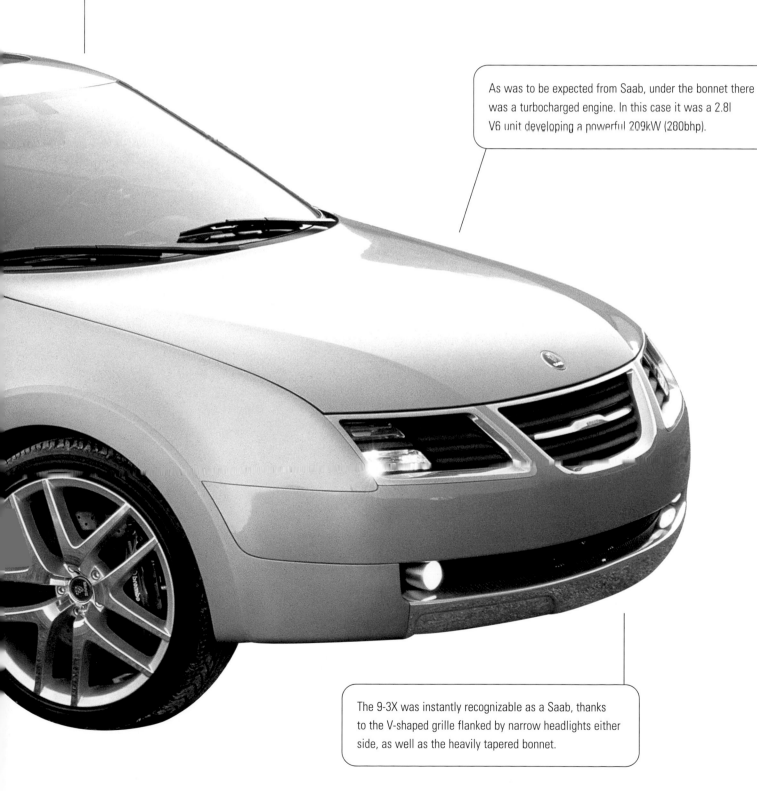

Saab had offered estate cars (station wagons) for
decades, but the most recent all had five doors. The Saab
9-3X harked back to the Swedish company's earlier 95,
which had just three doors.

As was to be expected from Saab, under the bonnet there
was a turbocharged engine. In this case it was a 2.8l
V6 unit developing a powerful 209kW (280bhp).

The 9-3X was instantly recognizable as a Saab, thanks
to the V-shaped grille flanked by narrow headlights either
side, as well as the heavily tapered bonnet.

With its combination of sporty, coupé bodystyling and off-road functionality, Saab's 9-3X finally brought the Swedish (but GM-owned) company out of the wilderness. Perhaps the only imageless car company in the world, Saab was the one car maker that nobody understood at the start of the twenty-first century. The 9-3X was an attempt to change that, putting Saab back on the map.

As was commonplace by the time the 9-3X made its debut at the 2002 Detroit motor show, the new car was a crossover coupé. Saab hoped to prove that a four-wheel drive vehicle with off-road capabilities could retain a strong, sporty, on-road appeal. This also marked the first time that Saab had shown a car with off-road abilities, and, most importantly, it formed the basis on which Saab would introduce its first sports utility vehicle (SUV).

Multitasking, multidynamic

The key word which Saab touted at every opportunity was 'multidynamic'. In other words, the 9-3X had to be able to deliver at lots of different levels. Whether it was an outright sporty drive or the ability to carry large and heavy loads – or anything in between – the car had to be able to dismiss it with aplomb. Although Saab had never before constructed a car within this

To reduce the amount of switchgear on the fascia of the Saab 9-3X, most of the buttons used to control the transmission and multimedia system were located on the steering wheel.

sector, the 9-3X had to incorporate the family look. That meant a sharply wrapped around windscreen, a high, wedge-shaped waistline and a strongly curved C-pillar. Added to this were disguised A-pillars and a more distinctive nose treatment than usual – and the end result was a particularly handsome car.

In part, this was thanks to a conscious effort, made from the start, to avoid the stylistic clichés that so often afflicted off-roaders. So there were no roof bars, bumper appendages or extra cladding down the car's flanks. Nor were there any unsightly overlarge wheelarch clearances. Such attention to detail gave the 9-3X a far cleaner look than was typical for the sector.

Inside was equally well thought out. The car was targeted at people with active outdoor interests, so its cabin was designed to be versatile, roomy and light. Intended to be a proper four-seater, it had a long wheelbase, allowing decent space in the back seats. The roof panels were made of glass, making the car feel even more spacious, while the choice of pale green leather for the upholstery gave it quality.

To get into the Saab 9-3X, the driver used a keyless entry system. Once inside, the most striking

Leather and aluminium were to be found in abundance in the cabin of the 9-3X. The use of light-coloured materials made the relatively compact interior feel more airy and spacious.

thing was how uncluttered the dashboard was. An important part of the design brief for the interior had been to remove as much as possible from the fascia, thus reducing the visual clutter so typical of a luxury car. So, in a break from tradition, there was no wraparound centre console, while the twin-dial instrument display was set in a gently curving narrow fascia panel, which was flanked only by a light switch and the main display screen. The steering wheel

Saab 9-3X	
Debut:	Detroit 2002
Engine capacity:	2.8l (170.9ci), turbocharged
Configuration:	Front-mounted V6, petrol
Power:	209kW (280bhp)
Top speed:	155mph (limited)
Transmission:	5-speed semi auto, 4WD
Length:	4380mm (172.4in)
Width:	1826mm (71.9in)
Designer:	Michael Mauer/Anthony Lo

The 9-3X had a far cleaner look than was typical for an off-road vehicle. Saab had made a conscious and deliberate effort to keep its design free of extraneous detailing.

featured buttons on its two spokes, which controlled the entertainment and information systems, along with the telephone and switches for gear selection of the semi-automatic transmission.

New engine

Mechanically the 9-3X also broke new ground for Saab because it carried an all-new 2.8l, V6 engine. With a turbocharger, four valves per cylinder, direct ignition and variable valve timing, this powerhouse was capable of generating 209kW (280bhp) and 41kg-m (295lb-ft) or torque. This was transmitted to all four wheels via a five-speed semi-automatic transmission, and, when left in fully automatic mode, this would adapt its gear shifting patterns to the driving style and road conditions prevailing at the time.

Considering most of its rivals had been creating four-wheel drives for years, Saab was rather slow in getting its act together with the 9-3X. Being one of the last, however, is not necessarily a bad thing: by the time Saab arrived on the scene, it had eliminated many of the shortcomings of its rivals.

SEAT Salsa

The Salsa was the perfect example of how to make an everyday, affordable mid-sized hatch into something that looked enticing and completely modern – if not futuristic.

Interior space was maximized by putting the wheels right out at each corner. Reducing overhangs to a minimum meant there was more room available for the cabin.

The SEAT Salsa's interior was luxurious without being over-the-top. There was plenty of terracotta with alloy highlights, while soft lighting provided real class.

There was a 186kW (250bhp), 2.8l V6 petrol engine tucked away under that steeply sloping bonnet. Feeding all four wheels, this powerplant endowed the car with a top speed of 245km/h (152mph).

2002 EDI

Pushing the wheels out to the corners also increased the wheelbase, which made the ride that much better and also helped to improve handling.

Until Volkswagen took a controlling stake in SEAT in 1985, the Spanish company did little more than build its own versions of Fiat's cast-offs. But with SEAT unveiling one concept after another from the early 1990s, it was clear that there was plenty of life in the company – and the Salsa demonstrated this better than anything. The VW Group was trying to make SEAT synonymous with sportiness, and the Salsa reinforced that, while also oozing character.

With hardly any overhangs at the front or the rear, the wheel-at-each-corner stance made the car look incredibly purposeful and also helped to keep the handling sharp, while making the ride as comfortable as possible. The windscreen started above the front axle line, which went some way to creating a monobox look, and the bonnet was heavily tapered so that headlights were positioned within the front wings, which swept round to meet the narrow grille.

Unconventional

At the back was a split tailgate featuring a bottom-hinged lower section and a top piece hinged at the top. Although this latter panel was conventional in the way it opened, what was less predictable was the fact that it opened up so far into the car's cabin – it was hinged above the back seats. The rear pillars were raked very sharply, to increase the amount of light

Built to reinforce SEAT's sporting image, the Salsa featured a pair of exhausts that exited from the centre of the car, subtle spoilers and a superbly aggressive stance.

SEAT Salsa	
Debut:	Geneva 2000
Engine capacity:	2791cc (170ci)
Configuration:	Front-mounted V6, petrol
Power:	186kW (250bhp)
Top speed:	245km/h (152mph)
Transmission:	5-speed auto/sequential manual, 4WD
Length:	4152mm (163in)
Width:	1777mm (70in)
Designer:	Walter de Silva

that entered the cabin, but there was no B-pillar. The cabin itself was very spacious, with plenty of room for four people, each of whom got their own heavily bolstered bucket seat.

Much of the interior was trimmed in blue, but the carpeting was terracotta by way of contrast, while most of the switchgear was in aluminium alloy, which was also used liberally around the cabin to indicate quality. A nice touch used for the Salsa's cabin was plenty of soft lighting, which was fitted within the floor as well as the roof panels. At night, this highlighted some of the alloy detailing, while also preventing the interior from being plunged into total darkness.

Among the switchgear were controls that allowed the driver to adjust the driving characteristics of the Salsa. As well as altering the suspension settings, it was possible to change the responsiveness of the throttle and the change-up points of the automatic gearbox. Besides this, the amount of instrumentation that was displayed could be adjusted – the satellite navigation could be shown or hidden, and which gauges were illuminated at night could also be set.

V6 power

Under the skin was the 2.8l V6 engine that was fitted to various cars within the Volkswagen Group. In the Salsa, this was tuned to produce 186kW (250bhp) and 26kg-m (191lb-ft) of torque, which SEAT claimed was enough to take the car up to a top speed of 245km/h (152mph), having completed the 0–100km/h (0–62mph) sprint in just 7.5 seconds. A Tiptronic gearbox should have allowed the driver to select the gears manually or let the car do it automatically –

The colour scheme chosen for the cabin was rather unusual, but it mirrored the exterior design. The black and silver trim was highlighted with red to echo the outside.

though there was no manual option in the one prototype that was built, and the driver simply chose between reverse and forward.

At the 2000 Paris motor show, the Salsa was developed further to become the Salsa Emocion – a jacked-up four-wheel drive version of the car designed to take on the likes of the Renault Scenic RX4. Thanks to flared wheelarches, the new arrival sat wider than the original and was also significantly taller due to a much-raised ride height (adjustable to give up to 700mm/27.5in of ground clearance), which gave it the urban off-road look that was becoming so popular.

Apart from a change of colour (to ivory), the only other significant change was the adoption of a Haldex four-wheel drive transmission, which also incorporated Audi's Tiptronic gearbox.

Volkswagen Microbus

Inside the Microbus there were seven liquid crystal displays to relay pictures from the on-board DVD player to the occupants. And these were additional to the one found on the dashboard!

Xenon lights were fitted, which were much more compact than the halogen units of the Microbus's ancestor, the Camper. They also allowed the car to look more modern – and more expensive.

Whereas the original VW Camper's engine was fitted at the rear, the 3.2l water-cooled V6 in the Microbus was fitted at the front.

Only Volkswagen could get away with building a concept that was essentially little more than a commercial van with windows. The Microbus was one of the coolest concepts ever, reviving the classic Camper of an earlier era.

There were plenty of subtle tricks used to make the Microbus look sporty, such as the heavily flared wheel arches with 50cm (20in) alloy wheels nestling underneath.

The original VW Camper must surely rate as one of the cars that best sums up the freedom and escapism of driving. Just throw a few bits and pieces into one, then set off for anywhere between a day and several years, tasting the open road. Even once the Camper was no longer officially available in most countries, it was still one of the most revered fun cars, which is why Volkswagen revived the formula with the dawn of a new millennium. A 21st-century interpretation of the

That single central exhaust of the Microbus borrowed nothing from the VW Campers of the 1960s – but it did make the Microbus look much more purposeful.

cult classic was unveiled at the 2001 Detroit motor show, then shown shortly after in Europe, at the Geneva motor show.

Using all the classic styling cues of the original, Volkswagen skilfully reworked the lines so that the Microbus looked utterly contemporary – just like it had done with the Concept 1, which was to become the new Beetle. Those slim headlights used the latest xenon technology and the flush-mounted door handles were activated electronically, by pressing the key fob. Once the button was pressed, they glided silently out of the bodywork, allowing the doors to be opened. The wheels were pushed to the very corners of the Microbus – just like the vehicle that inspired it. But this new car was fitted with 50.8cm (20in) alloy wheels shod with 245/45 R20 tyres, all of which nestled under flared arches to make the Microbus look much sportier than the original.

Although the Microbus looked purposeful, it was not a case of all show and no go – a 3.2l, V6 petrol engine was tucked away at the front. Producing a healthy 172kW (231bhp), the concept was blessed with easy

VW Microbus

Debut:	Detroit 2001
Engine capacity:	3.2l (195.3ci)
Configuration:	Front-mounted V6, petrol
Power:	172kW (231bhp)
Top speed:	N/A
Transmission:	5-speed semi-auto, FWD
Length:	4722mm (186in)
Width:	1909mm (75.2in)
Designer:	N/A

cruising capabilities, while the fitment of a Tiptronic gearbox made it even better to drive. This gave the choice of fully automatic operation of the five available gear ratios, or the opportunity to swap between them sequentially, but manually. Unlike the original car, the Microbus was both water-cooled and front-wheel drive.

Space and luxury

The Microbus was designed at Volkswagen's design centre in the Simi Valley, California. Although designed as a six-seater, the emphasis was on space and luxury, rather than outright people-carrying ability. To that end, there was plenty of leather and the whole car could be turned into a mobile cinema: there were no fewer than seven TV screens to relay pictures from the on-board DVD player, most set in the back of the front two rows of seats, with a pair of extendable monitors between the second and third rows.

As if all this were not enough, a 17.8cm (7in) screen was fitted to the dash, so that the front-seat passengers were able to join in the fun. There must have been a special offer at VW's screen supplier when the Microbus was being constructed because the displays did not stop even there. In place of a conventional rear-view mirror, a TV camera was set into the tailgate,

and this relayed pictures of what was going on behind the car, to another 17.8cm (7in) display above the windscreen, in the driver's line of sight.

Being a people-carrier, there was also plenty of interior flexibility, with the option of turning the middle row of seats through 180°. The rear pair of seats were individually sculpted (but were constructed as a bench seat), and the whole lot could be changed to all sorts of configurations thanks to a system of rails into which the seats were locked.

All this innovation was a far cry from the budget camper vans of the 1960s, which were invariably run on a shoestring and which were seen at pop festivals all over the world. This was a far more sophisticated device, aimed at trendy young families with money to spend and wanting something with a high specification and plenty of style.

Even better was the fact that Volkswagen created a whole family of Microbus variants, including a pick-up and a four-wheel drive version. You could say there was something for everyone – as long as they were well-heeled.

Cream leather is not the most practical upholstery in a people-carrier, but it certainly gave the Microbus an air of quality, especially when combined with so much fine alloy detailing.

Volvo SCC

The cleverest part of the Volvo SCC maximum visibility ethos was the way it sensed where the driver's eyes were, and adjusted everything accordingly – seat, pedals, gearstick and steering wheel.

In case the slim pillars and automatic adjustment of the driver's controls did not prove to be enough, there were also cameras and radar to warn of vehicles in the SCC's blind spots.

The best possible all-round visibility was the key to the SCC, which is why the A-pillars featured small, triangular glass panels. The other pillars were also very slim.

The SCC broke away from the usual Volvo boxy concept styling. Flowing curves were the order of the day, with just a hint of aggression towards the back.

The SCC, or Safety Concept Car, looked as though it were a three-door sporting estate (station wagon). But rather the vehicle was a hatchback/estate crossover and actually featured five doors.

If you were asked to name the car maker most likely to build a vehicle called the Safety Concept Car, the chances are that you would name Volvo. At the 2001 Detroit motor show, the SCC became a reality, making its debut at a show bristling with new concepts. As the name suggested, the aim of the Volvo SCC was to see how safe it was possible to make a car, without compromising the ergonomics, aesthetics or dynamics. Indeed, the SCC was made even safer by making sure that it was comfortable while also being as good as possible dynamically – in other words, active safety was designed in as well as passive safety.

Optimum visibility

The key to the way the SCC worked was the driver's eyes – when the driver's seat was occupied, a sensor worked out where the driver's eyes were and set everything up accordingly. First to adjust was the seat, which moved to the optimum position to benefit from the greatest all-round visibility possible. With the seat in position, the pedals, centre console, gearlever and steering wheel all then adjusted to suit the driver, ensuring that everything was within easy reach.

Visibility was further improved by the design of the car's bodyshell. To prevent the A-pillars becoming a blind spot, they were a boxed section with see-through Plexiglas, so the driver could see right through them. The B-pillars were curved inwards and followed the

Volvo SCC	
Debut:	Detroit 2001
Engine capacity:	N/A
Configuration:	Front-mounted
Power:	N/A
Top speed:	N/A
Transmission:	FWD
Length:	N/A
Width:	N/A
Designer:	Peter Horbury

contours of the seat frame to offer an unobstructed field of vision to the offset rear.

Despite all this effort, there was still the chance of a distracted driver getting into trouble, or falling prey to one of the few blind spots that the SCC had. To ensure that scraped paint and dented panels were as unlikely as possible, all sorts of other gadgets were fitted to keep the unwary driver out of trouble. The first of these was a radar unit, which measured the distance between the SCC and cars behind, as well as vehicles alongside.

Backing this up were rearward-facing cameras integrated into the door mirrors, which showed the driver what was in that blind spot. Added to these were

The relationship between the Volvo SCC and the classic 1800ES of the late 1960s is most apparent from this angle – the car really deserved to go into production, just for its original and stylish shape alone.

In typical Volvo fashion, all the safety angles had been carefully thought out. There were high-visibility pillars and even the seatbelts were a new design that offered much-improved restraint.

type of seat belt – a four-point unit that formed a V-shape across the wearer's front. But the car did more than protect its occupants – if the car collided with a pedestrian, the Volvo SCC would do its best to look after them as well. Hidden in the front was what Volvo called a 'cowl bag' – an air bag which inflated to afford any pedestrian unfortunate enough to come into contact with the car a degree of protection.

Security was also high on the SCC's agenda, with fingerprint-controlled locks and ignition systems. Once the car had been set up with the owner's fingerprints, it was possible for that owner simply to grasp the door handle and the car would unlock. In addition, no key was required to start the engine and because the owner's preferences were stored, everything would adjust automatically to suit that individual's requirements.

headlights that turned along with the front wheels, and an infrared light enhancer boosted night-time vision beyond the reach of the headlights. In case the driver ignored all this technology and was still intent on crashing the SCC, a forward-facing camera monitored the position of the car, alerting the driver if there was any tendency to veer off course.

Active safety

Should all this technology fail, the vehicle's active safety features came into play – these were the ones that protected the occupants in the event of a crash. The front seat frames formed a safety cage, a feature which was as effective in the event of a rollover or side impact collision as conventional B-posts. Also introduced was a new

The open panelled A-pillars seen in the SCC were just one way in which Volvo had improved visibility over conventional cars. There were also sensors and cameras to watch the car's blind spots.

Production Models

The whole point of a concept is to test public reaction to new ideas, so it only makes sense for some concepts to go into production after a spin on the floors of the world's motor shows. The great thing for car buyers is that, in recent years, it has often been the freshest and most exciting cars that have made the graduation from concept to the marketplace.

Not all concepts are destined to finish up in a warehouse somewhere; some of them actually make it to the showroom. These cars have all done that in some form, though some will require a close look to see the similarity to the original show car.

In theory, the hardest category to build a concept for is the production one because the car has to have its roots in the real world. But, in practice, things are less clear cut: a radical concept can make an appearance, then something which merely resembles it is what becomes available to paying customers.

The Citroën C3 and Renault Vel Satis on the following pages are two such examples. In the case of the Vel Satis, in particular, the overall silhouette may have been familiar when the car reached the showrooms, but otherwise there was relatively little crossover. Even upmarket manufacturers such as Porsche have

come unstuck taking this route. When its Boxster was shown, it contained some truly beautiful detailing and many buyers put their deposits down on the strength of that one show car. However, when the first pictures of the production car were shown, it was immediately clear that the designs had been watered down and many of the details lost in the process.

The real thing

The good news is that more and more concepts are making it into the showrooms, even if some of them are being toned down in the process. If it is known from the very start of a project that a car is destined for production, the maker will tend to exercise some restraint and resist the temptation to go overboard with the concept. After all, if buyers are not seeing what they will be able to purchase, how does the manufacturer know if the car will be popular when it reaches the showroom?

That is why Audi ensured its TT changed relatively little as it progressed from show car to showroom, just as Volkswagen stayed true to its Concept 1, which became the new Beetle.

When first shown at the 1999 Frankfurt motor show, commentators assumed that the BMW Z9 did not indicate a new design direction for the German car manufacturer. However, in 2004, the Z9 provided the foundation for BMW's new and very stylish 6 Series range.

Audi TT

Because the Audi TT was a serious design proposal, its motive power was strictly real-world stuff. That meant using the 1.8l turbocharged petrol engine already fitted to many VW Group cars.

Six-spoke alloy wheels have that typical Teutonic quality of being simple and stylish while also solidly engineered. Even these made it to production cars.

Inside was a tan leather interior with highlighted stitching – which was meant to be reminiscent of a baseball. The rest of the cabin design was more sober.

The smooth, dramatic design of the Audi TT was barely watered down when it became a production car. The biggest change was to be to the rear pillars, which gained quarterlights.

Unlike other concept cars which have made it to the showroom, the Audi TT has managed to remain desirable thanks to a combination of sharp looks, a great specification and a strong image – and the fact that it is great to drive also helps, of course. It also helped that the initial concept was barely changed in the transition from showpiece to showroom – what potential buyers saw when the car was first exhibited was more or less what they were able to buy when the car entered showrooms in 1999. But then, from the outset, it had been envisaged that the car would be more than a mere showpiece.

The first TT concept to be displayed (at the 1995 Frankfurt motor show) was a coupé, despite the fact that the first version to be exhibited was supposed to have been the open-topped TTS. Work was well under way on that car when the head of Volkswagen/Audi, Ferdinand Piech, realized that too many of the concepts at the forthcoming Frankfurt motor show were convertibles. The open car was thus held back for the next major motor show; when unveiled at the 1995 Tokyo event, it was badged as the Audi TTS.

Familiar interior

Unlike most concepts, the TT was built with the intention of entering production as quickly as possible if reaction to it was positive. So, although the interior was unlike any other production Audi of the time, it did feature a lot of switchgear already familiar to Audi owners. Designed by Romulus Rost, the aim was to

Although the roadster was probably the more flashy of the two cars, it was the TT Coupé which was the most eye-catching, thanks to the unusually pure lines of the exterior design.

Audi TT	
Debut:	Frankfurt 1995
Engine capacity:	1781cc (109ci)
Configuration:	Front-mounted in-line four, petrol
Power:	112kW (150bhp)
Top speed:	225km/h (140mph)
Transmission:	5-speed manual, FWD
Length:	4002mm (157in)
Width:	1751mm (69in)
Designer:	N/A

keep things as simple as possible, while also creating something that felt special.

Hence there was plenty of leather and aluminium inside the cabin. The TTS also featured what was termed a baseball interior – tan leather with contrasting stitching that was reminiscent of a baseball. This even made it to production, where it was an option – although you would be hard-pressed to find an example fitted with it. Detail design touches such as those air vents that sprouted out of the top of the dash were novel, just like the brushed aluminium locking rings that surrounded them, along with the gearstick surround.

The TTS (roadster) was strictly a two-seater, while the TT (coupé) was officially a 2+2, although in reality it was suitable for only two people. The key to the affordability of the TT (for both Audi and

potential buyers) was its foundation – the Volkswagen Golf. By sharing the platform of one of Europe's biggest-selling cars, it was possible to slash production costs. It was also possible to incorporate front-wheel drive or even Audi's much-respected quattro four-wheel drive system, though this required the engine to be positioned longitudinally. Hence the show cars used the VW Syncro all-wheel drive transmission.

Golf floorpan

Basing the car on the Golf floorpan also allowed the choice of a huge range of engines – in the event, it was the turbocharged 20-valve, 1.8l powerplant which would be the mainstay of the range. In the Audi TT, this was tuned to give 110kW (150bhp) while the TTS unit was tweaked to produce 157kW (210bhp).

To keep weight down, the bonnet, doors and boot (trunk) lid were made of aluminium, which was a

The cabin of the Audi TT did not offer any more equipment than any other car in its class. What it did offer was a design that pushed the boundaries, making it exciting.

technology that Audi was becoming synonymous with thanks to production of its aluminium-bodied A8. This technology made it possible to keep the weight down to around 1100kg (2425lb) for the TT and 1240kg (2724lb) for the TTS – enough to guarantee sprightly performance.

The wide C-pillars (the loss of which was the most significant change in the transition to production) suggested that the car was fitted with a mid-mounted engine. But it was that blunt nose which marked out the car the most – there was simply nothing like it and it looked incredibly svelte. The rear end was equally curvaceous and equally aggressive, its twin exhausts poking out of the rear valance.

Citroën C3

To help with load bay accessibility in tight spaces, the C3's tailgate featured a neat split-folding mechanism that allowed the top half to fold under the lower portion.

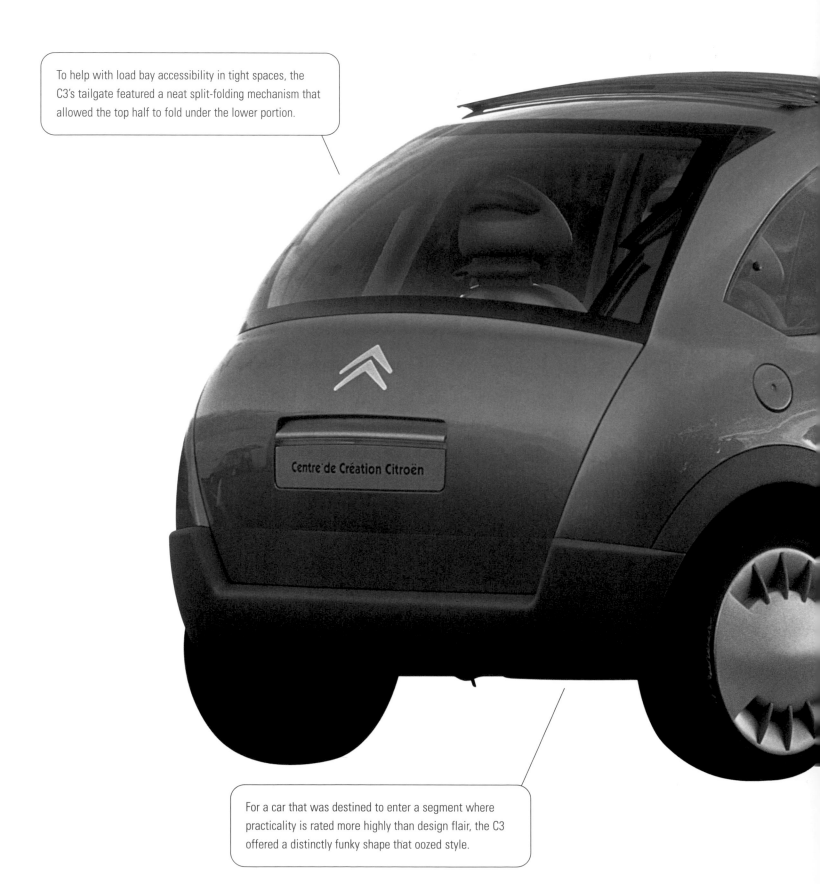

Centre de Création Citroën

For a car that was destined to enter a segment where practicality is rated more highly than design flair, the C3 offered a distinctly funky shape that oozed style.

There was plenty of glass in the car's roof and along its sides, to give the Citroën C3 a modern look, as well as to keep the cabin light and airy.

Citroën avoided the temptation to over-engine the C3, and instead installed the 1.6l petrol engine and clutchless manual gearbox that would be available in the production car.

The rear-hinged back doors made the interior more accessible, and to maximize cabin space the car was wider than normal and featured a high roofline for its size.

Take a look at the C3 first presented at the 1998 Paris motor show, and you will see that at first glance it is not dissimilar to the C3 which reached Citroën's showrooms around three years later. Much of the detailing may have been toned down for the production car, but the overall look of the car was retained. And this is exactly why companies such as Citroën show concepts in the first place – they need to gauge reaction to the car and see if it will be accepted by potential buyers. And in a segment that at the time was dominated by predictable and derivative designs, something fresh, exciting and innovative was desperately called for.

Sticking to the philosophy that it is more imaginative to create a completely new car than it is to try to re-create an old one, the aim of the C3 was to carry on

Despite the small proportions of the Citroën C3, its cabin felt extremely spacious, thanks to the huge amount of glass featured in the roof and the slim pillars.

from where the 2CV had left off when it went out of production in 1990. The reasoning behind the 2CV was that it provided simplicity, roominess, versatility and reliability – and the C3 was intended to have all those virtues, plus many more besides.

In reality, the C3 had to be far more complicated than its ancestor simply because of 21st-century safety and emissions requirements – but this did not mean it had to be overloaded with technology that would weigh it down.

Creative styling

The C3 was a product of Citroën's Creative Styling Centre and, when unveiled, featured a nose and tail that would clearly have to be elongated when the car progressed to production specification. Thankfully, though, this would not mean sacrificing the overall look. The rear-hinged back doors would, of course, have to be more conventionally attached to the B-pillars, but the whole point of a concept is to push the

boundaries. And it was a welcome change that Citroën did not feel the need to show the C3 concept in the form in which buyers would be able to purchase it.

The car was not very long at 3675mm (145in), but its height and width were unusually generous. Such proportions meant that the interior space could be maximized, and there were plenty of other tricks available to make the cabin feel even more spacious than it really was. The sunroof slid all the way back to allow huge amounts of light inside, and the lack of a B-pillar also made the interior feel bigger. The C3's cabin itself had a hi-tech feel about it, and it was also fairly minimalist so that the equipment that was fitted was not intrusive.

Citroën C3	
Debut:	Paris 1998
Engine capacity:	1587cc (97ci)
Configuration:	Front-mounted in-line four, petrol
Power:	67kW (90bhp)
Top speed:	N/A
Transmission:	5-speed clutchless manual
Length:	3675mm (145in)
Width:	1730mm (68in)
Designer:	N/A

Entry and exit were made as easy as possible with unique rear-hinged back doors. This design innovation did not make production, although other, more luxurious cars of the time did feature them.

Each seat was individually adjustable, with the front ones able to be turned through 180°. That allowed the interior to become a lounge when the car was not on the move, and to ensure the occupants were as comfortable as possible, while also remaining safe, a three-point seatbelt was incorporated into each seat.

Sharp colours

Another detail that was lost in the translation from concept to production model was the neat folding tailgate. The original Citroën C3 featured a tailgate in which the lower half folded under the top half, so that it could be handled more easily in tight parking spaces. Inside were four individual seats which could be slid the entire length of the cabin – something that was unlikely to ever be needed in reality. The seats themselves were trimmed in turquoise and green vinyl, and the floor was painted metal with a hardwearing resin coat.

There was no carpet or cloth anywhere to be seen, and ingrained in the resin were specks of sand. This looked bizarre, and as one of the C3's designers explained at the time – with refreshing honesty – it was an experiment that had not really worked. Once the sand had been sprayed into the resin, it was impossible to remove, so although few liked it, there was little that could be done!

Dodge Viper

The Dodge Viper followed where the legendary AC Cobra left off — power and torque aplenty, and with few driver aids to help tame the power.

The show car was a non-runner, but in time there was an 8l V10 truck-derived engine. Sophisticated it was not, but who could argue with 224kw (300bhp) and 62kg-m (450lb-ft) of torque?

The interior styling was very simple, with the minimum of switchgear and instrumentation. There was also no roof – all to keep the weight down and help increase power.

The exterior styling of the Viper was very clean – Dodge resisted the temptation to go overboard with scoops, slats and spoilers. Consequently, the car could be a handful at high speed.

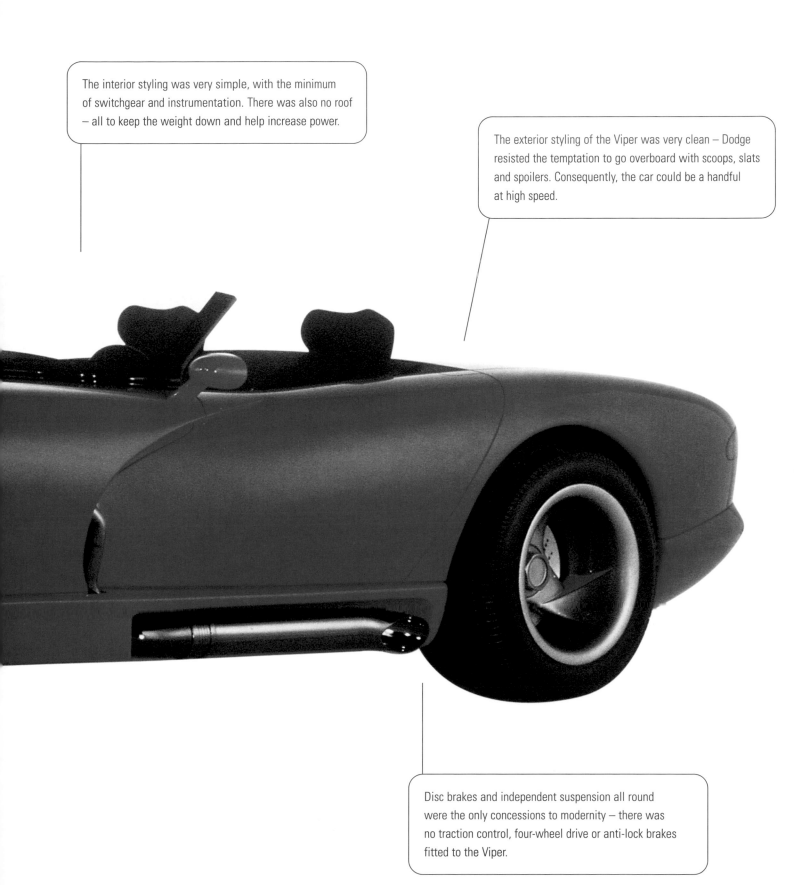

Disc brakes and independent suspension all round were the only concessions to modernity – there was no traction control, four-wheel drive or anti-lock brakes fitted to the Viper.

When the Dodge Viper RT/10 was first shown at the 1989 Detroit motor show, everyone went wild. There was no way the Chrysler Corporation was going to build anything as outrageous as this 8.0l V10 monster. With 224kW (300bhp) and 62kg-m (450lb ft) of torque on offer, it was just too mad to ever go into production. Except that it did, and by 1992 the car was available to buy; by 1996, a closed coupé version had been launched; and more than a decade after the original concept had been shown, a new Viper was to reach the dealership showrooms.

The first Viper RT/10 concept made was just a non-running mock-up, but the car that debuted was constructed from steel and featured the V10 engine, which had been developed for light truck use. The concept was an attempt to build in the same vein as the AC Cobra, the car that was the raw sports car of the 1960s, having huge power, but little in the way of comfort or refinement. Driver aids were also notably absent, although at that time, of course, all cars were far less sophisticated.

Raw driving experience

Carroll Shelby was the man responsible for the Cobra, so it was only natural that his help was enlisted to get the Viper project off the ground. Sports cars had become too comfortable, too sanitized and too sensible, and the team at Chrysler reckoned there was still a niche for something altogether more challenging. The Viper RT/10 was their answer. It also acted as a tool for Chrysler to demonstrate that it had

Dodge Viper	
Debut:	Detroit 1989
Engine capacity:	8l (488ci)
Configuration:	Front-mounted V10, petrol
Power:	224kW (300bhp)
Top speed:	233km/h (145mph)
Transmission:	5-speed manual, RWD
Length:	N/A
Width:	N/A
Designer:	N/A

not given up on cars for the enthusiast. The company had recently moved over to front-wheel drive exclusively, and no true enthusiast likes anything other than rear-wheel drive – with which the Viper RT/10 was equipped.

Although the Viper RT/10 used modern equipment such as disc brakes at the front and rear, along with independent rear suspension, there was little else to keep the driver out of trouble. Four-wheel drive,

The Dodge Viper's side-exiting exhausts pipes – here seen on a production coupé model – were reminiscent of the hot rods of the 1950s. Much of the technological inspiration under the skin also came straight out of the same era.

This was the second-generation Viper, in fixed-head form. With 226kg (500lb) per foot of torque, 500bhp and 8190cc (500ci) under the bonnet, it was even more of a beast than the original.

traction control and anti-lock brakes were all rejected because they diluted the driving experience too much. The truck-based engine was mechanically very simple, with overhead valves and a complete reliance on size rather than technology to provide those huge levels of power and torque.

When revealed, the Viper RT/10 was touted as the purist's alternative to technological *tours de force* such as the Porsche 959 and Jaguar XJ220, which were crammed with technology to make them go faster, yet were somewhat dull to drive.

Dramatic looks

Comfort came low on the list of priorities for the Viper. Air conditioning, electric windows and central locking were all left off the equipment list – anything that added weight unnecessarily was omitted from the specification. To that end, the interior was very simply laid out, with just a few bits of switchgear and basic instrumentation. There was also no roof, although a simple, tensioned piece of fabric to offer basic protection from the elements would not have taken much to engineer.

All this weight loss and power overload would have been in vain if the car's looks had been anything other than jaw-droppingly dramatic – and the Viper RT/10 was more than happy to rise to the challenge. In true hot-rod style, there were side-exit exhausts and also a massive bonnet to hide the V10 engine. Huge scallops ahead of the doors allowed hot air to exit from the engine bay, and the huge wheels and tyres showed that the Viper RT/10 meant business. There was not a straight line on the whole car – every surface was curved in at least one plane – and there was only the minimum of decoration both inside and out. There was no brightwork or fussy details such as scoops or spoilers, while the headlights sat behind eye-shaped lenses for an even less cluttered look.

Ford Ka

The Ka was the baby of the Ford range, but still carried all the 'New Edge' design cues with which its bigger siblings would be blessed.

It was hoped that motive power might be provided by a two-stroke Orbital engine, or maybe a small diesel. Electric power was even considered, but later rejected.

Unveiled as a non-runner, the Ka concept was envisaged to be an economy car, which meant that nothing more than a four-cylinder engine would be fitted.

The original concept, as shown at the 1994 Geneva motor show, was not fitted with an interior of any sort. The priority was to gain acceptance for the exterior.

The overall shape of the Ka changed little in the transition to production car, although the nose was made more aerodynamic — and arguably more radical in the process.

There are few examples of a concept car being less radical than the finished car that is eventually produced, but the Ford Ka is perhaps the best example. By the time the Ka concept was unveiled at the 1994 Geneva motor show, it had already been rejected as the car with which Ford would enter the segment below the Fiesta – or the sub-B sector, as it is known. Nonetheless, Ford decided to forge ahead with this baby car based on the Fiesta floorpan, and although the car would differ in detail when it reached the showroom, it remained more or less true to the original concept.

Unusual inspiration

Bizarrely, according to Fritz Mayhew (Ford's chief European small-car designer), inspiration for the design of the Ka arrived in a bottle of water. As he ate lunch at a London restaurant one day in early 1994, Mayhew noticed a bottle of Evian water. Jagged mountains etched along the top of the bottle reminded Mayhew of an edgy design that Ford's German studio had just proposed for a new European small car. Mayhew took the Evian bottle back to Ford's Dunton

Even without any facelifts or significant updates, the production Ford Ka has not dated since its introduction in 1996, although the original concept is now looking like it came from another era.

(England) design studio, and it became one of the influences of the sharp design theme of the Ford Ka.

The name 'Ka' may seem like just a play on words, but it actually comes from Egyptian mythology and means 'the vital spirit within man'.

Interestingly, far less evident in concept form than in the production car is the fact that this was one of the first cars to come out of Ford's styling studios, which were to showcase what Ford was calling 'New Edge' design. Instead of soft, flowing curves, the design consisted of intersections of straight lines – again, this was more evident on the final production car.

When the Ka was unveiled at in Geneva, this was to test the basic idea of a new entry-level car for Ford's range – the actual detail of the design was less important. Economy was becoming increasingly important for buyers across Europe, and even a Fiesta was too big and thirsty for some. The Ka was scheduled to weigh at least 100kg (220lb) less than its bigger brother, so it promised to be even more frugal.

All show, no go

The show car was not even fitted with an interior, just as there was no engine under that cute, curvy bonnet. Because the Ka was so small on the outside, the plan for the interior was to incorporate design touches which would open up the cabin as much as possible.

Unveiled at the 1996 Berlin motor show, the Ford Ka Step 1 was a three-cylinder lightweight research vehicle that was built to test direct injection diesel technology.

A simple, uncluttered dash would be joined by seats that gave up as much space as possible to the car's occupants without being uncomfortable. As this also heralded the beginning of Ford's New Edge design phase, there would be plenty of sharp lines bisected with yet more straight edges, although by the time the car reached the showrooms its dashboard was not quite as avant garde as it could have been.

The concept unveiled in Switzerland was no runner, so there were no fuel consumption or performance figures available. But the company envisaged that the car would be available with a choice of both petrol and diesel engines. Also available would be a new type of engine with which Ford was experimenting – the Orbital two-stroke. This was an engine that was more efficient than the typical internal combustion engine of the time, and the company even fitted some Fiestas with the engines to see how effective they were in practical applications.

However, with the advent of complex electronics, three-way catalytic converters and direct injection all as standard for even the most basic economy car, Ford made the decision that developing existing four-stroke powerplants would be the best way of progressing the Ka.

Production model

In the event, the Ford Ka went on sale in 1996 with just a conventional 1.3l petrol engine and no choice of a diesel – and certainly not an Orbital two-stroke engine. Even seven years later, when a larger (1.6l) joined the range, there was still no diesel option, just as there was no hybrid or electric offering, despite the electrically powered E-Ka prototype that had been shown in 2000.

It seemed that despite Ford's lack of concern about playing safe with the design of the Ka, the company was to take no risks when it came to the engineering. Perhaps that water had an even greater significance than even Ford realized!

Ford Ka

Debut:	Geneva 1994
Engine capacity:	Non-runner
Configuration:	Front-mounted
Power:	N/A
Top speed:	N/A
Transmission:	N/A
Length:	3350mm (132in)
Width:	1640mm (65in)
Designer:	Claude Lobo

Ford Mustang

The lineage of the Mustang concept was immediately apparent, with its short deck behind the rear window and the long bonnet complete with power bulges.

Anything less than a big V8 would have been unthinkable, which is why Ford installed its 4.6l unit in the new Mustang – complete with a supercharger and intercooler to produce a massive 298kW (400bhp).

Both convertible and coupé versions of the revived Mustang were shown, but the closed car featured a glass roof that was nothing like anything offered on the original.

Part of Ford's 'legends revival', the Mustang is the most iconic car that the American company could have brought back to life. The new Mustang looked as sensational as the 1964 original.

The engineering was thoroughly modern, with 350mm (13.7in) Brembo brakes discs visible behind the 50cm (20in) alloy wheels. Ducts in the front air dam and rear wings channelled cooling air to them.

Think of a motoring icon and the chances are that it will hail from Europe. Japan and America have produced relatively few collectible cars over the years, but there is one remarkable exception – the Ford Mustang. The fastest-selling car in history, it racked up more than a million sales within two years of its introduction in 1964. Unfortunately, Ford did not continue to enjoy such success, and by 2003 the company needed an injection of excitement into its range. Cashing in on its heritage, it looked to the original Mustang and re-created its greatest icon for the twenty-first century.

And so, at the 2003 Detroit motor show, two versions of an all-new Mustang were unveiled, the lines of which drew heavily on the original 1964 car. With both convertible and coupé Mustangs on show, it was only a matter of time before Ford would officially reveal that it was to put this reborn pony car into production. Within a year, the icon was back on the roads, following after the Mini and Beetle.

For some reason, the interior of a 1964 Mustang looked best when trimmed in red leather. Ford reckoned its 2003 counterpart would look just as good with the same styling.

Ford Mustang

Debut:	Detroit 2003
Engine capacity:	4601cc (280ci), supercharged
Configuration:	Front-mounted V8, petrol
Power:	298kW (400bhp)
Top speed:	N/A
Transmission:	6-speed manual, RWD
Length:	4623mm (182in)
Width:	1897mm (74.7in)
Designer:	J Mays and Richard Hutting

Modern classic

Although the Mustang concepts looked to the past for their design inspiration, they brought the whole personal sports car up to date with crisply styled, modern interpretations of the classic look. Both cars were two-seaters, featuring plenty of neat details that could easily be overlooked at first glance. An example

of this was the adaptive headlights, which featured a pair of concentric rings shielded behind a single lens. The rings rotated in a helix pattern to zoom in and out like a professional camera lens.

From a single light source, the Mustang GT concepts used fibre-optic ribbon to deliver adaptable light levels through their highly focused lenses, and, once the sun had gone down, the value of such technology became all too evident.

Signature exterior

On the outside, those classic cues ensured that the source of inspiration behind the new concept was never in doubt. With its signature long bonnet and short rear deck, the Mustang's design also incorporated several other classic themes: C-scoops in the sides, three-element tail lights, the galloping pony in the centre of the grille, and a silhouette that was unmistakably Mustang. The coupé was reminiscent of 1967 and 1968 Fastbacks, while the convertible had a distinct air of the early Shelby Mustangs about it.

The cars were displayed in coupé and convertible forms from the outset because the two had always been available alongside each other. While it may have made more sense to debut them separately, the reality was that Ford intended to announce within a year that they would be going into production.

Sitting on 50.8cm (20in) alloy wheels, the Mustangs looked every bit as aggressive as the production cars that sired them. Behind these wheels were 350mm (13.8in) Brembo ventilated disc brakes, and to add an extra degree of muscle was a hefty air scoop on the bonnet. This channelled cooling air to the 4.6l V8 that

The spare wheel mounted where the rear seat would normally be found in a coupé was evocative of the Mustangs used for circuit racing during the 1960s.

sat underneath – the only configuration that Ford could realistically have chosen for such a car. With the aid of a supercharger and a liquid to air intercooler, this powerplant was capable of churning out 298kW (400bhp) and 54kg-m (390lb-ft) of torque. Although no official performance figures were issued for either of the concepts, it is probably fair to say that it would have been no slouch …

Racing interior

Inside, the Mustang was every bit as tempting as the outside. With red and black leather interiors and plenty of alloy detailing, the cockpits nodded to the past without being overly retro. Four-point racing harnesses kept the occupants of the coupé in place, while the back-seat space was given over to the stowage of a spare wheel; this latter feature was used in some of the early Shelby Mustang racing cars. The convertible was rather more practical, without ever becoming dull. After all, the fact that something works well does not make it boring.

Inside the NeoSpace was plenty of brushed aluminium to give the car a thoroughly modern feel. Added to this was orange acrylic to mirror the exterior highlights.

The NeoSpace was only a small car, but the orange highlights in the grille and along the tops of the doors broke up the expanses of colour-coded bodywork.

NEOSPACE

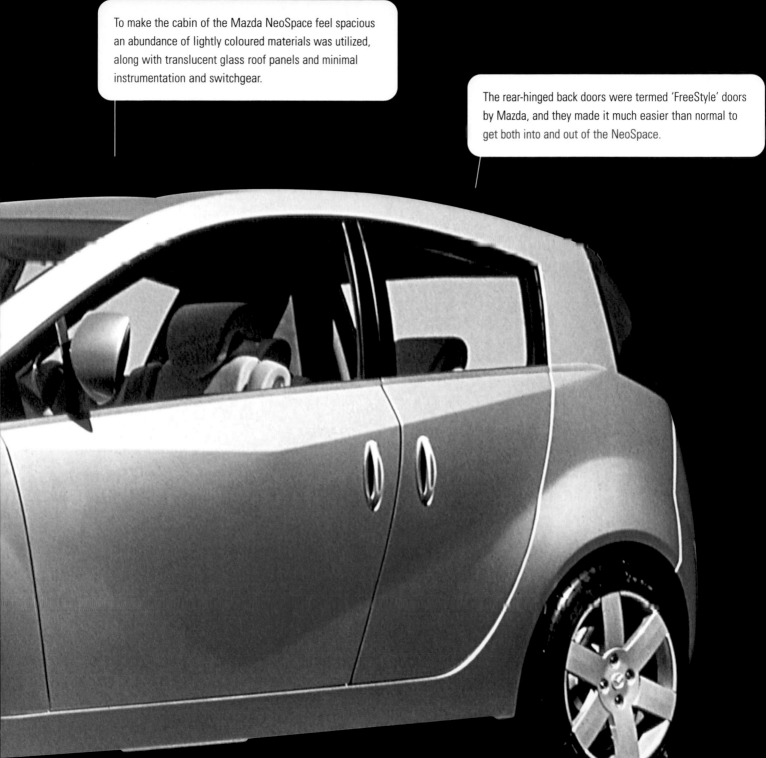

To make the cabin of the Mazda NeoSpace feel spacious an abundance of lightly coloured materials was utilized, along with translucent glass roof panels and minimal instrumentation and switchgear.

The rear-hinged back doors were termed 'FreeStyle' doors by Mazda, and they made it much easier than normal to get both into and out of the NeoSpace.

When the Mazda NeoSpace was unveiled at the 1999 Frankfurt motor show, it illustrated all too well the dangers of letting the marketing department get too close to a project – its fingerprints were everywhere. Do you fancy a car with an interior designed using a 'contrast in harmony' design theme? Or how about an exterior that was created on a 'dynamic strong wheel oriented' design theme? There was all this and more shoehorned into the tiny city car.

If you cut through the hype, though, the NeoSpace was a funky, space-efficient supermini that featured some really nice design touches – so it was a shame that when the car entered production as the Mazda 2 it was just another common-or-garden hatchback following the herd.

FreeStyle doors

The NeoSpace's silhouette was not especially revolutionary, but all the small design details added up to produce something that worked really well. The orange highlights in the front grille, shoulder line and door handles echoed interior highlights in the same colour. The rear-hinged rear doors – or 'FreeStyle' doors, as Mazda liked to call them – were *de rigueur* for a concept car of the time, and naturally were replaced by conventional units when the car reached production. What was not lost was the sharp suit that the car wore, and the rising shoulder line made the car look surprisingly dynamic while the rear light assembly, placed high up, gave it a very modern feel.

The interior was also very modern, and once again the marketing department had got too close: it was allegedly designed with a 'lightweight and floating'

Mazda NeoSpace	
Debut:	Frankfurt 1999
Engine capacity:	1498cc (91ci)
Configuration:	Front-mounted in-line four, petrol
Power:	78kW (104bhp)
Top speed:	N/A
Transmission:	Continuously variable transmission
Length:	3900mm (157in)
Width:	1695mm (67in)
Designer:	N/A

theme in mind. All this really meant was that the seats were fixed to the centre console rather than the floor, so that they appeared to be levitating – something which everybody else was doing at the time, and which worked especially well with the use of the FreeStyle doors.

As well as plenty of brushed aluminium highlights, there was plenty of orange acrylic to lift the interior of the NeoSpace, and to help bring the interior design into line with that of the exterior. Beige was chosen for most of the trim, to keep the cabin feeling spacious, and instead of a clear glass roof there were

In an age when even basic superminis were becoming funky, the Mazda NeoSpace aimed to outdo them all with its pillarless construction and neat styling details.

incorporated into the design as well, including air bags galore, and the lack of a central pillar ensured that visibility was optimized – although side impact protection must have suffered as a result.

By using Michelin PAX run-flat tyres, there was no need to accommodate a spare wheel in the Mazda NeoSpace, which freed up a lot of space in the load bay. This, in turn, meant that the boot (trunk) floor could be much lower than normal, which meant that much larger things could be carried than was usual for a supermini. In fact, there was so much space that it was possible to carry bulky items such as bicycles. To make things even easier when it came to load

The split rear tailgate featured on the NeoSpace was something usually found on much bigger cars. For added practicality, the luggage bay floor could be lowered to accommodate bulky items.

carrying, there was a split tailgate, the lower half of which was hinged at the bottom – which meant it could be used as a ramp up to the load bay. If a flat floor was needed, it was possible to fold the rear seats into the sunken rear half of the load bay, or just one seat could be folded away so that there were three seats and still masses of luggage carrying capacity.

Powering the NeoSpace was a 1.5l direct-injection petrol engine mated to a continuously variable transmission – as the car was primarily a city car, this meant that it would be easy to drive around town while also remaining as economical as possible. MacPherson struts were fitted at the front, while there was torsion beam suspension at the rear – and this layout meant that it was possible to reduce intrusion into the load bay as much as possible while ensuring that the car was fun to drive.

Mazda RX-Evolv

The five-door hatch that looked like a two-door coupé was popular at the time – and the Mazda RX-Evolv, as the RX-8, was the first such car to go on sale.

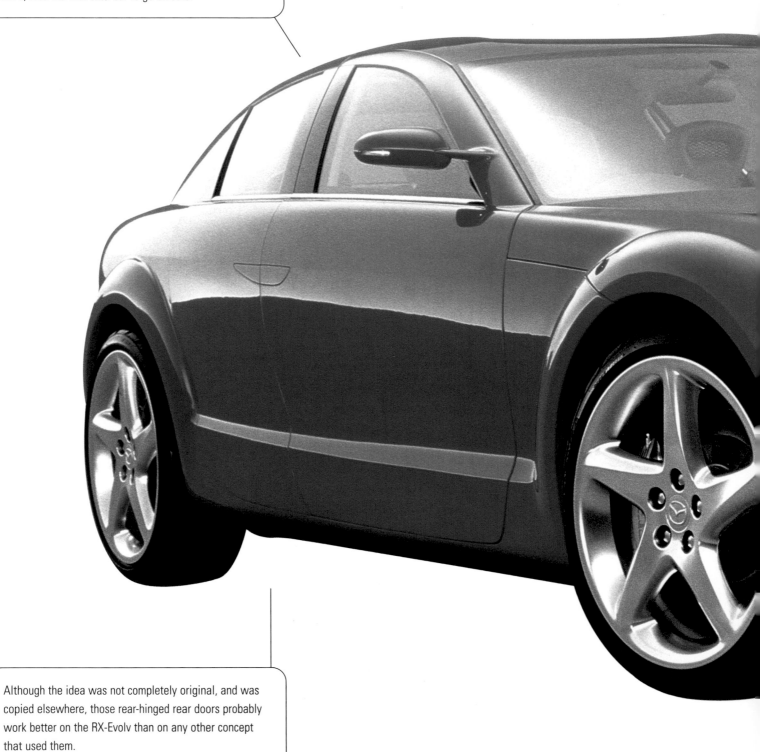

Although the idea was not completely original, and was copied elsewhere, those rear-hinged rear doors probably work better on the RX-Evolv than on any other concept that used them.

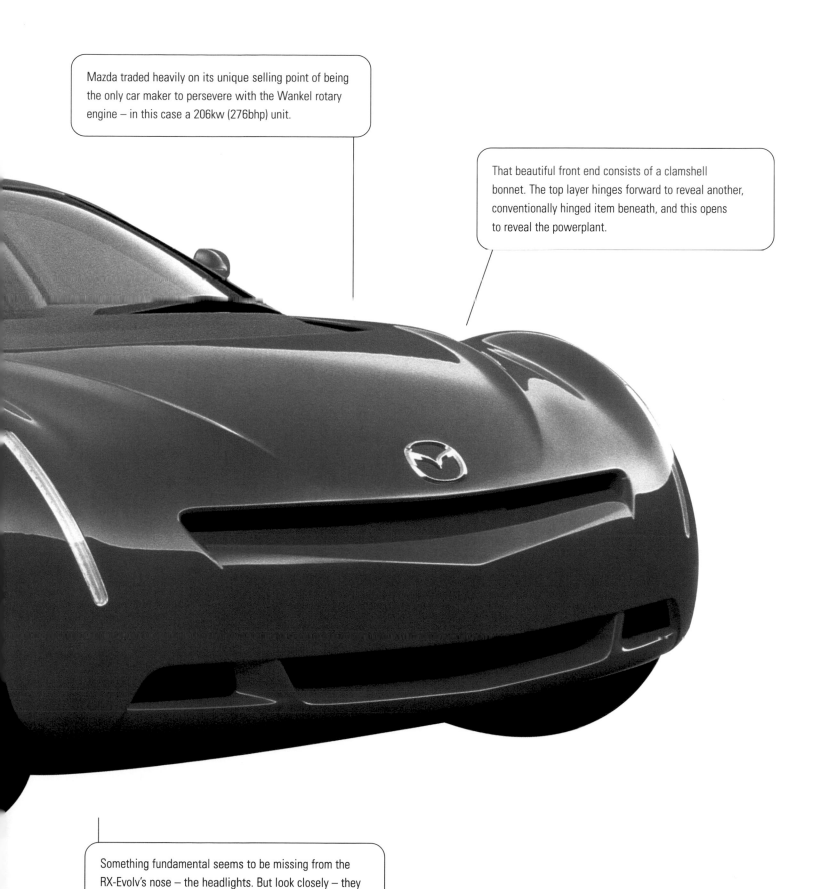

Mazda traded heavily on its unique selling point of being the only car maker to persevere with the Wankel rotary engine – in this case a 206kw (276bhp) unit.

That beautiful front end consists of a clamshell bonnet. The top layer hinges forward to reveal another, conventionally hinged item beneath, and this opens to reveal the powerplant.

Something fundamental seems to be missing from the RX-Evolv's nose – the headlights. But look closely – they are those strips along the front edge of the wings.

While unique selling points are hard to come by in the 21st-century automotive world, Mazda has one, and the RX-Evolv traded heavily on it. It was the rotary engine – a powerplant which had been abandoned by everyone else in the 1970s as being inherently thirsty and unreliable. Mazda, however, had stuck with it, developing it to the point where it was entering rotary-engined cars in endurance racing, and an outright 1991 Le Mans 24 Hours win proved that the engine could succeed. Having stopped producing the RX-7 – the company's only rotary-engined car – Mazda knew it made sense to revive the motive power for which it was famed.

Rotary revival

The RX-Evolv, which was tasked with reviving the rotary engine for Mazda, was first shown at the 1999 Tokyo motor show. At that stage, there were rumours that this could be a new combination of sports and family car which would see production in the new millennium, but nobody was sure. It was pretty radical, with its 'FreeStyle' rear-hinged back doors and tiny slitted front lights – but these were the type of details which would soon be dispensed with if the project went any further. Except that in the case of the door arrangement, the RX-8 did actually use the same system when it became a production reality.

Although the whole car looked fantastic, it was the front end which was the most futuristic, both overall

Although the overall shape of the RX-Evolv was not especially radical, the design concept certainly was. And the best thing was that this radical machine made it to production, virtually unchanged.

Mazda RX-Evolv	
Debut:	Tokyo 1999
Engine capacity:	654cc (40ci) x 2
Configuration:	Front-mounted rotary, petrol
Power:	206kW (276bhp)
Top speed:	N/A
Transmission:	6-speed sequential manual/auto
Length:	4285mm (169in)
Width:	1760mm (69in)
Designer:	N/A

and in terms of the detail. Sadly, it was also the front end which was changed the most as the project evolved – those headlights were perhaps just too revolutionary for the time. Measuring just 25mm (1in) by 300mm (11.8in), these carried the Micro-HID tag, short for High Illumination Discharge. At the rear were more conventional 'jewelled' light housings, and these, when illuminated, were meant to resemble the afterburners of a jet. Borrowing a classic styling cue from Zagato, there was a very subtle pair of bubbles in the roof, which Mazda dubbed an 'Aerowave' roof, and to increase the bodyshell's rigidity, there was a very thick rear pillar.

At the front was a double clamshell bonnet, with the top panel being front-hinged. This opened to reveal the most regularly serviced under-bonnet items, while the panel beneath this was

The Mazda RX-Evolv's dash struck just the right balance when it came to mixing contemporary materials and design with a retro feel. For safety reasons as well as practicality, the cut-off steering wheel was never going to last.

rear-hinged. By lifting this, the less frequent engine maintenance areas could be accessed. Quite why the two needed to be separate was not made clear.

By moving the wheels to the very corners of the car, and by mounting the engine well behind the front axle line, it was possible to attain the optimum 50:50 front:rear weight distribution needed for the best possible handling balance.

The result was a car which could be made to understeer or oversteer, depending on what was wanted at the time; this was to be one of the best-handling family cars ever when it went on sale.

A snug fit

Inside the RX-Evolv, things were equally neatly designed, and there were plenty of gadgets such as an electronic parking brake, a multimedia system and paddle shifts for the gears. As was common with Mazda concepts of the time, there was a design theme – in this case, a very brief phrase encapsulating what was being aimed for, 'Snug-Fit'. This meant

The Mazda RX-Evolv's dash struck just the right balance when it came to mixing contemporary materials and design with a retro feel. For safety reasons as well as practicality, the cut-off steering wheel was never going to last.

simply that whoever sat in the car, whether in the front or rear, would be able to feel at one with it. To that end, there were cosseting seats that would grip any of the four occupants during spirited driving, but it was not all about sportiness – there was a healthy dose of practicality thrown in for good measure, as one of the rear seats incorporated an integrated child seat.

For the RX-Evolv, there was a new generation of rotary engine dubbed the 'Renesis'. This normally aspirated powerplant developed a very healthy 206kW (276bhp), which was transmitted to the rear wheels via a six-speed sequential manual gearbox. The magnesium wheels were 50.8cm (20in) in diameter and, as was customary by now, the equipment list featured plenty of electronics, such as traction control and anti-lock brakes, to keep the driver out of trouble.

MCC Smart

Sitting at the back of the Eco-Speedster was a three-cylinder petrol engine, which drove through a sequential manual gearbox. The vehicle's top speed was just 140km/h (87mph).

To make the most of the limited interior space, the driver sat slightly ahead of the passenger, so that both were not trying to use the same shoulder space.

The Eco-Speedster was the open-topped version of MCC's Smart car. Also available was the Eco-Sprinter, a closed version that was more functional.

This was meant to be the ultimate city car. Hence its compact dimensions – just 2500mm (98in) long and 1500mm (59in) wide.

eco-speedster

Despite it being so small, the Eco-Speedster was designed to be safe in the event of an accident. Hence its three-layer chassis construction – which would cause problems later.

The problem with concept cars is that they always show what could be possible if risks were taken – risks with interior and exterior styling, packaging and the introduction of new technology. But the frustration is that they are always watered down and, by the time they reach the showroom, they are just a shadow of their former selves. Every rule, though, has exceptions, and in the case of the concept car, the MCC Smart is one of them.

The first fruits

The project began in 1990, when the Swiss company SMH, which was also behind the Swatch watch, teamed up with Volkswagen to come up with a microcar that would revolutionize city transport. But by 1993 Volkswagen had got cold feet and pulled out of the project, leaving SMH to continue alone. Without the money to develop the car, SMH teamed up with Daimler-Benz, which took a stake in the new venture known as Micro Compact Car, or MCC. The first fruits of this collaboration were unveiled in March 1993 – the MCC Eco-Sprinter and Eco-Speedster.

Although the first major European motor show of 1993 (the Geneva salon) was taking place when the two cars were unveiled, neither was displayed at the

Externally, the production Smart differed only in detail from the original concept. Other microcar concepts had come and gone; this was the first to make proper production.

event. This was rather a shame because these two cars represented quite a revolution in personal urban transport – at just 2500mm (98in) in length, this was no less than 600mm (24in) shorter than a Mini. And while the MCC cars were strict two-seaters, that did not matter in the end because most urban commuters travel solo anyway.

The targa-topped Eco-Speedster was a petrol-powered two-seater while the Eco-Sprinter was an electric version, which was also slightly narrower (at 1400mm/55in). The petrol car was rear-wheel drive, and the electric one was front-wheel drive. Both the Eco-Sprinter and Eco-Speedster featured rear-mounted engines, but at the time of the unveiling, MCC was very coy about revealing exactly what the motive power was in either of the vehicles.

Although the mechanical side of the cars was pretty unusual, it was the body structures which were the big news. Building a car which was so small, but which would also live up to the mandatory crashworthiness tests of the time, was quite a challenge – and Mercedes claimed that the MCC duo would not only meet these targets, but exceed them as well. The secret was in the underbody structure, which incorporated a sandwich construction so that the engine would be pushed downwards and out of the way of the occupants if the car was involved in a collision. In the case of the electric Smart, this centre cell also provided a safe location for the batteries.

With the wheels pushed right to the extremities of the car, the Smart rode surprisingly well, despite the very short wheelbase. But the narrow track caused stability problems.

Premium values

Being the baby of the Mercedes range, the Smart was always going to be a premium small car – in fact, there would be much larger cars available for less money. But MCC also argued that those cars also would not be so beautifully engineered.

The cabin of the cars featured leather trim and plenty of brushed aluminium, while the fascia was rather plain – by the time the car was available to buy, it would be much more funky, with the different pieces of equipment picked out as features within the interior.

Working on the basis that most people commuting within cities do so alone, the passenger seat of the Smart was positioned 300mm (12in) behind the driver's. This did produce something of an odd-shaped load bay (which was also extremely small), but it did also mean that the two occupants were not vying for the same shoulder space – a simple but very effective solution.

Because of the three-layer sandwich construction of the Smart's floorpan, the driving position was much higher than normal for such a small car – something which would cause problems later, when the cars were noted for being unstable. Once these problems were ironed out, however, the Smart made one of the trendiest – and most expensive – microcars around.

MCC Smart	
Debut:	March 1993
Engine capacity:	N/A
Configuration:	Rear-mounted 3-cylinder, petrol
Power:	N/A
Top speed:	140km/h (87mph)
Transmission:	Sequential manual/auto
Length:	2500mm (98in)
Width:	1500mm (59in)
Designer:	N/A

Mercedes-Benz SLK

The nose featured a mesh grille and especially large headlights, which would later be toned down to make the car much more subtle – as was the Mercedes way.

At the front of the SLK there was a 2.1l four-cylinder engine, but it was engineered to accept much bigger powerplants, including a 3.2l V6 unit.

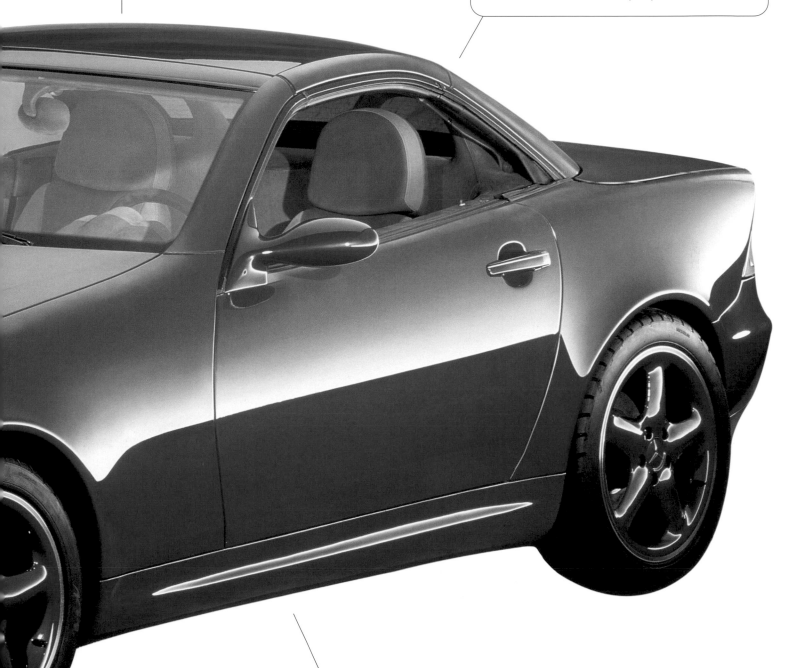

The SLK's folding metal roof was by no means the world's first, and the original concept had not been fitted with a roof of any kind.

Safety was high up the agenda, in keeping with Mercedes principles. A strengthened windscreen surround and pop-up rolls bars kept the occupants out of trouble if the car became inverted or rolled in any way.

This version was the second of two SLK concepts – the first one was painted silver. Although many of the details were changed for production, the essentials remained the same.

Although the Mercedes-Benz SLK is often credited with the introduction of the folding hard top, the concept first seen at the 1993 Turin motor show was not actually fitted with a roof of any kind. Moreover, the SLK was several decades behind cars from Peugeot and Ford that used the same roof construction. What the car did do, though, was introduce a folding metal roof that was also reliable, leak-free and easy to use. The concept was called the SLK Studie, where the S was short for 'Sporty', the L stood for 'Lightweight' and the K was an abbreviation for 'Kurz', the German word for short. In essence, the concept showed what a smaller and more affordable Mercedes SL would look like if it entered production.

Production ready

The SLK was one of those rare concepts that made it to production more or less unchanged from the car displayed at the motor show. Although there would be detail changes to the outside, such as a more rounded tail, smaller headlights and the deletion of the speedster-style humps behind the occupants, the overall shape was barely changed.

The mesh grille was also toned down (it reduced the air flow to the radiator so much that the engine overheated if it was kept in place), and the twin exhaust pipes became far more discreet. By the time an AMG-tuned SLK made it to the showrooms, the car was looking butch once again. The 43.1cm (17in)

Mercedes-Benz SLK	
Debut:	Turin 1994
Engine capacity:	2100cc (128ci)
Configuration:	Front-mounted in-line four, petrol
Power:	112kW (150bhp)
Top speed:	209km/h (130mph)
Transmission:	5-speed manual
Length:	4090mm (161in)
Width:	1720mm (68in)
Designer:	Peter Arcadipane

wheels on which the SLK concept sat were chrome-plated, which made them look rather more glitzy than Mercedes' usual customers were used to – but they certainly gave it presence.

The interior was also toned down rather a lot, with more conventional switchgear and instrumentation, even though the concept was fitted with standard Mercedes parts on the dash. There was a carbon-fibre

This is the production-ready SLK, with its folding hard top. The windscreen surround was strong enough to protect the occupants in the event of a rollover.

The first SLK shown was this example finished in silver. It was to introduce the idea of a lightweight, small and affordable Mercedes roadster, although that word 'affordable' is a relative one!

steering wheel, and red leather swathed the main sections of both the fascia and the centre console. The centre of the steering wheel was also clothed in red leather, and to mirror the composite steering wheel were other carbon-fibre details around the interior, such as the grab handles on the doors. Directly in front of the driver was a trio of dials, with the two outer gauges bisected by the large central speedometer.

Safety sells

If this first SLK concept had seemed a bit garish, the second edition, which was unveiled at the 1994 Paris motor show, was even more sudden. Although the details of the first car remained, such as the oversized headlights and mesh grille, the car was painted a bright blue this time. Not only that, but the alloy wheels were blue as well, as was the interior, which was fitted with orange highlights. Easy on the eye it was not! But the crucial difference between this and the earlier concept was that it was pretty much production ready, as it incorporated the folding hard top which was set to become the car's unique selling point, and which would be copied elsewhere.

The SLK was designed from the outset to take a range of four- and six-cylinder engines, and because this was supposed to be a sports car – albeit a highly civilised one – there would be no weedy powerplant

options. Even the basic car with a 2.0l engine would be capable of 209km/h (130mph), and although there would be no V8 units fitted, there would be V6 and supercharged in-line four-cylinder engines. Offering power outputs of well over 224kW (300bhp), these range-topping versions of the SLK would be able to top 241km/h (150mph) easily, but because of the gentlemen's agreement into which Mercedes had entered, they would always be restricted electronically to 249km/h (155mph).

By the time the SLK entered production, it had received typical Mercedes attention to detail, the roof mechanism being even more beautifully engineered – everything worked at the press of a button. With the roof down, there was little in the way of boot (trunk) space; this was a car built to look glamorous and cool, not to worry about such practicalities as how much you could carry. But carrying the three-pointed star meant the SLK had to be as safe as possible, which is why even the concept was fitted with air bags for each of the occupants (of which there were just two), along with roll bars and a massively strengthened windscreen surround to protect occupants in the event of a rollover.

Mercedes-Benz Vision A 93

The A93 showed the direction in which Mercedes was heading – its tiny size would allow the company to expand into markets it had not previously considered.

Three versions of the A93 were built – diesel, petrol and electric. When the car reached the showrooms, though, only the former two were offered.

S·LS 7068

The high seating position helped improve visibility, but also raised the centre of gravity. This led to instability problems later on, with some cars falling over.

Inside was flexible seating – the A93 was a cross between a city car and an MPV. This allowed it to carry any combination of luggage or people.

Beneath the passenger compartment was a dual-level chassis, in which sat the engine and gearbox. In a collision, these would stay out of the car's interior.

When the Vision A93 was first seen at the 1993 Frankfurt motor show, everybody knew just how significant it was; this was the car that was going to take Mercedes into market areas that it had never even thought about before. Mercedes was used to selling premium large cars – saloons (sedans), coupés, convertibles and estates (station wagons) – but not small hatchbacks. This was the car with which Mercedes was going to steal mass-market sales from the likes of Volkswagen.

Mercedes-Benz Vision A 93

Debut:	Frankfurt 1993
Engine capacity:	550v A/C
Configuration:	Electric
Power:	40kW (54bhp)
Top speed:	75mph
Transmission:	Automatic
Length:	3327mm (131in)
Width:	N/A
Designer:	N/A

This is what the A 93 became: the A-Class. The lines are significantly different between the two, but the overall concept remained the same – a small and practical supermini.

The Vision was also important because it was touted as the most innovative small car since the original Issigonis-designed Mini of 1959. That car had maximized passenger space by giving up just 20 per cent of its overall volume to the mechanicals. The Vision attempted to achieve something similar while also offering far better levels of safety, comfort and refinement. This was achieved by the use of a novel split-level floorpan, which strengthened the car's shell while also offering crash safety – in an impact, the side-mounted engine and transmission would slide under the high-level floor to prevent it coming into contact with the occupants.

Three of a kind

Three versions of the Vision A were built at concept stage – a diesel, a petrol and an electrically powered example. It was this electric car which the world's media drove when reporting on the Vision, and, although it suffered from the usual electric car problem of a lack of range, Mercedes had managed to introduce a type of battery that was four times more efficient than conventional lead-acid batteries. They would last up to 153km (95 miles) on a charge and the battery pack would last 96,560km (60,000 miles) before having to be replaced – but they were still very heavy and accounted for nearly a third of the car's weight.

Although the electric car never made it into production (and was always unlikely to), the turbodiesel and petrol cars were quite close to what customers would actually be able to buy. Alongside the 56kW (75bhp) petrol, there was a 45kW (60bhp) diesel, both with three cylinders – though by the time the production car was launched, each powerplant had gained a cylinder.

Sitting high

It was the rest of the car that garnered most attention. The double-floorpan meant the seating position was rather higher than normal – something that meant visibility was much improved over normal production cars. It also meant the centre of gravity was higher, and this led to problems when early cars fell over. A Swedish magazine journalist tried to swerve sharply in an A-class, and the car ended up on its roof – something of a marketing disaster for a new car that was supposed to sell in huge numbers and which was made by a company renowned for the safety of its cars.

The aim of the Vision A was to take up as little road space as possible while also offering more space in the interior than a conventional four-door saloon. The A-class was just 33.2m (131in) long (shorter than a Fiat Panda), but had more cabin room than a Mercedes C-class – a car which was more than 1m (39in) longer. It also had huge amounts of head room, while innovative and flexible seating made it possible to adjust everything to fit in any combination of people and luggage.

On the outside, everything was colour-coded, with large headlights and a stylized grille that made the car look very smooth, if rather bland. Lots of glass gave the cabin an airy feel and also ensured great visibility for everyone. Something which failed to make production was the window arrangement – the over-large glass area meant the windows would have been too large to open. The answer was to have smaller windows within the main glass area, with only these opening. Not only did this unnecessarily complicate things, but it also gave the car a distinctly odd appearance.

The Mercedes-Benz Vision A93 concept looked more radical than the car that made it to production, but the stance was just the same: a narrow track and high roof.

Porsche Boxster

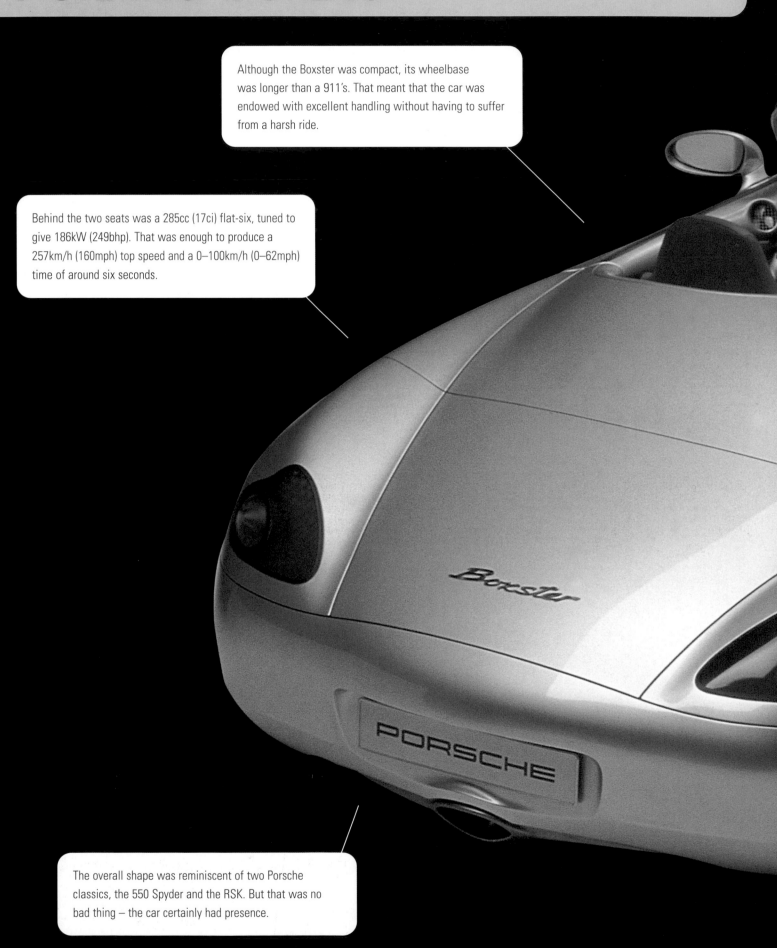

Although the Boxster was compact, its wheelbase was longer than a 911's. That meant that the car was endowed with excellent handling without having to suffer from a harsh ride.

Behind the two seats was a 285cc (17ci) flat-six, tuned to give 186kW (249bhp). That was enough to produce a 257km/h (160mph) top speed and a 0–100km/h (0–62mph) time of around six seconds.

The overall shape was reminiscent of two Porsche classics, the 550 Spyder and the RSK. But that was no bad thing – the car certainly had presence.

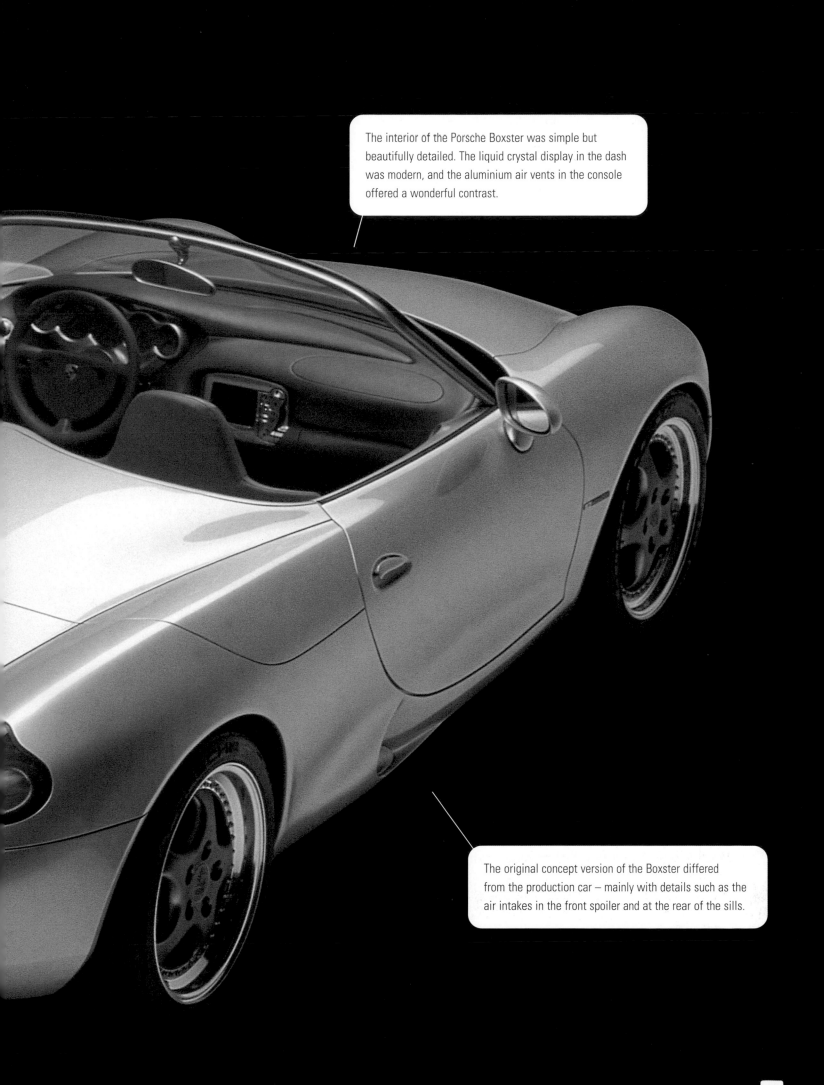

The interior of the Porsche Boxster was simple but beautifully detailed. The liquid crystal display in the dash was modern, and the aluminium air vents in the console offered a wonderful contrast.

The original concept version of the Boxster differed from the production car – mainly with details such as the air intakes in the front spoiler and at the rear of the sills.

The overall shape remained when the Boxster went into production, but, as this photograph shows, some of the finer details, especially the polished air scoops, were lost on the way.

As soon as the Porsche Boxster was shown as a design study at the 1993 Detroit motor show, it was clear that this was actually much more than just a design study. Porsche was going to put the car into production as long as enough interest was shown – and, sure enough, the deposits came in thick and fast.

However, many of those who put their cheque in before the final production car was shown were disappointed. Between the concept and production stages, the Boxster's design was watered down, and there were many who decided the road car was just too tame after such a beautifully detailed show car had been displayed.

Classic Porsche styling

That first Boxster concept had incorporated some fantastic details, such as the polished air intakes at the front, and another one at the rear of each sill. A single exhaust in the centre of the rear valance was also neat, but it was the interior which was changed the most in the transition to production car – the loss of the red leather was no hardship, but the production Boxster looked less futuristic.

Incorporated into the dashboard was a liquid crystal display, which was at that time something quite revolutionary. It also helped to keep the fascia uncluttered while offering the right balance of futurism and retro to discerning sports enthusiasts.

Under the skin, the Boxster featured double wishbone suspension all round, with 43.1cm (17in) wheels being fitted front and rear. There was a 2.5l flat-six engine capable of producing up to 186kW

(249bhp) – enough for the car to crack 257km/h (160mph), while despatching the 0–100km/h (0–62mph) dash in around six seconds.

Many of the external styling cues were borrowed from the classic 550 Spyder, RSK and even the 911. Cashing in on heritage was a common theme that ran throughout many concepts during the 1990s, and, with such a rich past to trade on, Porsche was not going to miss a trick. But the Boxster was also very compact, with its mid-mounted engine sitting behind just a pair of seats. Yet despite its lack of length, the car sat on a wheelbase which was longer than a 911's – something which would make its handling less edgy, while also giving it a more comfortable ride. At the front was a new design of headlight, which would later be incorporated into the updated 911 (and later still the Cayenne), while at the rear the tail lights were beautifully integrated. Also very neatly incorporated was the large central exhaust, which sat flush with the valance beneath the number plate.

Although the Boxster's lineage was immediately apparent, its shape came in for criticism because it was so rounded at the front as well as the rear. When fitted with an optional hard top, the car was accused of looking as though it did not know if it were coming or going. What was really needed was something to break up that huge expanse of panelling behind the two seats – but instead there were featureless planes

Porsche Boxster

Debut:	Detroit 1993
Engine capacity:	2855cc (174ci)
Configuration:	Mid-mounted flat-six, petrol
Power:	186kW (249bhp)
Top speed:	257km/h (160mph)
Transmission:	Manual, RWD
Length:	4115mm (162in)
Width:	1778mm (70in)
Designer:	Grant Larson

which just gradually fell away. Apart from those air scoops at the back of each sill, there was nothing to show where the powerplant was positioned – the 911 had made a feature of this for many years, and it seemed appropriate for the Boxster to do the same.

Interior simplicity

The interior was designed by Stefan Stark, and he opted for something that was simple but very high quality. To that end, there was a single instrument cluster, but those dials were beautifully crafted, featuring an aluminium surround that echoed the alloy detailing seen elsewhere around the cabin. In a very neat reversal of standard design, these instruments featured the calibrations on the glass, rather than the dial itself – something which did not make it to the production model, unfortunately.

The gearstick protruded from an alloy surround, and the gear linkage itself consisted of an exposed rod – very retro. There was a liquid crystal display in the centre of the fascia, and this incorporated a TV, stereo, satellite navigation system, on-board computer and telephone. The alloy trim running down the centre console also incorporated ventilation fans and the controls for the heating and cooling systems – another superb piece of design that failed to move from concept to production.

However, these were all quite obvious design touches – what was less obvious was the use of some quite unusual materials both inside and outside the Boxster's bodyshell. Several of the cabin's details along with the exterior badging were made of the same tortoise-shell acetate from which spectacle frames are made.

The Boxster could not fail – it reduced the price of entry-level Porsche ownership by half while still looking every bit as sensational as the iconic 911 that had arrived over 30 years earlier.

Renault Vel Satis

The nose also introduced people to Renault's new corporate look. Although not immediately obvious, this was based on Renaults of the 1920s.

In keeping with the luxury theme of the car, the Vel Satis was fitted with a 3l V6 powerplant, which drove the front wheels via a five-speed automatic gearbox.

Although the cabin used traditional wood and leather, both were used in a way that was unpredictable. And although the cabin was not fussily designed, it was well equipped.

The rear of the Renault Vel Satis offered an introduction to the company's new look – Renault's production cars would feature similarly distinctive curves and be equally controversial.

Although the Vel Satis was a luxury four-seater, it featured just two doors. But by the time it reached production, it had a more conventional four doors.

Renault's Vel Satis is a classic case of how a concept can be so watered down when it becomes a production car that it is a shadow of its former self. Despite this, even the Vel Satis that reached the showroom has a bold style far more adventurous than most of its rivals – if, indeed, any other cars can claim to be direct rivals. The name is taken from the words 'velocity' and 'satisfaction', which may seem like an odd pairing, but which hint at the speed and comfort that are the car's

Innovative interiors were the order of the day when it came to late twentieth-century concepts, but nobody could pull it off in quite the same fashion as Renault did.

foremost attributes. There was never any secret that the Vel Satis was intended as an illustration of what Renault's range-topping models would be like in the future. Whereas most manufacturers of prestige and luxury cars are very conservative in their design (just as the buyers of such cars tend to be anything but adventurous in their tastes), Renault, with typically Gallic flair, decided it could teach its rivals a thing or two when it came to building a luxury car.

Front garde design

Termed a four-seat coupé de ville by Renault, the Vel Satis was avant-garde in both concept and design. Most luxury cars of the time were conventional three-box saloons (sedans), but Renault's aim was to move towards a monobox design. So where most executive cars were equipped with a boot, Renault's take on the genre was that there should be a silhouette more akin to a people carrier or estate car (station wagon).

Although not immediately apparent, the inspiration for the front of the Vel Satis was the series of pre-war Renaults which was typified by the 40CV. Either side

Renault Vel Satis	
Debut:	Paris 1998
Engine capacity:	2946cc (180ci)
Configuration:	Front-mounted V6, petrol
Power:	157kW (210bhp)
Top speed:	225km/h (140mph)
Transmission:	5-speed sequential
Length:	4680mm (184in)
Width:	1880mm (74in)
Designer:	N/A

of the large badge, which sat in the centre of the bluff nose, there was an air intake. At each corner was a very slender layered headlight, and these, like the rear lights, were stacked vertically. To facilitate Renault's move towards a one-box profile, the rake of the windscreen was barely different from that of the bonnet, while the back of the car finished fairly abruptly to maximize the amount of space available within the car's length. Because the Vel Satis was a full four-seater, the doors – due to the fact that there were just two of them – had to be massive. Each door, at 1780mm (70in), was nearly twice the normal length of a car door. Yet despite this, when opened, they needed no more space than the doors of Renault's smallest car, the Twingo. This was managed by using a neatly designed hinge to move the door forward as it was opened, allowing easy access to the rear seats.

The interior itself was truly luxurious, with Renault holding nothing back when it came to choice of

The next best thing to a full convertible is a car with a roof that is made almost entirely of glass. This gave the Renault Vel Satis a sense of space, but with refinement.

materials or equipment fitted. To keep the cabin feeling spacious, all the materials used were either beige or silver/grey. Leather and wood were also used, though not in the conventional way by which everything is covered in one material or the other. Inside each door was a pair of cabinets, hidden behind vertical sliding covers, and opening to reveal crystal champagne glasses. The instrumentation was kept to a minimum so that it was easy to read, and all the heating, ventilation and air conditioning systems were reduced in size over conventional units so that interior space was freed up. But the neatest feature was the steering wheel, which was fitted with a hub that did not move. Instead, just the rim turned while in the centre of the hub there were built-in controls.

Being at the top of the Renault range, the company fitted the Vel Satis with a 3.0l six-cylinder engine, capable of producing 157kW (210bhp). As was expected for this sector, the car featured a five-speed automatic gearbox, but with the option of sequential manual shifting – a feature that allowed the driver to feel in control, even though this was a car that never offered a particularly sporting drive.

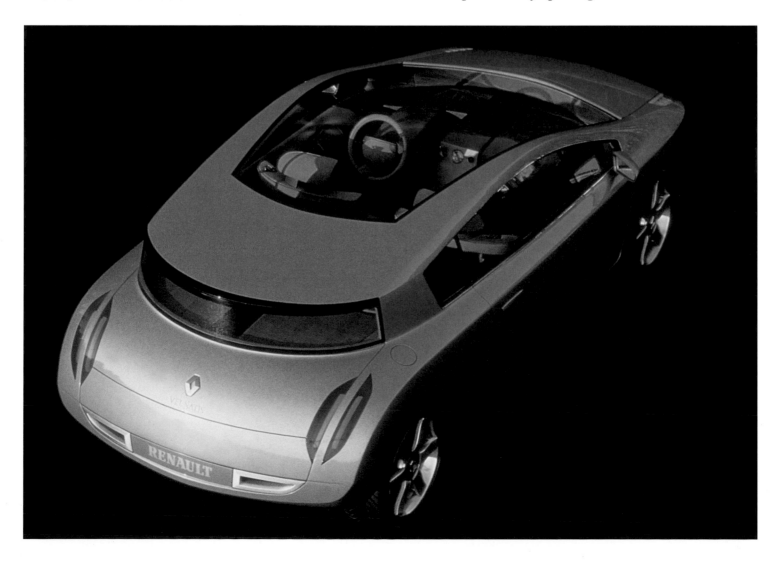

Volkswagen Concept 1

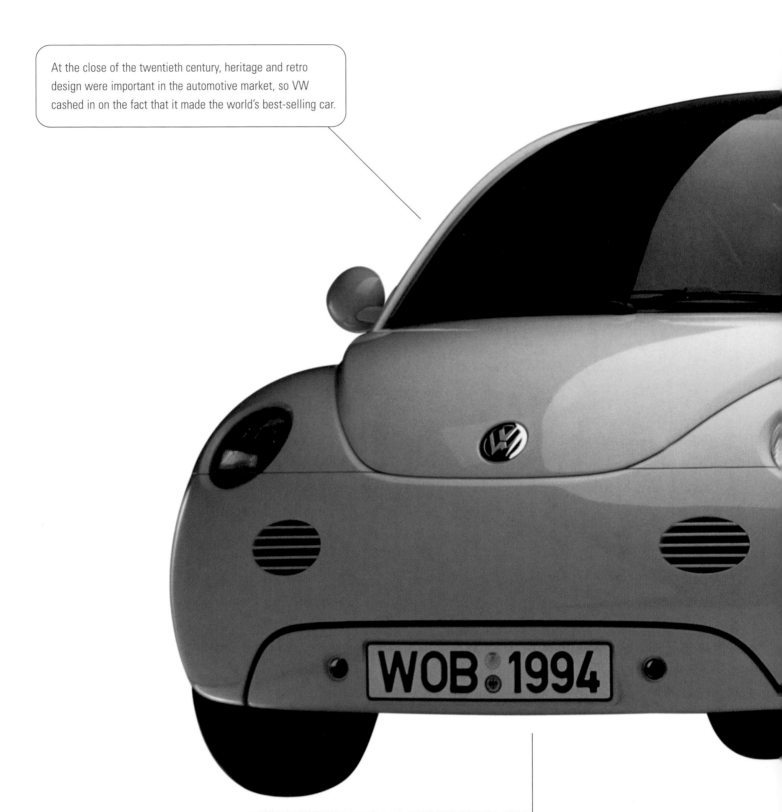

At the close of the twentieth century, heritage and retro design were important in the automotive market, so VW cashed in on the fact that it made the world's best-selling car.

The first concept was a non-runner, but it was to feature four-wheel drive and a water-cooled engine, which was to be mounted at the front, under all those curves.

WOB 1994

Inside, the retro design was very understated, although the equipment count was high, including air bags, air conditioning and a stereo system.

The design roots of the Concept 1 were plain for all to see and, although the mechanical configuration of the new car was completely different, it worked.

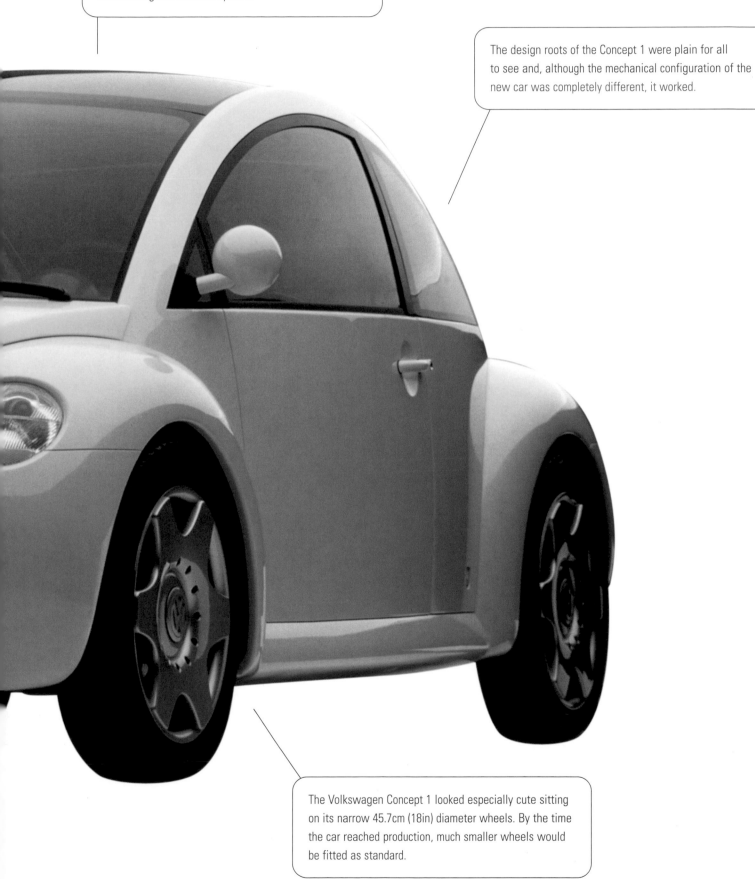

The Volkswagen Concept 1 looked especially cute sitting on its narrow 45.7cm (18in) diameter wheels. By the time the car reached production, much smaller wheels would be fitted as standard.

When the Concept 1 was first seen at the 1994 Detroit motor show, the original Beetle was still in production, in Mexico. But although the rear-engined air-cooled classic was still rolling off the production lines, it was not available – at least, not officially – in many markets around the world. What was needed was an updated version with the cheeky looks of the classic Beetle, but with modern standards of driveability, crash safety and environmental friendliness. Indeed, this latter reason was the driving force behind the first Concept 1 – Volkswagen's sales were falling in the United States and a zero emissions vehicle was at the time just what the company thought it needed to put itself back on the map. People had simply forgotten that the company was still selling cars!

Stunning debut

The Concept 1's debut also took place at the Detroit motor show because the concept had been designed in Volkswagen's American Design Centre, at Simi Valley in California. It was J Mays who came up with the exterior design, and the first car, which came together in 1992, was based on an electric golf cart.

Ultimately, Volkswagen would offer a full convertible, but in the meantime it was possible to order a glass roof that opened up the whole of the Concept 1's interior.

Volkswagen Concept 1	
Debut:	Detroit 1994
Engine capacity:	1896cc (116ci) turbocharged
Configuration:	Front-mounted in-line four, diesel
Power:	75kW (110bhp)
Top speed:	179km/h (111mph)
Transmission:	5-speed Ecomatic
Length:	3824mm (150in)
Width:	1633mm (64in)
Designer:	J Mays

That said, the production car was only ever intended to use conventional internal combustion engines, with the possibility of a diesel/electric hybrid if there was enough demand. By 1994 and the time of the Concept 1's debut, the electric power had been replaced by petrol, although there was also talk of diesel power because Volkswagen had access to an excellent oil-burning powerplant in the form of its 1.9 TDi unit. If the hybrid system had been used, it was envisaged that

The mechanical configuration was completely different, but there was no doubt where the influence for the Concept 1's design lay. Volkswagen even called the new car a 'Beetle' – unlike the original, which had been nicknamed after the insect by affectionate owners.

it would consist of a three-cylinder 1.4l turbodiesel engine, which worked in tandem with an electric motor. The internal combustion engine would have developed 50kW (67bhp), while the motor added another 18kW (24bhp), and the car would have been good for just over 160km/h (100mph).

As soon as the Concept 1 was shown, there was much clamouring for the car to be put into production. Despite the probably humble underpinnings (Volkswagen did not disclose what the concept was based on or what powered it), this was a car with character and practicality that would appeal to both American and European buyers.

Beetle tradition

The look of the old Beetle was reproduced quite faithfully – or, at least, many of its styling cues were – but it was thoroughly modern underneath and inside. That meant it featured front-wheel drive in place of the previous rear-wheel drive, and the 45.7cm (18in) wheels looked just right for this type of car.

The Golf floorpan on which the car would be based led to economies of scale that made it feasible to put

the car into production and also allowed much more efficient packaging. But despite all this, the Beetle continued to be seen as a car that was priced at a level above the Golf on which it was based, without offering the same degree of practicality or space efficiency.

Inside the Concept 1 was a solitary round gauge that echoed the look of the original car's. There was also automatic transmission, air conditioning, a pair of air bags and anti-lock brakes – all items of equipment that buyers of such a car would expect.

So well received was the Concept 1 that when the next major motor show of 1994 opened (the Geneva event) a development of the car was on display – the convertible version. Once again, this aped the original car, with a pram-style folding roof. Once again, the car went down a storm. Now there was no going back – the car just had to get into the showrooms. Before the production version of the Beetle was shown, however, a further development of the Concept 1 was shown at the 1995 Tokyo motor show.

This was different from the 1994 cars, being both longer and wider, as well as featuring integrated bumpers and larger headlights. Whereas the original car was painted yellow and the convertible was red, this new version was black with a glass roof. But the glass was heavily tinted so that it matched the paintwork from the outside, while also letting light in to keep the cabin feeling more spacious.

GLOSSARY

A/B/C/D-pillars

Each of the pillars supporting the roof are named in sequence, from front to back. So the leading pillar – usually the windscreen surround – is known as the A-pillar. The B-pillar is the one between the front and rear doors and the C-pillar usually sits behind the rear door. It is normally only estates that have a D-pillar, as only this type of car has four roof supports.

Active ride

By using electronics it is possible to calculate the loadings at each corner of a car as it travels along. By measuring the various forces acting on the car at any given point, it is possible to prevent the car from rolling in corners as well as to counteract the dive and squat that are inherent in braking and accelerating respectively – thus levelling out the ride and making it corner, accelerate and brake in a more flat manner.

Brake horsepower (bhp)

The measure of an engine's horsepower without the loss in power caused by the gearbox, alternator,

differential, water pump and other ancillaries. The horsepower delivered to the driving wheels is always less than the engine is capable of generating because of these transmissions and ancillary losses.

Cab-forward

Usually a characteristic of two-door, two-seater supercars, a cab-forward design is one that puts the car's occupants towards the front of the car, normally with the engine tucked away behind them.

Continuously variable transmission

Instead of a car's gearbox using fixed gear ratios, this type of transmission uses metal bands on conical gears which produce infinitely variable ratios between two fixed points. This allows the optimum ratio to be chosen for any situation, hence maximising engine efficiency.

Drag co-efficient

How aerodynamic a car is, and also known as the drag factor; an unusually slippery car will have a drag

Designed as a clean alternative to the traditional family saloon, the 1991 HX3 from General Motors featured a monobox design and a powertrain that could be switched between petrol (gasoline) and electric power.

factor of, say, 0.25. Things such as flush-fitting glazing and tighter shutlines between panels have reduced the air resistance around a car – the limiting factors are now accommodating people and mechanicals.

Drive by wire
Most of the controls of a car are connected to mechanical linkages. For example there is the pedal box for the accelerator, brakes and clutch as well as a steering column from the steering wheel. By getting rid of all these linkages and relying on electronics instead, huge advances can be made. Cars become safer, better packaged and easier to tailor to a driver's individual requirements. But the technology needs to be failsafe, and so far it rarely is.

Fastback
A car that has an unbroken line from the top of the rear of the roof to the rear bumper; this line is usually at a relatively shallow angle.

Glass house
The amount of glass within a car – that is, the volume of window space taking into account the windscreen, back window and side windows. It also often refers to the depth of the side windows, and the proportion of them relative to the overall height of a car.

GT/ Grand Tourer
From the Italian Gran Turismo. A car combining saloon and sports car qualities in which effortless power is the dominant feature. Combines excellent road handling with high levels of comfort and is the perfect type of car to enjoy a long-distance (usually fast) journey.

Header rail
Usually only applicable on a convertible, the header rail is what runs across the top of a windscreen. In an open-topped car, the folding roof will close flush with the header rail.

Kamm Tail
If a car features an abrupt ending it has a Kamm tail, named after the German aerodynamicist W. Kamm. He discovered that drag begins to increase after the rear of a car's cross-sectional area is reduced to 50 percent of the car's maximum cross section.

The 1954 Cadillac El Camino concept showed the trend for fins, which was evocative of the jet age that was about to come. It would be another five years before fins were deemed to be passé.

Lean burn
An engine runs on fuel mixed with air. The ratio in which the fuel/air mixture is burned depends on various things such as the operating temperature of the engine and how much load the unit is under (i.e. whether or not the car is accelerating or cruising). A lean burn engine attempts to reduce the amount if fuel being burned while still allowing enough power to be produced for the car to accelerate cleanly.

Monobox design
In profile a car is made of varying numbers of boxes. For example, the classic saloon is a three-box design while the typical hatchback or estate is a two-box design. By sloping the bonnet sharply, at roughly the same angle as the windscreen, it is possible to create a monobox design. The most common cars that feature this are people carriers and the new breed of hatchbacks.

Monocoque
Whereas cars used to be built with a separate chassis (and some specialist cars still are), for many years the standard method of car construction has been the monocoque. Otherwise known as unitary construction, this way of building a car features a bodyshell onto which everything is attached directly; engine, suspension and transmission.

Normally aspirated
The opposite of turbocharged (which is also known as forced induction). Instead of forcing the fuel/air mixture into an engine, it is injected in at atmospheric pressure.

The Pontiac Stinger of 1989 was effectively an update of the beach buggies of the 1960s and 1970s. It featured all-wheel drive, carbon fibre body panels and, with the exception of the windscreen, removable glass panels.

Pillarless construction

Cars do not generally have a truly pillarless construction, because there would be no protection in the event of a roll over accident and there would also be no way of supporting a roof or holding a windscreen in place. But some cars (whether it has two doors or four) sometimes has no B-pillar behind the front doors. This is popular with two-door coupés and is becoming increasingly common on four-door saloons; especially those with rear-hinged back doors.

Roadster

An open car of sporty appearance, also known as a convertible, cabriolet or drop head. Rag top, drop top and spyder are also names for these open-topped cars. While originally they were all slightly different, they have tended to be lumped together in recent years.

Targa

A removable-roof body style popularised by Porsche that is similar to a convertible, except that it incorporates a fixed rear window.

Transmission

This refers to the gear shifting system through which engine power is transferred to the wheels. The purpose of the transmission is to keep maximum engine power applied to the wheels at all times for all conditions, from start-up to high speeds. Most transmissions have 3-6 ratios or 'speeds'. The engine (via the crankshaft) spins too fast to drive the wheels. The transmission reduces the revs and allows the engine to drive the wheels. Generally speaking, the fewer ratios a transmission has, the less efficiently the engine operates.

Tumblehome

This term that describes the convex curvature on the side of a car body, when viewed from straight ahead or directly behind.

Wheelbase

This refers to the distance between the centres of the front and rear wheel axles as viewed from the side of the vehicle.

INDEX

Earl, Harley 6, 7, 8
ECC, Volvo *190–1*, 192–3
Eco 2000, Citroën 12
Eco-Speedster, MCC 291, 292
Eco-Sprinter, MCC 291, 292
Ecos, Fiat 11
electric cars
    BMW E1 170, 172–3
    Fiat Ecos 11
    Ford Ka 274, 277
    General Motors Hy-Wire *168*, 169, *178–9*, 180–1
    MCC Eco-Sprinter 291, 292
    Mercedes-Benz Vision A93 298, 300–1
    Renault Zoom *236–7*, 238–9
    see also hybrid cars
Elise, Lotus 65, 67, 199
Eltec, Ford 195, *204–5*, 206–7
Envall, Bjorn 117
Escort Mk5, Ford 204, 206
ESR, Mitsubishi *186–7*, 188–9
ESX3, Dodge *174–5*, 176–7
EV-1, Saab *114–15*, 116–17
Evoq, Cadillac *36–7*, 38–9
Exner, Virgil 8

F
F-Type, Jaguar 15, *44–5*, 46–7, 150
F1, McLaren 63, 88
F300 Lifejet, Mercedes-Benz 15, *48–9*, 50–1
Feline, Peugeot *56–7*, 58–9
Ferrari
    512S 9
    Pininfarina Mythos *110–11*, 112–13
    Testarossa 111, 112, 113
Fiat 8
    Ecos 11
    Panda 301
    see also Alfa Romeo; Lancia
Fiftie, Renault 195, *232–3*, 234–5
Fioravanti Vola *40–1*, 42–3
Firebird, Pontiac 7, *8*
Ford
    E-Ka 277
    Eltec 195, *204–5*, 206–7
    Escort Mk5 204, 206
    Fiesta 276
    Ghia 8, 9
    GT40 86, 88
    GT90 73, *86–7*, 88–9
    Indigo *90–1*, 92–3
    Italdesign Maya 12
    Ka *274–5*, 276–7
    Model T 210
    Model U *208–9*, 210–11
    Mustang *278–9*, 280–1
    Probe 207
    RS200 26
    Shelby Mustang 281
    Sierra 207

    Thunderbird *11*
    see also Jaguar; Land Rover
Formula, SEAT 15, *64–5*, 66–7
fuel cells *168*, 169, 178–9, 180, 181
FXS, Toyota *68–9*, 70–1

G
gas turbine, Volvo ECC 192–3
General Motors 6
    Autonomy 180
    Harley Earl 6, 7, 8
    Hy-Wire *168*, 169, *178–9*, 180–1
    Motorama 7
    see also Opel; Saab
Ghia 8, 9
Golden Rocket, Oldsmobile *9*
Golf, Volkswagen 265, 313
GT40, Ford 86, 88
GT90, Ford 73, *86–7*, 88–9
GTV, Alfa Romeo 18, 40, 41, 42

H
Harada, Norihiko 125
Hartnell, John 92
Hatton, Adam 47
Helfet, Keith 46
Honda Dualnote *182–3*, 184–5
Horbury, Peter 258
Horrell, Paul 6
Hubbach, Bob 143
Hunaudières, Bentley *78–9*, 80–1
Hutting, Richard 280
Hy-Wire, General Motors *168*, 169, *178–9*, 180–1
hybrid cars 169
    BMW E1 170, 173
    Dodge ESX3 *174–5*, 176–7
    Ford Model U *208–9*, 210–11
    Honda Dualnote *182–3*, 184–5
    Mitsubishi ESR *186–7*, 188–9
    Nissan Yanya *216–17*, 218–19
    Volkswagen Concept 1 312–13
    Volvo ECC *190–1*, 192–3
    see also electric cars

I
IAD Alien 12, *94–5*, 96–7
Indigo, Ford *90–1*, 92–3
International Automotive Design *see* IAD
Issigonis, Alec 300
Italdesign
    Asgard 100, *101*
    Aspid 100
    Aztec *98–9*, 100–1
    Bugatti EB 18/3 Chiron 84
    Maya 12
    Nazca *102–3*, 104–5
    Volkswagen W12 120

J
Jacob, Benoit 235
Jaguar

E-type 44, 45, 46, 149, 150
F-Type 15, *44–5*, 46–7, 150
R Coupé 150
R-D6 *148–9*, 150–1
S-type 148, 150
X-type 150
XJ 150
XJ220 87, 89, 273
XK8 46
XK180 46, 150
Junior, Opel *220–1*, 222–3

K
Ka, Ford *274–5*, 276–7
Kim, Yuntae 134
Kucera, Phil 230, 231

L
LaCrosse, Buick *132–3*, 134–5
Lamborghini
    Countach 27, 94, 95
    Diablo VT 82, *84–5*, 123, 124
    Gallardo 120
    Marzal 9
    Murciélago 120
    VW/Audi ownership 80, 81, 84
Lancia
    Appia 154
    Aurelia 154
    Dialogos *152–3*, 154–5
    Thesis 155
Land Rover 214
    Range Rover 157, 158, 159
    Range Stormer *126*, *156–7*, 158–9
Larson, Grant 305
Lawson, Geoff 46
Le Mans
    Bentley 80, 81
    Mazda 288
    Mercedes-Benz CLK GTR 120
    Volkswagen W12 120
Le Sabre, Buick 7, *10*
Lexus
    LS430 68
    SC430 71
Lincoln
    Navicross *160–1*, 162–3
    Sentinel 162
Lloyd, Mark 146, 202, 203
Lo, Anthony 247
Lobo, Claude 277
Longmore, Martin 96
Loquendo Automatic Speech Recognition System 23
Lotus Elise 65, 67, 199

M
M1, BMW 102, 103
Marzal, Bertone 9
Matra, Renault Zoom 238
Mauer, Michael 247
Maxx, Opel *224–5*, 226–7
Maybach, Mercedes-Benz 138

PICTURE CREDITS